The Democratic Collapse

Civil War America

PETER S. CARMICHAEL, CAROLINE E. JANNEY,
and AARON SHEEHAN-DEAN, editors

*This landmark series interprets broadly the history and
culture of the Civil War era through the long nineteenth
century and beyond. Drawing on diverse approaches
and methods, the series publishes historical works that
explore all aspects of the war, biographies of leading
commanders, and tactical and campaign studies, along
with select editions of primary sources. Together, these
books shed new light on an era that remains central to
our understanding of American and world history.*

The Democratic Collapse

HOW GENDER POLITICS
BROKE A PARTY AND A
NATION, 1856–1861

Lauren N. Haumesser

THE UNIVERSITY OF NORTH CAROLINA PRESS
Chapel Hill

*Published with the assistance of the Authors Fund
of the University of North Carolina Press.*

© 2022 Lauren N. Haumesser

Designed by Richard Hendel
Set in Miller, Sentinel, and Antique No 6
by Jamie McKee, MacKey Composition

Manufactured in the United States of America

Cover illustration: Library of Congress,
Prints and Photographs Division, LC-DIG-pga-04866.

Library of Congress Cataloging-in-Publication Data
Names: Haumesser, Lauren N., author.
Title: The Democratic collapse : how gender politics broke a party and a nation,
1856–1861 / Lauren N. Haumesser.
Other titles: Civil War America (Series)
Description: Chapel Hill : The University of North Carolina Press, [2022] |
Series: Civil War America | Includes bibliographical references and index.
Identifiers: LCCN 2022017103 | ISBN 9781469671420 (cloth ; alk. paper) |
ISBN 9781469671437 (paperback) | ISBN 9781469671444 (ebook)
Subjects: LCSH: Democratic Party (U.S.)—History—19th century. |
Male domination (Social structure)—Political aspects—United States—
19th century. | Slavery—Political aspects—United States—19th century. |
Feminism—United States—History—19th century. | Racism—United States—
History—19th century. | United States—History—Civil War, 1861–1865—Causes. |
United States—Politics and government—1849–1861.
Classification: LCC E459 .H35 2022 | DDC 973.6—dc23/eng/20220608
LC record available at https://lccn.loc.gov/2022017103

For Mom and Dad

Contents

Illustrations

Acknowledgments

I am indebted to a number of people for their help over the course of this project. First among these is my dissertation advisor, Elizabeth Varon. She encouraged me to focus on gender and partisanship. She listened carefully to my ideas, distilled their essence, and sent me away with both more leads to follow and the renewed sense of excitement I would need to see them through. She offered astonishingly thoughtful, incisive comments at every stage of every chapter, and even after I finished the PhD, she continued to provide feedback on the book manuscript and on my career goals. Brilliant, hard-working, mind-bendingly efficient, fair, and compassionate, she modeled how to be a woman and a professional in academia. This book is far better off for having had her on my side.

I am also grateful for the rest of my dissertation committee: Justene Hill Edwards, Corinne Field, and Gary Gallagher, all of whom provided thoughtful feedback on this project. The members of the Civil War Seminar at the University of Virginia played a similar role. Over sandwiches and after some good-natured banter about baseball, they helped me set the scope and understand the value of my research. I appreciate their thoughtfulness and their collegiality.

My work benefited from the support of a number of archives and historical societies. The Virginia Historical Society, the South Caroliniana Library at the University of South Carolina, the Dolph Briscoe Center for American History at the University of Texas, the Kentucky Historical Society, the Filson Historical Society, and the Huntington Library all generously funded my research. (I have particularly fond memories of the two sunny months I spent at the Huntington.) Trips to the South Carolina Historical Society, the Massachusetts Historical Society, the Special Collections Research Center at the University of Chicago, the Historical Society of Pennsylvania, and the Southern Historical Collection at the University of North Carolina, Chapel Hill, were also productive. In every location, the archivists were knowledgeable and generous with their time.

The support I have received from UNC Press has been second to none. Mark Simpson-Vos and Aaron Sheehan-Dean shepherded me through the publishing process with patience and grace. And the feedback from anonymous reviewers was immensely helpful.

The most important support I received was from friends and family. When I arrived at the University of Virginia, Swati Chawla, Alex Evans, Alexi Garrett, Melissa Gismondi, Kimberly Hursh, Rachael Givens Johnson, Scott Miller, and Brian Neumann were strangers to me. Now they are my dear friends. Swati offers sage advice with a side of killer wit. Alex fields my all-hours text messages. Alexi is my very best cheerleader and makes me laugh in even the darkest of times. Melissa, Rachael, and Kimberly and I talked through personal problems and pop culture on weekend long runs; Kimberly—who is wise and patient—also showed me around Mexico when it was time for a break. Scott has gone out of his way for me (and out for beers with me) more times than I can count. Brian shared his exhaustive knowledge of Civil War historiography on bike rides through the Virginia countryside. These people were the best part of my time in Charlottesville.

Friends and family outside of academia provided additional moral support. My aunt, Marcia Griffiths, and her son, Daniel Miller, grounded me with good conversation about feminism, writing, and creativity. My friend Lindsay Gumley is lovably weird, deeply kind, and believes in me when I do not. Maribeth Crane, Victoria Ryan, and Laura Apgar buoyed me with weekend visits and regular check-ins. Michael O'Brien's sense of humor is unmatched. Tyler Nicholas is as good an egg and a friend as there is. (He also helped me settle in with my rescue dog, Zoey, whose insistence on daily runs and nightly head rubs I happily oblige.) And to my best friend and soul's mate, Rachel Goodman: for me, you're it.

Finally, I have the pleasure of thanking my parents, to whom I owe everything. My dad, David, inspires me with his intellectual curiosity, his voracious reading habits, and his appreciation for the perfect word or well-turned phrase; I get my love of a good argument from him. When I have felt frustrated or stuck, he has gotten my mind off things by reciting Wordsworth or Shakespeare—both from memory—or telling me stories about Juan Marichal and Willie Mays. He nearly died of a heart attack while I was finishing this book; I am unspeakably grateful that he is still alive to see it published. My mom, Mary, demonstrates by quiet example discipline, professionalism, independence, and utter reasonableness. She has always left me completely free to be my own person, but the older I get, the more I simply want to be like her. Together, my parents provided every kind of love and support I could wish for. With a heart full of gratitude and without any hesitation, I dedicate this book to them.

The
Democratic
Collapse

Introduction

In the summer of 1856, Democrat Louis Maurer, a staff lithographer for the popular New York printmaking firm Currier and Ives, published a political cartoon depicting Republican presidential candidate John C. Frémont surrounded by a motley crew of supporters. Nearest to Frémont stands a free Black man wearing an outrageous cravat. He says, in Maurer's stereotypical rendering of Black dialect, "De Poppylation ob Color comes in first; arter dat, you may do wot you pleases." Two places behind him stands an unattractive old woman—"the sourest, leanest, most cadaverous, long-nosed, long-chinned . . . old maid," as one Democratic paper later described her. She tells Frémont, "I wish to invite you to the next meeting of our Free Love association, where the shackles of marriage are not tolerated & perfect freedom exist[s] in love matters and you will, be sure to Enjoy yourself, for we are all Freemounters." Behind the free love advocate stands a woman wearing bloomers, boots, and spurs, with a cigar in her mouth and a whip in her hand. She demands "the recognition of Woman as the equal of man with a right to Vote and hold Office." To these supposedly radical figures—a free Black man, a free love advocate, and a women's rights activist—Frémont promises, "You shall all have what you desire . . . if I get into the Presidential Chair."[1] The cartoon perfectly illustrated the Democratic Party's strategy in the election of 1856: to associate the fledgling Republican Party with the conjoined evils of abolition, women's rights, and free love. Frémont went on to lose the election to Democrat James Buchanan.

In the presidential election of 1860, Democrats again deployed gendered rhetoric against the Republican nominee, this time Abraham Lincoln. The same Democratic cartoonist portrayed Lincoln astride a rail borne by *New York Tribune* editor Horace Greeley. Lincoln's followers—the same set of radicals who appeared in the Frémont cartoon—line up behind him to march into an insane asylum. With apparent longing, a free love activist sighs, "Oh! what a beautiful man he is, I feel a 'passional attraction' every time I see his lovely face." A free Black man in another ostentatious cravat declares, "'De white man hab no rights dat cullud pussons am bound to spect' I want dat understood." And a thin, old, hook-nosed woman demands, "I want woman[']s rights enforced, and man reduced in subjection to her authority."[2]

Maurer's reuse of such imagery notwithstanding, this election differed dramatically from the previous one. In 1860 northern and southern Democrats nominated different candidates—Stephen A. Douglas and John C. Breckinridge—who used gendered arguments not only against Lincoln but against each other as well. Southern Democrats argued that gender radicalism had poisoned the entire North—Democrats and Republicans alike. A typical southern newspaper warned that a "white slavery . . . dominates in the North . . . a slavery which ostracizes and expels from the community the man who does not think with the majority—who will not submit to be led by demagogues and masculine women." And a pamphlet warned that if Lincoln were elected, southerners stood to lose "the domestic altar; patriarchal and conservative institutions; the family circle around the hearthstone; and mothers who . . . devote themselves to their children in principle, as their chiefest jewels."[3] The gender tactics that had bolstered Democratic unity in 1856 intensified the sectional schism over slavery by 1860.

The issue of slavery proved the undoing of the Democratic Party. In 1856, northern and southern Democrats alike supported the popular sovereignty plank in the party's platform. But this unity belied fundamental differences in how northern and southern Democrats hoped popular sovereignty would work. Most northern Democrats simply expected that westerners would decide the slavery matter for themselves. Southern Democrats, meanwhile, hoped to guarantee and promote slavery's westward expansion. In 1857, initial—fraudulent—elections in Kansas raised southerners' hopes that they would get their wish. Instead, northern Democrats insisted on a fair vote and, given the chance, Kansans rejected slavery. Southern Democrats felt betrayed. To them, it seemed northern Democrats had snatched a new slave state out of their hands. In 1859, John Brown's raid on Harpers Ferry only confirmed southerners' doubts: in Virginia, as in Kansas, northern Democrats had failed to protect slavery. By the election of 1860, southern Democrats had come to see northern Democrats as unreliable allies. They also had come to believe that protecting slavery required an activist, proslavery federal government. To that end, southerners insisted on a southern nominee and a proslavery platform, a gambit that split the party in two, precipitating Lincoln's election and southern secession.

This book argues that gender politics exaggerated and exacerbated the Democratic Party's internal disagreements over slavery. Northern and southern Democrats used gender to make powerful arguments about slavery at each successive juncture in the gathering sectional crisis, from the emergence of the Republican Party, to the Lecompton Constitution in Kansas, to John Brown's raid at Harpers Ferry, to the 1860 convention, and finally to secession. Gender turned slavery in the territories, which for Democrats had been a political and economic matter, into an intractable cultural debate. Gendered charges and countercharges raised the stakes of every dispute and made compromise ever more elusive.

By "gender politics," I mean two things. First, Democrats made gender—images and conventions of masculinity and femininity—an issue unto itself. Second, they used gender to make powerful arguments about slavery. Between 1856 and 1861, these two broad tactics took a variety of forms. Democrats cast their political opponents—first Republicans, and then Democrats from the other section—as either radical themselves or as associates of gender radicals. They analogized slavery to marriage to make arguments about the government's role in regulating domestic institutions. As the ties between northern and southern Democrats frayed, men on both sides denounced compromise as emasculating. And finally, southerners justified their demands for increased protections for slavery by maintaining that those measures were necessary to defend southern women, children, families, and homes from northern influence and slave insurrections. Because Democrats derived their personal and political rights from their status as white men, in opposition to white women and enslaved Blacks, all of these gender tactics were inextricable from racial concerns.

Regulating sexuality was a near-constant preoccupation in Democratic politics. Democrats fixated on candidates' wives. They fretted about protecting monogamy against the assaults of free love activists in New York state's Oneida Community and Latter-Day Saints in Utah. And they worried about interracial sex—which they associated with the specters of consensual "amalgamationism" in the North, and the rape of white women by enslaved Black men in the South. The frequency of these concerns in Democratic politics spoke to white men's much deeper fears about maintaining social and racial control.

The Democratic Party promised to defend white men's roles as protectors, providers, and patriarchs. For most of the antebellum era, this helped unite the party. Northern and southern men alike believed they should be in charge of their own households; they should feed and protect their families; and they should govern their cities, their states, and their country as they saw fit. In 1856, Democrats from both sections saw Republican antislaveryism and gender radicalism as the greatest threat to their personal and political independence.

But ultimately, the Lecompton crisis and John Brown's raid exposed the irrepressible conflict between northern and southern Democrats' world-views. According to the dominant southern definition of manhood, woven into proslavery propaganda, being a protector meant a man must defend the sexual purity of his wife and daughters against potential assault at the hands of enslaved men. Being a provider meant working the land with whatever labor he wanted—his own, his wife's, or his slaves.' And being a patriarch meant managing his household and governing his community as he saw fit. The Lecompton crisis and John Brown's raid convinced south-ern Democrats that protecting these rights would entail more than just asserting the sovereignty of their own states: it would require an active, proslavery central government.

Northern Democrats saw things differently. They too believed that male heads of household should guard their families against the threat of race mixing and social equality. But in the overwhelmingly white North, that threat seemed less immediate. They wanted to provide for their families, but slavery was not essential to their success. Indeed, in northern free labor ideology, slavery was an obstacle to economic progress. Primarily, they were concerned with maintaining the core prerogatives of patriarchy: presiding over their households and their local governments. So when southern Democrats tried to push through a fraudulent proslavery constitution in Kansas—which would effectively gut popular sovereignty and disfranchise northern men who had qualms about the slave power's agenda—northern Democrats balked. Surrendering their right to vote on slavery was akin to surrendering their manhood.

During the election of 1860 and the secession winter, southern Dem-ocrats highlighted these diverging ideas about manhood and slavery to generate support for splitting the party and leaving the Union. Empha-sizing the supposed differences between a radical northern culture, with its free soil and free women, and southern slave society, where white men sat atop the social hierarchy, helped construct a southern national identity. Championing white patriarchy had strengthened the Democracy's position as the party took on the emerging Republicans in 1856. But over the next three years, northern and southern Democrats came to see each other's gender systems as mutually antagonistic.

This argument relies on and contributes to the literature in four distinct fields of inquiry. First, this work expands on the literature on women, gender, and antebellum politics. Scholars have long recognized women's role in antebellum reform movements. In the late 1970s, historians such as Nancy Cott began to examine the nature and emergence of a cult of domesticity in the antebellum era. Increasingly, Americans—especially middle-class northerners in urban areas—began to articulate the notion that men and women were fundamentally different and therefore should inhabit different spheres: men should be out in the world, and women should remain within the home. Ann Douglas and Ellen DuBois investigated how women flipped this paradigm, harnessing it to justify their presence in the public sphere or their demands for equal rights. These works typically examined women's roles in benevolent reform movements. And in the 1990s, scholars demonstrated that women became involved in partisan politics even before they had the vote.[4]

More recently, historians have expanded the scope of their research from women's political history to gender and politics more broadly. LeeAnn Whites argues that the Confederate war effort altered the system of white women's dependence and enslaved people's subordination that formed the basis of southern men's free and independent political status. White women resolved this gender crisis by reinterpreting the Confederate cause—and southern manhood—as a defense of home and family, rather than a defense of slavery and whites' social, racial, and class privilege. Stephanie McCurry has shown that yeomen and planters alike derived their status as free men from their mastery over their households. Amy Greenberg has demonstrated that two distinct masculinities encouraged men to support America's westward expansion. And Michael Pierson has shown that antislavery political parties articulated cogent positions on gender issues, and that "many people who assumed a partisan identity did so in part because they . . . imagined themselves with that worldview." These works have shown how gender debates were interwoven with sectional politics in nineteenth-century America.[5]

This book builds on such work, with a focus on masculinity. It argues that the Democratic Party's use of gendered political tactics played a critical role in exacerbating the slavery issue, splitting the Democratic Party, and sundering the South from the Union. Between 1856 and 1860, northern Democrats came to see their southern counterparts as overbearing patriarchs who, if left unchecked, would exert the same brutish control over the national party—over white northern Democrats—that they did over their slaves.

This language reflected real differences in northern and southern Democrats' conceptions of manhood—a changeable yet powerful concept in the antebellum era. To many Republicans, being a man meant demonstrating restraint in their personal lives, making Republicans more likely to support using the law to shape behavior. Northern Democrats revolted at this idea. To them, the alpha and the omega of manhood was being able to act as they saw fit, entailing total autonomy over their homes and their government. Southern Democrats shared this vision—to a point. When slavery appeared under threat, they pushed to protect it by restricting northern men's sovereignty. The increasing recriminations over gender roles discouraged compromise, diminished trust, and brought into relief northern and southern Democrats' increasingly divergent understandings of manhood and political independence. Thus, as works by Whites and McCurry have done, this book claims that the "private" sphere of domestic relations had a profound effect on the "public" sphere of politics, and vice versa, and seeks to illuminate the interplay between gender and race. White men wielded gendered and racial images and aspersions to justify their policies, malign enemy politicians, and forewarn voters of the dangers of voting for the other side. It was almost impossible for politicians to talk about the issue of gender without saying something about the issue of race.[6]

In taking this approach, this work owes a great debt to gender theorists. In 1986, Joan Wallach Scott famously called on historians to examine "gender as an analytic category"; soon after, Judith Butler declared that gender was a performance—its "'naturalness' constituted through discursively constrained performative acts." This book takes up Scott's call to analyze how gender creates and reinforces power relationships. Democrats both invoked and reified their particular, conservative definitions of masculinity and femininity through their political speeches, their partisan newspapers, their out-of-doors politics, and their private letters. R. W. Connell has pushed beyond seeing gender's construction as a process that occurs in a masculine-feminine binary, arguing that men define their masculinity in relation to other men. Readers will see the influence of this theory on my work: much of this book examines how Democrats and Republicans, and later northern and southern Democrats, competed to define themselves as model patriarchs in contrast with opponents who, for one reason or another, were not so ideally suited to leadership.[7]

This book uses gender analysis to build on a third body of literature: the long-standing debate over the origins of the Civil War. In the 1920s, Charles A. and Mary R. Beard argued that the economies of the industrial North and the agrarian South were incompatible, rendering war between the two sections unavoidable. In the 1930s and 1940s, other scholars countered that agitators—abolitionists in the North, and fire-eating secessionists in the South—whipped up popular sentiment, resulting in a "needless" war between the two sections. Later scholars took up this debate, dividing into two camps: "fundamentalists" and "revisionists." Building on the pioneering work of W. E. B. Du Bois, fundamentalists such as James M. McPherson and Eric Foner contended that slavery was the root cause of the Civil War: it created two fundamentally different and ultimately antagonistic societies.[8] Contemporary revisionists do not deny that slavery played a critical role in the outbreak of the Civil War. But they insist that historians must also look at other factors—such as the breakdown of a cross-sectional party system—and they argue that the rise of a major antislavery political party was not inevitable. They also confound the idea of a fundamental antagonism between the two sections by pointing out the commonalities between northerners and southerners and the divisions within northern and southern society.[9]

This book builds on the work of scholars who have broken free from the fundamentalist-revisionist debate. These scholars acknowledge that slavery created two profoundly different societies, but they seek to understand what factors made slavery particularly divisive in the mid-nineteenth century.[10] This work argues that the Democratic Party's gender demagoguery was one of these factors. Slavery gave rise to a southern culture that was more hierarchal than in the North. This, in turn, created distinct sectional visions of men's and women's roles. The Democratic Party mined these differences for electoral gain, inflaming the slavery issue and ultimately splitting the party and the country in two.

Finally, this book contributes to the literature on the Democratic Party. In the 1850s, more than half of Americans were Democrats—yet scholars have most often portrayed the Democratic Party as the backward foil to the ascendant Republicans. Historians have conducted serious studies of the Republican Party, but no similarly complete work exists for the Democrats. Various scholars have studied the Democratic Party in the context of northern politics and northern culture. Southern Democrats are less studied.[11] And the literature on the national Democratic Party—of northern and southern Democrats combined—is thin. This gap is ironic, given that, by the mid-1850s, the Democratic Party was one of the country's last surviving national institutions. The only book-length study of the national Democratic Party, Michael Woods's recent work demonstrates that a conflict between defenders of slaveholders' property rights and advocates of popular sovereignty tore the party apart. Woods argues that racism and negative partisanship sustained the Democracy more than ideological uniformity, and that these forces could not hold the party together in the face of such a profound internal conflict over slavery.[12] This book complements Woods's work, arguing that gender politics exacerbated the divisions Woods describes.

As the last remaining national political institution in 1860, then, the Democratic Party allows us to test the theory that diverging conceptions of gender inflamed the slavery issue that Woods describes and alienated northerners from southerners. Gender was important yet epiphenomenal in the conflict between the Democratic and the Republican Parties, which held such vastly different positions on slavery. Within the Democratic Party, however, the slavery issue seemed easier to reconcile, with northern Democrats endorsing popular sovereignty and southern Democrats supporting slavery's expansion. Northern and southern Democrats also had a shared enemy in the Republican Party—a powerful motivator in politics. Ultimately, however, just as popular sovereignty had papered over Democrats' differences on the slavery issue, Democrats' general support for white patriarchy belied meaningful differences in their understandings of masculinity.

This study of gendered political discourse relies heavily on antebellum newspapers. Thanks to a growing American population, the advent of new printing and communication technologies, and federal subsidies for newspaper postage, the newspaper industry flourished in early nineteenth-century America. In 1840, the U.S. Census counted 1,631 newspapers; by 1850, that number had reached 2,526. In big cities, many newspapers published daily with circulations in the tens of thousands; in small towns, newspapers came out weekly and boasted far fewer subscribers. Americans often read newspapers aloud at post offices, taverns, and other public spaces, so newspapers big and small reached more people than their subscription numbers would indicate. As to the content of the papers, nearly all were unabashedly partisan: one editor described them as "literally drenched in politics." Political parties sustained the newspapers through direct subsidies and government printing contracts, and the newspapers, in turn, sustained the parties, working to convert swing voters and shore up the party faithful by printing editorials and speeches. This book takes those words seriously: trends in language reflect common assumptions and values. High literacy rates amplified newspapers' influence. Regional variations persisted—literacy was higher in the North and the mid-Atlantic than it was in the South—but by 1860, 93.4 percent of white men and 89.9 percent of white women knew how to read.[13] Taken together, newspapers' ubiquity, partisanship, and reach make them a critical source for any study of gendered political discourse; they reveal what politicians and editors thought and how those ideas spread.

Newspapers also tell us about the values of their readers. The broad republication of congressional speeches in local newspapers allowed

INTRODUCTION

Americans to follow political debates more closely than ever before. As a result, historians have argued, congressmen began crafting their speeches to please their constituents. As one historian describes it, politicians linked their "audience in an immediate, emotional way to events, principles, or policies." Put simply, the speeches "were designed to please" constituents.[14] I extend this argument to include newspaper editors. These partisans wrote their own commentary and selected which letters and speeches to publish. In a partisan media environment, papers that did not reflect the views of subscribers would not sell: people chose the news that matched their beliefs. In sum, newspapers both created and revealed deep divides between Republicans and Democrats and northerners and southerners.

This book elaborates on these arguments over the course of five chapters. The first deals with the election of 1856. During that campaign, Democrats used gender in three distinct ways to paint the Republican Party as illegitimate and sectionalist: they pilloried Republican John Frémont's appearance and the independence of his wife, Jessie. Second, they associated the Republican Party with the women's rights and free love movements. Third, they argued that abolitionism was at once the source of all Republican gender radicalism and its most terrifying manifestation. These tactics defined Republicans as the party of women's rights, free love, abolitionism, and disunion, and the Democrats as the party of patriarchy, conservatism, and Union, and contributed to the election of Democrat James Buchanan.

The second chapter reveals that Republicans and Democrats used gender tactics in an attempt to gain the upper hand in the debates over popular sovereignty in Kansas and Utah. In 1856, Republicans claimed that popular sovereignty had created chaos and social immorality in Kansas, with its "domestic institution" of slavery, as well as in Utah, with its "domestic institution" of polygamy. Republicans had cleverly turned one of slaveholders' common arguments against the Democrats. Common law had long recognized both slavery and marriage as "domestic institutions" that gave white men legal control over the bodies, labor, and property of white women and enslaved Blacks who lived in their household. Americans also used the term "domestic institutions" as a proxy for states' rights—for the right of men in each state to decide for themselves on a host of matters, from elections to slavery to marriage. White southerners had long argued that northern interference in slavery infringed on men's power over their states' politics and their households' relations. And so northern and southern Democrats alike squirmed as Republicans demanded to know whether the Democratic doctrine of popular sovereignty—the right of men to decide on the domestic institutions of their state—meant that

Democrats supported Mormons' right to choose polygamy. But in 1857, northern Democrats fought against the ratification of Kansas's fraudulent Lecompton Constitution by reaching for the same weapon Republicans had used: analogizing slavery to marriage. If southerners would not hinder a man's right to make laws regarding marriage, why did they now reject Kansans' right to make laws regarding slavery? The whole Kansas controversy revealed that gendered language could not resolve the Democrats' profound internal disagreements over the purpose and practice of popular sovereignty.

The third chapter examines how Democrats responded to John Brown's raid. Seeking to make electoral headway in the North and to shore up support in the Border and Upper South, northern Democrats blamed Brown's actions on Republican radicalism. They linked Brown's outspoken supporters, such as women's rights activist and abolitionist Lydia Maria Child, to the Republican Party as a whole, and denounced the whole lot as race and gender traitors. But in the wake of the raid, Border and Upper South Democrats—including many white women—became more susceptible to secessionist fearmongering that emphasized the dangers of slave rebellion to white southern women and homes. Ultimately, Democrats' racialized and gendered reactions to the raid deepened the fissures within the party.

The fourth chapter analyzes the rupture of the Democratic Party in 1860. In that year's election, northern and southern Democrats nominated and ran separate candidates, splitting the vote and handing the election to Republican Abraham Lincoln. During the nominating conventions, both sides equated compromise with dishonor. Since honor was such a powerful motivator, and since a man's honor was often tried in the court of public opinion, this was an effective tactic to forestall compromise. Democrats also expressed alienation from each other in highly gendered political language that emphasized the social and cultural incompatibility of North and South. Taken together, these tactics made Democrats' disagreements seem more profound and compromise seem dangerous.

The last chapter contends with the secession winter of 1860–61. For four years, Democrats had caricatured Republicans as social radicals who wanted to impose a program of women's rights, free love, and abolition on the South. After Lincoln won the election, northern Democrats frantically tried to walk back this rhetoric. Through the winter and spring of 1860–61, northern Democrats sought a peaceful resolution to the secession crisis—trying, as ever, to inhabit a middle ground between northern Republicans and southern Democrats. But it was no use: already, Deep South Democrats had come to believe their slave society was profoundly different from, superior to, and under threat by northern free society. They also began to construct a conservative southern national identity that idealized white southern womanhood. Elite white southern women—who were just as invested in maintaining slavery and patriarchy—lent their support to the cause. After Lincoln's call for troops, Upper South Democrats finally accepted secessionists' appeal to quit the Union and fight for slavery, southern women, and southern homes. Meanwhile, northern Democrats rallied to support the war effort. By the night of April 25, 1861, when Stephen Douglas addressed the Illinois State Legislature, he was ready to proclaim, "I believe in my conscience that it is a duty we owe ourselves, and our children, and our God, to protect this government and that flag from every assailant, be he who he may."[15] The Democratic Party's collapse demonstrates the danger of deploying hyperbolic claims to gender in politics. Unable to resist the electoral power of gender hyperbole, Democrats North and South split their party and the Union in two.

1

Free Women, Free Land, Free Love, and Frémont

THE 1856 CAMPAIGN

By 1854, Senator Stephen A. Douglas of Illinois—a champion of western expansion—had spent ten of his eleven years in Congress pushing for the construction of a transcontinental railroad. And for ten years, congressmen could not agree on a route. Northerners complained that federal money should not subsidize a southern railroad because it would run through the state of Texas. Southerners blocked a northern route because they worried that an influx of people into the lands west of Iowa and Missouri, which lay north of the Missouri Compromise line, would lead to the addition of new free states to the Union. So Douglas brokered a compromise. Congress would organize the Kansas and Nebraska Territories, with the understanding that the railroad would extend west from Chicago through Kansas to the Pacific. But settlers themselves would decide whether to allow slavery in the new territories. This bill effectively repealed the Missouri Compromise, which many Americans—including Douglas—had long regarded as permanent.[1]

Many northern congressmen were incensed by the Missouri Compromise's repeal. In the months following the Nebraska bill's passage, northern Whigs joined with free-soil Democrats to form a new political organization: the Republican Party. Republicans opposed the extension of slavery, calling for the federal government to ban the institution in the territories. This antislavery position attracted support from a broad spectrum of northerners. The majority were men who dreamed of moving west and working the land without having to compete with slave labor. Others hoped restricting slavery would set slavery on a path to gradual, peaceful extinction. And a very small minority wanted to abolish slavery immediately.

Northern and southern Democrats, meanwhile, united in support of the Kansas-Nebraska Act. But they did so for different reasons. Southern

Democrats saw a chance to carve slave states from land previously slated to be free. Northern Democrats thought the law would devolve the slavery question from Congress to the territorial legislatures, ending national debates about slavery and smoothing westward expansion. It also did not hurt that popular sovereignty seemed so irreproachably democratic, since Democrats had long vaunted local rule and white men's autonomy.[2]

By 1856, Republicans were ready to contest the presidency. Gathered at the Musical Fund Hall in Philadelphia, Republicans avowed their opposition to the "repeal of the Missouri Compromise . . . [and] to the extension of Slavery into Free Territory"[3] and celebrated western explorer John C. Frémont as their standard-bearer. Republican newspapers declared the convention a triumph—"a complete success," according to Horace Greeley's *New York Daily Tribune*. They crowed about their nominee, describing Frémont as "a young man of energy and action, of tried courage, and of a nice heroic sense of honor." They gushed over Frémont's wife, Jessie, approving of her personality—"a free hearted, free spoken, independent woman"—and of her sexual relationship with her husband—"the fusion of one man with one woman, of John C. Fremont with Jessie Benton." And they extolled the party's platform of "free speech, free land, freedom, and Fremont." The platform, its dashing standard-bearer, and his beautiful wife gave the impression of a party that was young, fresh, and forward-thinking.[4]

But forward-thinking to some is radical to others. Democrats saw a political opportunity and quickly moved to paint John, Jessie, and the Republican Party as fanatical, abolitionist, and disunionist. Contrasting the Republican Party's exclusively northern support with their own national electorate, Democrats cast the election as a battle between the forces of disunion and the forces of Union. Transforming the Republican slogan with a racial slur, the *Richmond Enquirer* ridiculed Republicans as the party of "free [n—], free women, free land, free love, and Fremont."[5] The Democrats' hyperbolic and racist language typified nineteenth-century political campaigns. But gendered accusations—that Republicans supported women's rights and free love, in addition to abolition—had never before been deployed as tirelessly and effectively in a national campaign.

By using partisan newspapers to analyze public rhetoric and perception, this chapter argues that in the election of 1856, Democrats deployed gender politics in three distinct but related ways. First, they criticized Frémont's marriage and his physical appearance. Second, they associated the Republican Party with the women's rights and free love movements. Finally, and most critically, Democrats contended that Republicans' gender radicalism dovetailed with Republicans' support for abolition: both movements grew out of an excessive commitment to individual freedom at the expense of social stability. This portrayal of the Republican Party was an absolute caricature. Though women's rights activists and many abolitionists supported the Republican Party, and though the Republicans did offer a slightly more progressive gender vision, mainstream Republicans supported neither women's rights nor abolition. But the accusations spoke powerfully to men's fears that abolition and women's rights—with their implied threats to white men's autonomy—were gaining ground in the North. The attacks also worked by uniting northern and southern Democrats around a vision of cultural conservatism. If Republicans stood for women's rights, free love, abolition, and disunion, then Democrats must stand for white patriarchy, social order, racial hierarchy, and the Union.

The Radical Frémonts

When Republicans nominated John C. Frémont as their standard-bearer, they nearly guaranteed that gender would become an issue in the campaign. Young and handsome, Frémont had made his name as an explorer of the West and served briefly as California's first U.S. senator. Republican newspapers described the forty-three-year-old's good looks—his "eagle eye," his "classic head, delicate but firm features, mild yet determined expression, [and] his profusion of wavy dark hair." They also waxed poetic about his bravery, describing him as the leader of expeditions "filled with romance, daring, and suffering," a "gallant explorer" to whose "valor and conduct we owe the possession of California."[6] Frémont lacked significant political experience: he served less than a year as senator and then failed to win reelection. So Republican papers played up the romantic aspect of his personal story—his youth, his good looks, his dangerous expeditions in the West—to capture the imagination and the votes of the Republican rank-and-file.

Where Republicans saw Frémont as the handsome explorer, Democrats saw a candidate who offered more style than substance—a man whose foppish attention to his appearance emasculated him and made him unfit for leadership. Frémont parted his thick, wavy, brown hair in the middle— an unconventional look in an era when only women wore middle parts. Democrats attacked his supposedly feminine hairstyle. On September 24, Pennsylvania Democrat and academic William Reed gave a speech in support of Buchanan's campaign. Reed claimed he would try to "avoid personal reference to Mr. Fremont." "I have neither time nor taste for such insignificant details," Reed claimed. But a publisher who printed copies of

Reed's speech for distribution could not avoid the temptation to add his own paragraph-long description of Frémont's look—"heavy, waving, dark hair, sprinkled slightly with white, part[ed] . . . in the middle." An article in the *Brooklyn Daily Eagle* added that "owing to the feminine arrangement of his locks," Frémont was "the most distinct and *sui generis* in the Union." But Democratic voters did not want a man who distinguished himself by wearing his hair like a woman. "The old farmers and laboring men in the country are not going to vote for the son of a French dancing master, who . . . parts his hair in the middle (*a la Marie* [Antoinette]) for President," the *Cincinnati Daily Enquirer* insisted. It might seem incredible that Frémont's center part became a campaign issue. But as Craig Thompson Friend and Lorri Glover point out, in antebellum America, "manhood did not exist except in contrast to womanhood."[7] Democrats attacked Frémont's hairstyle both to argue that his femininity disqualified him for the presidency and to encourage voters to think of Democrats as the party for real men. Democrats aligned the binary of femininity and masculinity with the binary of America's two-party system. If Republicans were feminine, then Democrats must be masculine.

Frémont had also married well, having eloped with the beautiful Jessie Benton, the daughter of Missouri senator Thomas Hart Benton. A slaveholder and lifelong Democrat, Benton had nonetheless fallen out of favor with the party due to his opposition to the Compromise of 1850 and the Kansas-Nebraska Act. Jessie was an astute political observer and thus a great asset to her relatively inexperienced husband. Republican strategists recognized Jessie's potential for generating enthusiasm in the election. Party papers published breathless, romantic descriptions of the couple's elopement. One writer described the young Jessie as possessing "every charm calculated to produce a profound and lasting impression on the ardent and appreciative nature of Lieut. Frémont." Another compared Frémont, who had captured the heart of a famous senator's daughter, with Democratic nominee and lifelong bachelor James Buchanan. If Democrats said, "Fremont ran off with a respectable man's daughter. He is a thief!," the Republican paper suggested the "spunky" reply: "He had better steal a wife than live a bachelor!" If Democrats countered, "If you mean to insinuate Buchanan ain't married, I can tell you that he married his Country over forty years ago, and has taken good care of her," the paper offered the riposte, "Fremont did run off with Tom Benton's daughter, and next November he will run off with Jim Buchanan's wife!"[8] The interest in the young couple's elopement and marriage testifies to the public's broader preoccupation with politicians' sexual relationships, which partisans mined to better understand the men on the ballot. If Frémont had been man enough to "steal" a senator's daughter, then surely he was man enough to be president.

Republican fascination with Jessie extended beyond the Frémonts' initial elopement. Socially conservative Republicans depicted her as the charming, domestic wife adorning the arm of their handsome candidate. A typical Republican campaign song described Jessie as "sweet" and "bright," while a newspaper report on the Frémonts described her as "plain in dress, simple and unaffected in manners[,] domestic in feelings and pursuits, [and] warm and earnest of heart and purpose . . . the very type of American woman in her highest and noblest sphere." More progressive Republicans praised Jessie's political acumen and her support for the Republicans' antislavery platform. One song told voters that Jessie would help John as president: "for the Chieftain's White Mansion she's better than [one]." The *Burlington (Vt.) Free Press*, an antislavery paper with abolitionist sympathies, went so far as to claim that "Col. Fremont . . . has owed much of his success to the counsels and aid of his wife, and her reputation as a free hearted, free spoken, independent woman." The paper recounted how while southern women in California insisted they needed enslaved labor to manage their households, Jessie had done "the work of her household with her own hands," which "silenced the appeals of the women for slavery, and strengthened the hands of her husband and his free state associates who were fighting the battle for freedom." Republican women even formed "Jessie Circles" to foster partisanship, promote antislavery causes, and organize events. Indeed, Republicans invoked Jessie so frequently that one scholar has remarked that "'Frémont and Jessie' seemed to constitute the Republican ticket rather than 'Frémont and [vice presidential nominee William] Dayton.'" [9] Republicans of all stripes projected their ideas about womanhood and their hopes for their party's nominee onto Jessie Frémont. Conservatives saw her as a paragon of domesticity—the beautiful wife of a manly explorer. More progressive Republicans saw her as an independent woman with abolitionist tendencies, which in turn reinforced their belief in John as an antislavery crusader.

To Democrats, Jessie symbolized something different altogether. Democrats had encouraged women's involvement in their political campaigns since the 1830s. Democratic women attended mass meetings, listened to debates, baked cakes for party barbecues, and even marched in torch-light parades.[10] When it was their party, their cause, and their supporters, Democrats welcomed women's political participation. But when Jessie stumped on behalf of the Republican Party, Democrats retrenched, seeing her behavior as proof of the gender disorder in her marriage and in the

Republican Party as a whole. Democratic newspapers reported indignantly on each of Jessie's campaign appearances. In July, a crowd of Republicans gathered outside the Frémonts' lodgings in New York, cheering and crying out for the couple to make an appearance. John made a brief speech and then retired. After a short wait, Jessie came out onto the balcony and was greeted by the roar of the Republican supporters below. The *Cincinnati Daily Enquirer* sneered that the interval before Jessie appeared had been a "pretense of holding back—a sham of coyness." The public appearance showed Jessie lacked the modesty, deference, and domesticity expected of women of her time. On the contrary, she relished her role as "the feminine partner in the business."[11]

Some Democrats even claimed that Jessie had masterminded John's bid for the White House and would be the power behind the curtain if he were elected. Holding forth at an outdoor meeting one August night in New York's Lower East Side, Democrat Isaiah Rynders claimed that Frémont's election would render Jessie president "*de facto*," because she was the "*best man* of the two." A subscriber to the *Boston Post*, meanwhile, mailed a song to the paper, asking readers to "imagine Jessie singing [it] to her darling spouse." This fictional Jessie dreams of sharing power with her husband. "How happy we shall be / When you and I, my darling John / Shall rule the land and sea!" one verse goes. In another, "Jessie" disparages "the people" as "great ninnies"—a jab at Republicans' supposed elitism—and then goes on to promise, "And this we'll let them know / When you and I are president / John C. Frémont, my jo." Like Rynders's speech, the song exaggerated Jessie's control over her husband's politics, portraying her as aggressive and political—and therefore masculine and subversive. This language was endemic. It appeared in dozens upon dozens of Democratic newspaper articles; over the course of only two months, one paper published seven articles decrying the gender disorder in the Frémont's marriage.[12]

Jessie's involvement in the campaign impugned John's masculinity as much as it did Jessie's femininity. Why, Democrats wondered, would a man allow his wife to speak in public? Perhaps he did not approve of his Jessie's campaigning but could not control her—exposing him as a failed patriarch. Did voters really believe that a weak husband would make a strong president? Alternatively, perhaps John did approve of Jessie's campaigning. If that was the case, it revealed the depth of the Republican Party's gender radicalism: even the Republican presidential nominee believed women belonged in public life. To Democrats, either scenario laid bare the fact that John—whom they frequently emasculated as the "husband of Jessie"—was unfit to be president.[13]

Democrats were quick to amplify stories claiming that Frémont had failed to protect and provide for his dependents. The *Brooklyn Daily Eagle* harped on Frémont's neglect of the men he commanded during an expedition across the Rocky Mountains. In the winter of 1848–49, Frémont had led a group of thirty-five men through Colorado in search of a passable route for a transcontinental railroad. As the weather deteriorated and the Sangre de Cristo mountains became increasingly difficult to navigate, Frémont—eager to restore his reputation after a court-martial during the Mexican War—had insisted that his men forge onward. Ten men in Frémont's command died in the expedition, some as they went back to find help. According to the *Brooklyn Daily Eagle*, "No man"—no real man— "with an American heart would desert his comrades while life lasted."[14] Here again, Democrats saw an example of Frémont failing to protect and provide for those who depended on him.

Closer to home, Democratic papers scandalized readers with claims that Frémont had abandoned his mother. Frémont had become a wealthy man when Mexican miners discovered gold on his California ranch. Despite these new riches, the *Richmond Enquirer* reported, Frémont's mother was widowed, destitute, and alone in Charleston. She had become a washerwoman for "several benevolent ladies in the neighborhood," who had given her work to "lessen . . . the humiliation of her condition."[15] Whether or not it was true, the claim that Frémont had deserted his mother sent three messages to readers. For one, it told readers that since Frémont had not taken care of his mother, they should not expect him to take care of the country. Second, it indicated that Frémont did not share their values: he did not provide for his family like they did. And third, it revealed that he was not the man he claimed to be—and certainly not man enough to be president.

Not only had Frémont deserted his family, but he had allegedly encouraged his wife to leave hers. On September 29, a Democratic speaker in Cambridge, Massachusetts, described for listeners how Frémont "induced a confiding daughter"—that is, Jessie—"while within her teens, to trample on the commands of her parents, and consummate a marriage, without their knowledge and consent." Jessie's parents had indeed initially opposed the match. The couple eloped, and later, her parents embraced John as a member of the family. Michael Pierson has shown how Republicans used the story of the Frémonts' elopement to argue that John was bold, manly, and decisive.[16] Here, however, we see Democrats arguing that the very same story revealed John's defiance of patriarchal norms. Democrats believed that a father had the right to manage and control his daughter's life. When a woman married, the father willingly transferred that prerogative to her new husband. By eloping with Jessie, John had disrespected her father and the patriarchal system as a whole.

Drawing a contrast between Republican and Democratic views of marriage, Democratic outlets published articles about marriages that went sour when wives sought equality with their husbands. In a typical story, titled "Three Ways of Managing a Husband," a wife's desire for autonomy nearly destroys her marriage. At first, the woman asserts her independence, claiming the "right to say and do a little as [she] pleased." This results in her husband's being unable to "bear anything from [her]." Then the woman pushes for equality with her husband, "struggl[ing] fiercer than ever for the ascendency." This behavior precipitates a fight, causing the husband to withdraw and the couple to live estranged from one another for a year. Finally, the wife abandons her dreams of independence and equality. She relinquishes her "pride, self-will, [and] anger," accepting that, as a "weak woman in the hands of a strong-minded man," she must simply "obey." In deference, the woman finds peace. Tying up her own will "with a silken fetter" miraculously transforms her marriage into a happy one.[17] For Democrats who read the story, the moral was clear: a happy marriage depended on a man's control over his wife.

Democrats believed patriarchal control over families played an important role in ensuring the stability and durability of the nation. The *Richmond Enquirer* looked back to the Roman Empire to prove the point. When Roman husbands "relaxed their rule . . . wives, children, and slaves had lost much more in protection, guardianship, affection, and even supervision and control, than they had gained by the larger liberty in which they were permitted to indulge." This, the *Enquirer* told readers, critically weakened the Roman Republic, leaving it "disgraced and lingering to her fall."[18] Democrats believed in political independence and equality among white men, but a corollary of that belief was the political dependence and inequality of women and people of color. In this vision of society, white men were responsible for exercising steady control over their families, since obedient wives, children, and enslaved people would result in a stable and prosperous America.

In principle, Democrats believed that men should exercise this white masculine prerogative with benevolence and generosity. The horrors of spousal abuse in the North and slavery in the South reveal that men most often failed on this account. Still, short stories and poems in Democratic periodicals reinforced paternalistic ideals. One story told readers what happens to the families of neglectful husbands. The man lords over his wife with "selfish, arbitrary, and implacable" mastery. His wife, who at the time of their marriage had been like a "confiding, dependent child"—the ideal wife—becomes a "self-possessed woman" as a result of her husband's mistreatment. Physical illness follows quickly on the heels of moral decay, and the woman dies of consumption. Another story emphasized the positive effects of a husband's generosity. The husband in the story has the power to grant his wife's every wish, and he usually does. His benevolence pleases him and makes her "happy in the possession of a complying husband and pleasant anticipation of future gratifications."[19] In this story, both husband and wife fulfill their obligations: the husband by providing for her, and the wife by submitting to him. These stories appeared in Democratic publications alongside partisan editorials, and indeed, their implications stretched beyond the household. The stories reminded men that they derived their political power from their status as patriarchs; governing a family was a dress rehearsal for governing the country.

The Democrats' nominee, however, was not a successful patriarch. Sixty-five-year-old James Buchanan had won the Democratic nomination on account of his deep government experience—over the previous forty years, he had served as a member of the Pennsylvania House of Representatives, member of the U.S. House of Representatives, minister to Russia, U.S. senator, secretary of state, and minister to Great Britain—and his cross-sectional appeal. As one historian put it, Buchanan "was the only potential contender who offended no one." Yet unlike Frémont, who had eloped with beautiful Jessie, Buchanan was a lifelong bachelor and had no children of his own—a shortcoming Republicans enjoyed bringing up at rallies and in the partisan press. At one rally, a Republican asked "whether it was not better to send to the White House one who had . . . marr[ied] an accomplished woman, than to send there the rusty old bachelor Buchanan." The party's papers mocked Buchanan as a "withered up bachelor" and a "bachelor peculiarity," and suggested that he be sent to Utah to find a wife among the Mormons. A Republican voter in Cincinnati even wrote to his local paper proposing that "it ought to be *unconstitutional* for a bachelor to be President."[20]

Having ridiculed Frémont's marriage in the partisan press, Democrats scrambled to respond to the inevitable countercharges against Buchanan's bachelorhood. Some Democrats maintained that Buchanan's empty nest was an asset. On the eve of the election, Indiana lawyer Charles Denby promised voters that without a wife to distract him, "Buchanan, so long a bachelor, would be married to the Constitution and the Union." As Joshua Lynn has demonstrated, Democrats argued that Buchanan's bachelorhood enhanced his conservative, cross-sectional bona fides. Democrats pointed to his sexual moderation as proof that he would lead with his head and to his empty nest as an indication he would not be prejudiced toward northern or southern families.[21]

Other Democratic papers, recognizing their candidate's bachelorhood as a political weakness, tried to justify why Buchanan had never married, explaining that he had never recovered from a nearly four-decade-old heartbreak. As a young man, Buchanan had been engaged to marry Ann Coleman, the daughter of a wealthy Philadelphia family, but the wedding was called off, and Coleman died soon after. Democratic papers transformed the story of the broken engagement into a Shakespearean tragedy, complete with an ambitious mother of the bride, separated lovers, mixed messages, and Coleman's ultimate death from heartbreak. Buchanan was not a bachelor "because of indifference to woman," one paper explained, "but really from the highest appreciation of one of the loveliest of the sex." The *Brooklyn Daily Eagle* agreed: "An early and unfortunate attachment was the cause of his celibacy, and none but the prowling hyenas would tear up the grave of buried affections." But the *Eagle* also pushed back against the very notion that a candidate's personal life should factor into a political campaign. "The investigation into the claims of candidates for public office is no longer limited to their public acts and qualifications," the paper complained, "but extends . . . to their own family arrangements." The fascination with candidates' private lives, the paper clucked, was "disgraceful to a people . . . believing in the good old doctrine that every man's house is his castle."[22] If voters supported men's control over their households, they could not question a man's choice to remain single—even if that man was running for president. As hypocritical as any political operatives, Democrats had made Frémont's marriage a political issue, then protested when Republicans did likewise to Buchanan.

Still other Democrats sought to cast Buchanan as a responsible patriarch by demonstrating that he had provided for his community and protected his friends. The *Richmond Enquirer* reported that Buchanan had given $4,000 to create a trust for the "relief of poor and indigent females in the city of Lancaster," Buchanan's hometown in Pennsylvania. Buchanan's generosity toward the impoverished women, the paper assured readers, was "only one of the many evidences of Mr. Buchanan's judicious and warmhearted generosity." A Democratic campaign pamphlet repeated this story, adding that the interest on Buchanan's donation continued to fund the purchase of fuel for the women's homes. The same pamphlet also recalled how in 1828, on the floor of the House of Representatives,

Buchanan defended John Quincy Adams's wife against disrespectful insinuations made by another congressman. "I believe that the person to whom he has alluded is not only a lady by courtesy, but a lady by nature and education. I shall not credit one word derogatory to her reputation. The man who attempts to destroy the character of a woman, destroys his own," Buchanan scolded.[23] Buchanan had no wife or children, so Democrats told readers these stories to assure them that he was indeed a model patriarch, whose steady but firm guidance would hold the Union together.

In Democrats' eyes, the Frémonts' marriage embodied the irrational, destructive nature of the Republican Party as a whole. Jessie's independence made her seem masculine, while John's appearance and his inability to control his wife or support his mother made him seem weak and feminine. Even by themselves, these traits worried Democrats, who could not imagine that a man who exercised so little control over his wife would be strong enough to lead the country. But the Frémonts' relationship also seemed to confirm Democrats' fears about the increase in women's rights activism over the previous decade. Apparently, voters were prepared to elect a man who treated his wife as his equal. Moreover, Democrats worried that Frémont's unconventional marriage was a harbinger of a creeping social disorder that would breed political instability.

The Danger of Women's Rights

On July 19 and 20, 1848, about 300 people attended a convention in a small town in New York State, roughly thirty miles south of Lake Ontario. Modeled on the Declaration of Independence, the Declaration of Sentiments that the convention produced declared "that all men and women are created equal," listed the "repeated injuries and usurpations on the part of man toward woman," and insisted that women "have immediate admission to all the rights and privileges which belong to them as citizens of these United States." The Seneca Falls Convention was not the beginning of the women's rights movement in the United States: women including Sarah and Angelina Grimké, Margaret Fuller, and Lucretia Mott had demanded equal rights from within and outside the abolitionist movement.[24] Yet the convention gathered that momentum, inspiring a similar meeting in Rochester a few weeks later and annual, national women's rights conventions beginning in Worcester, Massachusetts, in 1850.

Broadly, the movement called for women's political, legal, and social equality with men. Activists articulated what Nancy Isenberg has described as "ingenious arguments for women's full entitlement as citizens." Women demanded property rights, educational opportunities, the rights of citizenship, and equality under the law. They also exposed the oppressions of nineteenth-century family life, fighting to reform marriage so that it would recognize women's "mutual consideration and equal interest" in the relationship.[25] These women battled for space in public life despite their formal legal exclusion from it.

Though their conventions received significant attention, women's rights activists made almost no serious progress in achieving their goals over the ensuing decade, and they and their movement remained intensely unpopular with the general population. Indeed, women's rights seemed so extreme that even abolitionists—themselves a progressive fringe group—split over whether to welcome women into leadership roles within their movement. Nonetheless, in 1856, Democrats took up condemning the women's rights movement as a campaign tactic, portraying this movement as a growing force and a threat to patriarchy that would be emboldened and empowered by a Republican victory.

Sometimes, Democratic journals decided that merely describing the activists' demands would frighten their readers. The *Richmond Enquirer* wrote that "women deem the throwing off the restraints of modesty and marriage, a '*sine qua non.*'" In their radical social circles, the "women wear masculine attire, preach infidel sermons, abuse the constitution and the marriage tie, and yet do not lose caste in society." In another article, the *Enquirer* incriminated the women's husbands, as well, implying that their failure to provide for their wives had led the women to seek independence. "No wonder the women are rebelling," the *Enquirer* sneered. "It is shameful and disgraceful to leave wives and children unprotected."[26] Woman's rights activists did hope to liberalize divorce laws and expand opportunities for women beyond the home. But Democrats found even these modest demands deeply troubling. Changes in divorce laws would undermine men's power at home, while increasing women's participation in religious and political life would challenge men's power over the public sphere. By describing and exaggerating the women's demands, the *Enquirer* fanned the flames of these fears.

More frequently, Democratic papers claimed that the Republican Party secretly supported women's rights. This was a gross mischaracterization of the Republican Party, which, for the most part, opposed the movement. In 1856, Republican Samuel A. Foot served as chairman of the New York Assembly's Judiciary Committee. From that post, Foot ridiculed women's rights activists and blocked all attempts at reform. Throughout the late winter and early spring of 1856, women's rights committees had been sending suffrage petitions to the New York Assembly. The House referred the petitions to the Judiciary Committee. They languished there until mid-March, when Foot finally addressed the matter—though not in the manner women's rights activists would have hoped. Foot joked that on women's rights, the single men on the committee had deferred to the married men, since those men had more "knowledge and experience" on the subject. According to Foot, women's gender granted them special privileges: "Ladies always have the best piece and choicest titbit at table. They have the best seat in the cars, carriages, and sleighs; the warmest place in winter and the coolest place in summer." Men, not women, were the benighted party. "If there is any inequality and oppression in the case, the gentlemen are the sufferers," Foot quipped. He ended his report by lampooning men who signed the women's petitions. "The Committee have concluded to recommend no measure except [those] . . . several instances in which husband and wife have both signed the same petition. In such case, they would recommend the parties . . . change dresses so that the husband may wear the petticoats and the wife the breeches, and thus indicate . . . the true relation in which they stand with each other."

A Republican newspaper in Illinois reported that Foot's report was "so humorous, that the House was kept in a roar of laughter while it was being read."[27] Not content to simply table the petitions, the Republican Foot ridiculed the notion of women's rights and emasculated the men who supported the movement. Was this really the party of women's rights?

Republican newspaper editors joined Republican politicians in mocking the women's rights movement. In June, the *Carlisle Weekly* published a fictional story about a women's rights activist who travels to an imaginary land in which men and women enjoy equal rights. The woman is first surprised, then disappointed, then upset, and finally disgusted by the disordered society gender equality has created. When the activist's ship arrives in Utopia, she finds that the "decks were crowded with a motley crew of porters and . . . portresses—women! Struggling, quarreling, cursing, and trampling." She thinks to herself, "Woman, angelic woman, stooping to a life like this: surely, surely, these are the Pariahs." But from there, Utopia only gets worse. No man on the horse-drawn bus to the hotel gives up his seat for her; when a bump in the road pitches her onto a man's lap, the man cursed and reminded her that "ladies are our *equals* in Utopia, and must take care of themselves." Upon arrival at the hotel, she witnesses a political argument between a man and a woman that escalates into fisticuffs. Hoping to escape the chaos, the activist goes to visit a friend but finds the woman's home "betokened" with signs of "indolence and neglect," and her friend quarrelling over household chores with her husband. It was the final straw: the activist resolves to leave Utopia. The experience "ended my bright visions of woman's rights," the activist reports. "By the returning steamer, I resolved to . . . [be] content to live and die where woman's sphere is the fireside and the domestic circle." This story would have been perfectly at home in a Democratic newspaper. And like their Democratic counterparts, Republican editors never failed to rebuke the real women's rights activists in their midst. A typical article praised "the moral" of a recent anti–women's rights lecture—but warned against describing women as exercising a powerful moral influence over men, since "that is the doctrine of Mrs. Stone Blackwell and all the host of the advocates of Woman's Rights."[28] To these Republicans, even domestic feminism—the notion that women should wield a certain amount of control over the home—represented a threat to patriarchal control of households.

Other Republican editors adopted a benevolently sexist stance toward the movement.[29] One Republican newspaper in Ohio published a letter justifying opposition to women's rights by claiming that women were not intellectually inferior to men—they simply had different intellectual strengths. The letter explained that "woman is man's moral superior, and man is woman's intellectual superior"—and therefore neither had the better character overall. These supposed differences, however, left men better suited to rule. "Had woman's intellect been equal to man's from the first, she never would have been subjugated by him," the paper concluded.[30] Modern readers see through this post hoc fallacy. But in its time, this was a moderate take on women's rights. These Republican men would happily grant women power over the home, so long as men retained exclusive control over government and business.

Only a few Republicans truly supported the women's rights movement. In late November 1856, about a thousand activists met at the Broadway Tabernacle in New York City. Whereas all Democratic and most Republican papers typically included snide commentary alongside their reports on women's rights meetings, the *New York Tribune* gave the activists a fair hearing, reporting on the proceedings in three densely packed columns. The report reflected the views of the *Tribune*'s famous editor, Horace Greeley, a founder of the Republican Party, who by 1856 had come to support women's economic empowerment, even as he remained lukewarm on women's suffrage. And in one singular case, a Republican-controlled legislature even came close to enfranchising women. Following a talk by women's rights activist Amelia Bloomer, Nebraska's territorial legislature considered a bill that would "give women, or in other words, all white persons . . . a right to vote." The bill made it out of committee, passed the lower house by a vote of fourteen to eleven, and was sent to the upper house, which did not have enough time to consider the bill before the legislative session ended. A newspaper reported, however, that the "Council contained a majority in [the bill's] favor, and could it have been brought to a vote, would have passed that body also." As Michael Pierson has explained, some men voted Republican because it identified them as a "champion of female morality, male restraint, and sentimental marriage while stating [their] opposition to tyrannical marriages in the North and patriarchal abuses in the plantation South."[31] The Republican gender vision dovetailed with the party's antislavery ethos. Slavery hurt Black and white marriages: enslaved men and women could not marry legally, and when a white slaveholder raped an enslaved woman, he violated the sanctity of her union and of his own. Slavery also prevented enslaved women from exercising full control over their homes, instead forcing them to work alongside men.

Republicans' ambivalence about women's rights is thrown into relief by abolitionists' genuine support for the movement. Many abolitionists backed the women's rights movement, and many women's rights activists championed abolition. Both groups fought against institutions that were fundamentally illiberal and unequal. Woman's rights advocates reasoned that both wives and slaves lacked the right to self-ownership of their labor and their bodies. Southern slaves did not profit from their work; wives could not keep any of their earnings. A southern slave had to fend off her master's sexual assaults; a wife's consent to marriage forced her to consent to her husband's sexual advances.[32] Abolitionists, meanwhile, had long felt particular sympathy for Black women in the South, who were bound in slavery based on their race and subjected to reproductive labor and rape due to their gender. And they appreciated that both women's rights and the abolition of slavery would provide greater freedom to more people.

Among abolitionists, Frederick Douglass endorsed the women's rights movement from the start. In 1848, following the Seneca Falls Convention, Douglass published a supportive editorial in his newspaper, the *North Star*. "Standing as we do upon the watch-tower of human freedom," he wrote, "we cannot be deterred from an expression of our approbation of any movement, however humble, to improve and elevate the character of any members of the human family." He continued, "In respect to political rights, we hold woman to be justly entitled to all that we claim for man . . . and express the conviction that all political rights that it is expedient for man to exercise, it is equally so for woman." In 1851, Sojourner Truth gave her famous "Ain't I a Woman" speech at a women's rights convention in Ohio; she authorized the *Anti-slavery Bugle* to print it in full.

The prominent abolitionist newspaper the *National Era* also supported women's rights, publishing in the fall of 1856 a long article analogizing husbands to jail-keepers. "This, then, is marriage," the article concluded. "On the one side a gaoler, on the other a prisoner for life, a legal nonentity, classed with infants and idiots. . . . Neither property nor legal recognition, neither liberty nor protection has she—nothing but a man's fickle fancy, and a man's frail mercy, between her and misery." Abolitionist support for women's rights was never unanimous. Leading abolitionist Arthur Tappan resigned from the American Anti-slavery Society over the issue, and Marius Robinson, editor of the *Anti-slavery Bugle*, penned an anti–women's rights editorial only five years after printing Truth's speech.[33] But on the whole, more abolitionists supported women's rights more enthusiastically than did rank-and-file Republicans, most of whom barely tolerated the movement.

In typical campaign hyperbole, Democrats told voters that the entire Republican Party was under the sway of the women's rights movement. After printing the demands that a women's rights convention made on the Republican Party, a Democratic newspaper in Ohio mockingly asked "how [Republicans] can resist the demands of these 'strong-minded women.'" The women had called for the Republican Party to support their cause. From there, the Democratic paper leapt to the conclusion that Republicans had incorporated the activists' "ridiculous . . . nonsense and fanaticism" into their "creed."[34] Never mind that the paper did not prove that the Republicans reciprocated women's rights activists' support. The mere association was powerful enough to damn the whole Republican Party in the eyes of Democrats.

Democrats even peddled the false claim that John Frémont himself supported the women's rights movement. The *Brooklyn Daily Eagle* reported that attendees at a Frémont meeting in New Hampshire had hung John and Jessie banners, including one that said "Jessie for the White House." "It is evident," the paper intoned, "that our opponent fully sympathises [*sic*] with the women's rights movement." This intentionally misconstrues the banners' meaning: these Republican supporters were simply adapting the "give 'em Jessie" refrain that had circulated since the start of the campaign. Similarly, the *Richmond Enquirer* warned readers that "Frémont is run . . . as the anti-marriage and anti-female virtue candidate." The North was already "a vast magazine of explosive vices and corruptions," another *Enquirer* article reported. If Frémont won the election and women's rights were imposed on conservative men, the ensuing divorces would threaten the very "fabric of [the] Union."[35] Northern and southern Democrats alike worried about the advance of the women's rights movement, and not just because of its potential to liberate women. An advance in women's rights would undermine men's control over their households—whether that be over their wives in the North or over their enslaved laborers in the South. By fabricating the notion that Frémont supported women's rights, Democratic papers fanned the flames of these fears and encouraged conservative men to vote the Democratic ticket.

While damning all Republicans as women's rights supporters, Democrats portrayed their party as the defender of an idealized, domestic femininity—the opposite of the "pantalooned Amazon[s]" who supported women's rights. Northern and southern Democratic newspapers alike glorified this vision of womanhood during the 1856 campaign. One fictional story published in the *Brooklyn Daily Eagle* in the fall of 1856 traced the vicissitudes of a couple's married life, from the first night home after their honeymoon, to the loss of their first-born son, to the marriage of their children. Though the marriage was marked by "agony" as much as "intense joy," the wife found fulfillment in the "duties of married life."[36] Unlike women's rights activists, this woman would not run out on her family or demand equality with her husband. Conservative readers would have felt satisfied that the woman had guaranteed the happiness of her family and, in turn, the social stability of her community.

Democratic newspapers in the South also praised women who were domestic and unassuming. An obituary eulogized a Richmond-area woman as a loving wife and excellent homemaker. "She was . . . the cherished wife, the devoted mother," the obituary read. "Her rural home was remarkable for the most unbounded, generous, and refined hospitality to the many visitors who thronged it." In her loving relationship with her husband and her precise care for her home, the woman had developed "all the graces which beautify the female character." Similarly, a book review in the same paper praised a female author as a "beautiful specimen of that modest, shrinking, feminine nature."[37]

Democrats admonished women's rights activists for their involvement in public life. But Democrats themselves had embraced women's political participation, within certain limits. Party newspapers published paeans to the women who appeared at Democratic campaign rallies. At one meeting in Providence, Rhode Island, "The young ladies on the platform sung the Star-spangled Banner, and Miss Shea, a beautiful young lady, sung a good song to the tune of 'Wait for the Wagon.'" The *Boston Post* article continued to describe a parade that followed the meeting: "The procession was a large and fine one, consisting in part of . . . thirty-one oxen drawing a car containing 300 ladies!" Unlike Jessie Frémont or the women's rights activists, these women did not speak in public. In an era when public speech was a distinctly masculine prerogative, this represented an important distinction that preserved the women's femininity. But they did sing, and by participating in the event, they indicated their enthusiastic support for the Democratic Party. It seems, then, that despite their praise for women's "shrinking" nature, Democrats embraced women's public activism, as long as that activism supported the Democratic Party.[38]

The Threat of Free Love

In addition to John and Jessie Frémont and the women's rights movement, Democrats also targeted free love activists during the election of 1856. At its most basic level, the free love movement held that adults should be free to end a marriage or other sexual relationship when they no longer felt affection for their partner. Members of utopian communities that practiced free love, such as the Oneida Community in upstate New York, subscribed to the even more radical notion that any adult should be free to have sex with any other consenting adult, without possessiveness or exclusivity. Members of these communities raised the resulting children communally. In most parts of America, the movement was unwelcome. But in corners of Ohio and New York where reform movements had already gained a toehold, lecturers were able to convert some families, and adherents spread word of their doctrine through polemic tracts and periodicals.[39]

The idea that people could enter and leave sexual relationships when they chose struck Democrats as a radical assertion of women's independence and a direct challenge to patriarchy—especially since women owed their husbands access to their bodies. And collective child-rearing threatened the family as the fundamental unit of society.[40] Free love also represented an implicit threat to slavery. Slaveholders had long argued that slavery was a familial institution. But if men lost control of their wives and children, they also stood to lose control over their enslaved workers.

As they did with their descriptions of the women's rights movement, Democratic papers affirmed their readers' prejudice against free love by describing its supporters as unattractive and its demands as utterly radical. According to Cincinnati's *Daily Enquirer*, the men at "free-love meetings" in New York were "nasty, blear-eyed, sallow-faced, long-haired things" who "h[u]ng round the skirts of" "loose," "strong-minded women." The men and women alike were "lewd and dissolute."[41] Democrats used this description of gender-bending activists—of weak men and strong women—to discredit the free love movement as a whole.

Democratic papers also criticized the doctrines that the activists espoused. According to the *Richmond Enquirer*, free love would "cut clear asunder every social, domestic, and religious tie that binds man to man, and keeps society together; to banish religion, law, order, female virtue, parental authority, and separate property, and to inaugurate no-government, the unrestricted 'sovereignty of the individual' and the unbridled gratification of every passion."[42]

Free love activists did not wish to abolish religion, law, and order; they did not want to establish an anarchy. They simply rejected marriage and the family unit that came with it. But by challenging white men's absolute control over their wives and children, they implicitly questioned the white man's command over every other aspect of family life, from his right to control his family's labor to his right to own slaves. In so doing, they also challenged the system of white women's dependence—and, in the South, enslaved people's subordination—that undergirded white men's free and independent political status.

As they did with the women's rights movement, Democratic newspapers linked the free love movement to the Republican Party, falsely equating free love activists' support for the Republican Party with the Republican Party's supposed support for free love. The *Brooklyn Daily Eagle* reported that "Mrs. Nichols, a prominent advocate of free love and a member of the free love clubs of New York, has taken the stump for Frémont." Frémont did not support free love, but Nichols's support was sufficient to condemn him in the eyes of conservative northern voters. Indeed, these claims must have resonated with readers, because the paper received a letter to the editor from a Democrat incensed by Republican plans to undermine civil society by giving Americans too much of all kinds of freedoms, including "free love and a large number of other freedoms of appetite and action too numerous and unsuitable to mention."[43] This New York Democrat did not separate free love from any of the other freedoms Republicans called for: all were radical Republican policies that sought to undermine social order.

In another example of this tactic, Democratic cartoonist and lithographer Louis Maurer depicted a group of radicals lining up to offer Frémont their support. The group included a temperance advocate, a socialist, a women's rights activist, a Catholic priest, and an advocate of free love. Maurer portrayed the free love activist as an old woman, with a long, hooked nose, pointy chin, spectacles, and poorly made, narrow hoops holding up her skirt—not the nineteenth century's image of feminine beauty. She asks Frémont to join the "next meeting of our Free Love association, where the shackles of marriage are not tolerated & perfect freedom exist[s]

"The Great Republican Reform Party," 1856.
Library of Congress, Prints and Photographs Division, LC-DIG-pga-04866.

in love matters." "You will, be sure to Enjoy yourself," she continues, "for we are all Freemounters."[44] The bawdy pun made a serious point: Republicans and their supporters were not committed to sexual monogamy. To Democratic editors and readers alike, it apparently did not matter that there was no evidence that Frémont or any Republican on the ticket supported the free love movement. The mere association of the two was enough to damn the Republican Party in the eyes of any Democrat who wished to preserve men's control over their households and the political order that patriarchy sustained.

Democrats in the South overstated the relationship between the Free Love movement and the Republican Party, as well. The *Richmond Enquirer* scoffed that Frémont's "bad morals" made him "the appropriate leader of a party that . . . from Oneida . . . to the free-love saloons of New York and Boston, makes open war on female virtue and filial obedience." A similar article in the same paper accused the Republican Party of "making open war" on "morality and religion" and "attempting to inaugurate in their stead anarchy, agrarianism, infidelity, and licentiousness." The paper even warned that the South would secede to protect its moral purity from Republican influence if Frémont were elected—not an uncommon threat among Democrats during the election of 1856. While the ensuing war would be terrible, the editorial read, "licentiousness, and agrarianism, and infidelity, and anarchy, are far worse."[45]

Drawing a contrast between themselves and their Republican opponents, Democrats pitched their party as the protector of women's Christian morality—and, implicitly, of monogamy. Democratic newspapers published poetry and anecdotes that emphasized women's religious virtue. The author of one poem in the *Richmond Enquirer* dedicated his work to a certain Annie, of Charleston, South Carolina. The poet extolled the girl's "soul," which "searches for higher, better things" and encouraged her to develop her natural religious inclination by following the "One who lived for thee." Another poet fixated his recently departed beloved's moral purity. "Her body was the Temple bright, In which her soul dwelt full of light," he remembered. But because she had been so virtuous, he was sure that she "looks down on me from Heaven above."[46] These poems seem unrelated to the partisan fare that filled Democratic papers like the *Enquirer*. But the editorial decision to publish these poems tells us that Democratic newspapermen knew this vision of women's religiosity appealed to their readers' beliefs about women's social role. President Franklin Pierce affirmed this view at an October 1856 political event. "We all know," he declared, "no man who listened to his wife ever went astray, and no young brother ever gave a listening ear to his sister . . . without being the better for it." Indeed, "there is no good man who does not feel his heart made stronger through [women's] influence."[47]

This collection of poems and compliments helps us understand the prescriptive ideal of Democratic womanhood. Unlike women's rights activists, who used their morality to justify their intrusion into the public sphere, Democratic women were content to restrict their influence to their homes and their families. Democratic men embraced women's positive influence on the home because it did not fundamentally threaten men's control: wives could set a moral example, but husbands retained all the real power. Compared to Republican women, who supposedly demanded women's rights and free love, and Republican men, who purportedly supported the women's demands, Democratic women were religious and submissive, and Democratic men embraced their role as patriarchs. This vision of family life appealed to northern and southern white men who wished to maintain control over their families and preserve their vaunted political independence.

The Menace of Abolitionism

Most powerfully, Democrats linked arguments about gender roles and morality to the central issue of the campaign: slavery. Since the 1830s, women had supported abolition in ever more public and political ways. In 1837, sisters Sarah and Angelina Grimké set out on a speaking tour of New England, determined to convince listeners that antislavery activism was a Christian duty and a moral imperative. In 1838, a group of female abolitionists assembled at a national convention at Pennsylvania Hall in Philadelphia. In 1839, the abolitionist William Lloyd Garrison appointed Abby Kelley to a leadership role in the American Anti-slavery Society. In 1848, Jane Grey Swisshelm began publishing an abolitionist newspaper, the *Pittsburgh Saturday Visiter*. In 1851, Harriet Beecher Stowe's *Uncle Tom's Cabin* began its serialization in the *National Era*, an abolitionist newspaper. Beginning in 1854, these antislavery women found a home in the Republican Party, focusing particular attention on the sexual abuse of enslaved women.

Each move by these brave women wrought an unequal and opposite reaction by southerners and antiabolitionist northerners, who were horrified by the women's involvement in politics and their public speechmaking. Massachusetts clergymen issued a letter and delivered a series of sermons condemning the Grimké sisters' public activism. An antiabolitionist mob burned down Pennsylvania Hall to intimidate the abolitionist women who had spoken there. Lewis Tappan and his followers left the American Anti-slavery Society to protest women's increasing role in that organization. And southern critics disparaged Stowe for inserting herself into public life as much as for her antislavery message.[48]

In 1856, Democrats leveraged the existing connection between women activists and the abolitionist movement to forewarn voters about the gender and racial threat posed by the Republican Party. Democrats decried abolitionism as both the cause and the most horrifying example of Republicans' gender radicalism. This accusation required Democrats to claim that all Republicans were abolitionists—even though abolitionists were few in number compared to the Republicans, and the relationship between the two groups was highly ambivalent. Once they had established that point, Democrats argued that Republicans' gender radicalism could not be separated from their determination to abolish slavery: Republican radicalism, whether in support of women's rights, free love, or abolition, grew out of an excessive desire for individual freedom.[49]

Democrats frequently castigated abolitionists themselves as gender-bending radicals. The *Brooklyn Daily Eagle* called abolitionists sacrilegious "[n—] worshippers," lambasting them as "men who ought to be women, and women who ought to be men." The *Washington Union* informed readers that Harriet Beecher Stowe's husband, Calvin Ellis Stowe, "is simply known now as the 'husband of Mrs. Beecher Stowe'"—a title that called out her mannishness and his emasculation. The *Southern Banner*, the Democratic newspaper in Athens, Georgia, raised the specters of interracial sex and independent women in its report on an antislavery meeting in Chicago. Free Black people attended the meeting alongside socially prominent whites, and white men attended with their "wives and daughters." Worse, "fair white maidens" at the event cheered the blurring of "the distinction between the white and black races."[50] Stories that described mixed-race, mixed-sex meetings emphasized the radical nature of abolitionism. According to Democrats, abolitionists wanted freedom for slaves, freedom for women to participate in politics, and the freedom for white women to marry Black men. The stories also worked to discredit abolitionism among the newspapers' readers. Abolitionists were not respectable men and women—fellow countrymen—who simply supported a movement to free slaves. Rather, they appear in these newspaper articles as radical and dangerous—almost foreign. Democrats could not trust them or the party they supported.

In contrast, Democrats praised their own female partisans as supporters of patriarchy and white supremacy. The *Richmond Enquirer* proudly reported that fifty-four women, dressed in pure white, attended a Democratic rally in Concord, Ohio. The women carried small white flags emblazoned with "BUCHANAN and BRECKINRIDGE," and the wagon they arrived in was hung with a pink canvass on which was printed the motto "WHITE HUSBANDS OR NONE." "That is the way to say it," the reporter editorialized. The rebuke against "the present disgusting attempts to elevate the negro to . . . equality" was "well-timed" and likely to put the "wild fanatics" in their place. The event apparently made an impression on Democratic editors, who reprinted the story in their papers in North Carolina, Pennsylvania, Massachusetts, and Washington, D.C.[51] Democrats' praise for this incident reveals how they understood women's role in sustaining white supremacy. The law could attempt to uphold racial purity and social boundaries by forbidding interracial marriage. But the case of Massachusetts, which had repealed its antimiscegenation law in

1843, reminded Democrats that those laws required the people's continued support. If white women had sex with Black men, cracks would form in the foundation of white supremacy. Property could pass from white women to mixed-race children. And white men would lose their exclusive sexual access to white women. Democratic papers praised the women of Concord because the women supported the racial hierarchy that Democratic voters wished to uphold.

Democrats also argued that abolitionism represented Republicans' broader tendency toward radicalism. According to Democrats, Republicans wanted to free everybody and everything—from slaves to women to land to religion—from legal restraints and social norms. One article in Richmond charged Republicans with "crush[ing] one species of property"—slaves—"and in the very abuse of freedom cry[ing] out for everything to be free—love, marriage, lands, houses, possessions in every form." Republicans' supposed support for abolition represented just one more symptom of a disease that had spread throughout the party: the desire for individual freedom at the expense of society's conservative, stabilizing institutions. The *Charleston Mercury* expanded on this logic for its readers. "An extremist would assert that women and minors are enslaved because they are excluded from the ballot box," the paper editorialized. "But who but a radical or madman would change this state of things for a mere abstraction?" That "abstraction"—the belief in human freedom and equality—also led Republicans to support abolition. "Again, in theory, the abstract idea of equal rights has been run into Abolitionism." "In short," the *Mercury* concluded, "all the radicalism which clogs the civilization of our day, is but the derivative of acknowledged rights, urged to an extreme."[52]

In another case, the *Richmond Enquirer* warned its readers that Republicans would assail everything "valuable, moral, or sacred" in the South's "domestic institutions" with their "multitudinous isms." According to the paper, a vote for Frémont was a vote for "an infidel and licentious world . . . a Free Love World." This editorial testifies to the deep connection between slavery and marriage in the South. White southerners believed that both were familial institutions and were therefore best regulated—if at all—by local or state governments. But the relationship between slavery and marriage also made southern Democrats nervous: an abolitionist attack on the domestic institution of slavery could quickly lead to a free love attack on the domestic institution of marriage. The *Enquirer* warned that if Frémont won the election, he would use the power of the federal government to abolish both institutions.[53]

Democrats contended that Republicans harbored a desire to free women from marriage and slaves from slavery. A month after the election, the *New York Herald* accused the Republican *New York Tribune* of overzealous support for "justice, freedom, and humanity," which the *Herald* maintained would result in "some such general blow up as a servile war or social war." Despite never having been committed to the cause of free soil, *Herald* editor James Gordon Bennett had endorsed Frémont during the campaign. Now, having "scorched [his] fingers badly when [he] took up the cry of 'Fremont and Freedom,'" as one Democratic paper put it, he had thrown his support back to the conservatives, damning Horace Greeley's *Tribune*—and by connection the Republican Party—as radical rabble-rousers whose program would bring "servile war" upon the South.[54]

In private, Democrats voiced these same concerns about Republican radicalism. In late September, as Election Day approached, Virginia congressman Charles James Faulkner received a letter from a Massachusetts man who despaired that his "County, Congressional District, and State will all go for Frémont I think beyond a hope—Massachusetts is the hotbed of all the Isms of the day[,] and we must look beyond this state for help in this crisis." For years, northern Democrats had forged compromises with their southern counterparts in an effort to hold their party together. In the election of 1852, those compromises had paid off. Democrats ran on a platform that promised to "abide by and adhere to a faithful execution of the acts known as the compromise measures settled by the last Congress—'the act for reclaiming fugitives from service or labor' included."[55] Their unity had allowed them to triumph over the divided Whig Party. More recently, however, northern Democrats' concessions to the southern wing of the party had cost them dearly in the midterms. So, in 1856, Faulkner's correspondent still saw the alliance with southerners as a source of strength—as electoral votes that could prevent Republicans and their "isms" from taking the White House.

Southern Democrats, for their part, presented slavery as a necessary conservative counterpoint to all of the interrelated forms of Republican radicalism. A conservative stance on slavery could safeguard the country against any number of radical doctrines. Like the *Richmond Enquirer*, Democrats argued that free society's radicalisms, including "infidelity . . . anti-marriage doctrines, [and] free-love doctrines," were "express assertions, that free society is neither natural, rightful, or even tolerable." "The absence of these evils in slave society," the article continued, "shows that it is the better system." Another article in the same paper argued that a "united and conservative South"—that is, one that kept its slaves—would be "looked to as an . . . anchor of hope and security" by both "m[e]n of property" and every "Christian of the North."[56] Only the conservative institution of slavery could counterbalance Republican radicalism and save the country from moral ruin. This logic revealed a shade of difference between the northern and southern answers to radicalism. Northern Democrats believed that beating back the Republican Party would defend conservative social norms. Southern Democrats estimated that preserving slavery would have the same effect. At least at the moment, however, electing James Buchanan and instituting popular sovereignty served both northern and southern Democrats' purposes.

By arguing that Republicans wished to dismantle slavery and patriarchy, Democrats mischaracterized Republican thinking on abolition, antislavery, and gender norms. In reality, most Republicans saw free labor not as a challenge to white manhood but rather as an important way of performing white masculinity. Republican newspapers published paeans to farmers and laborers who made their living by the sweat of their brow. One poem, "The Man of Toil," extolled this idealized man. "He is the monarch of the soil / His reign the work of manly toil . . . His people are the loving herd / The ox alone attends his word."[57] In this depiction, the northern farmer was manly because he worked hard and because he was his own master; this, in turn, gave him the right to lead his family—his "loving herd." Inasmuch as it exalted white men's ultimate control over their system of labor and their families, this paradigm was, ironically, quite similar to the southern slaveholding ideal.

But the Republican Party made sure northern voters did not see it that way. Republican papers described the South as a place where slavery had made slaveholders indolent and yeomen submissive. The Republican *Indiana Herald* asked readers to compare the two types of men living in the territories west of the Mississippi. On the one hand was "the honest laborer . . . the young man . . . the mechanics . . . Nature's noblemen . . . wending their way westward, to plant their homes and cultivate the productive lands." On the other hand stood the southern slaveholder. "A tyrant drives before him a gang of weary captives . . . there to toil out their own lives . . . that their oppressors may sit in luxury and indolence." But no matter how hard he worked, the "honest laborer"—the free white man from the North— could not compete with the slaveholding southerner. This forced northern migrants into an impossible position: "The poor white man may either consent to be degraded to the level of the enslaved negro, or submissively retrace his steps to . . . New England."[58] According to free labor ideology, honest farmers could never compete with slave labor in the territories. This would force them to choose between hiring out their labor—a humiliating prospect for free white men, who believed only Black men worked for other people—or admitting failure and moving back to the Northeast.

Representative Bayard Clarke of New York, a member of the antislavery Opposition Party, echoed this view in a letter to the *New York Tribune*. Clarke believed that by pushing to expand slavery westward, southerners had intentionally forced upon northern men an impossible choice: move west and submit to southern men, or surrender any claim to the western territories. Clarke wrote, "The surrender of our Free Territories to the blighting curse of Slavery, thus virtually excluding the free laborer from their broad acres, except upon conditions to which he could not submit without the sacrifice of his entire manhood, is obviously calculated to restrain the immigration of all whose capital consists solely in strong muscles and resolute wills."[59] Clarke thought that northern men would rather remain in the East than be forced to eke out a substandard living alongside wealthy slaveholders.

Though Republican papers played to northern resentment of the slave power, they took umbrage when southern Democratic papers pandered to their readers' anxieties about free society. Republican organs quoted liberally from southern papers that scoffed at northern farmers and laborers. "The South say that the mechanic, the worker, is but a miserable thing, and unfit to [be] the companion of *gentlemen*," explained the *Alton (Illinois) Weekly Telegraph*. By way of example, the *Telegraph* shared a clipping from a Democratic paper in Georgia that exclaimed, "Free society! We sicken of the name. When it is but a conglomeration of greasy mechanics, filthy operatives, small fisted farmers, and moonstruck theorists?" This, the *Telegraph* concluded, "shows what the noble toiler must expect from the Southern aristocracy." Another Republican paper reprinted a quote from the *Herald* of Muscogee, Alabama. "All the Northern and especially the New England States, are devoid of society fitted for well bred gentlemen. The prevailing class one meets is that of mechanics struggling to be genteel, and small farmers who do their own drudgery; and yet who are hardly fit for association with a Southern gentleman's body-servant," the *Herald* sneered.[60] Republican voters believed that providing for their families by picking up a plough or working as a mechanic marked them as real men. Southern Democrats' ridicule for their hard work moved Republicans to self-righteous anger. Who were these slaveholders, who had never done an honest day's work, to insult them?

Republicans fanned the flames of these fears—of slavery's westward expansion, of slaveholders' money and power, of southern arrogance

and condescension, of the threat to white farmers' and laborers' masculinity—to mobilize voters for the November elections. In a race for
the House seat representing two Illinois counties across the river from
St. Louis, the local Republican paper did not so much encourage men
to vote for the Republican candidate as to vote against the Democratic
one. "[Wright] Casey," the Democratic candidate, "was a member of that
infamous Cincinnati Convention, which declared that slavery should
go everywhere, and that free laborers should be degraded to the level
of slaves," the paper reminded readers. Democrats in Cincinnati had
announced their support for popular sovereignty, not for slavery, and
they certainly had not called for white laborers to be "degraded to the
level of slaves." But a falsehood served the Republican paper better than
the truth. After manufacturing an insult to free white men, the paper
called on those men to go to the polls and "teach [Casey] that free labor
and free men are not to be wantonly degraded by such servile tools of the
slave power."[61] Free white men were jealous of their independence. The
paper weaponized that pride by claiming that Democrats would extend
slavery everywhere, forcing white farmers to humiliate themselves by
competing with slave labor.

Republican papers alleged that Democrats would put northern men
under the boot of southern aristocrats. In an article none-too-subtly titled
"The Buchanan Democracy Hate Freedom," the *Holmes County (Ohio)
Republican* quoted southern Democrats and their newspapers as they
argued for restricting democracy. "The great evil of Northern *free* societies,
is, that it is burdened with a *servile* class of *mechanics* and *laborers, unfit
for self-government,* and yet clothed with the attributes and powers of
citizens," one southern paper had written. The *Republican* then quoted,
out of context, a speech by Senator Andrew Butler of South Carolina.
Butler had said, "Men have no right to vote unless they are possessed of
property . . . no man can vote unless he owns ten negroes, or real estate to
the value of ten thousand dollars."[62] By the end of 1856, almost every state
had eliminated property requirements for the franchise. This represented profound change in American self-government. It also made voting a
mark of white manhood—which, in turn, made whiteness and masculinity
the wellspring of political power. According to the *Republican*, southern
Democrats now seemed to want to reverse that revolution: they would
reinstate property requirements, putting southern aristocrats in charge and
disenfranchising the mechanics and laborers of the North. Just as Democratic papers mischaracterized the Republican position on free soil, so too
did this Republican paper misrepresent southern Democrats' position on

white men's democracy. Democrats would disenfranchise northern men; therefore, northern men should vote Republican.

Republicans also tried to damn northern Democrats by tying them to their most radical southern counterparts. Taking the argument that slavery was a positive good to its logical conclusion, a very few southern Democrats had argued that slavery might benefit the white workers of the North. Republican papers made sure to quote from these arguments liberally. In one instance, the *Buffalo Daily Republic* cited a *Richmond Examiner* article that averred, "Slavery is right, natural, and necessary, and does not depend upon difference of complexion." The *Republic* then pointed to a Buchanan paper in New York City that had proposed "to enslave poor Americans, Germans and Irish who may fall into poverty and be unable to support their families."[63] For years, northern Democrats had walked a political tightrope, holding that the Democratic Party was the only national party while at the same time avowing that they were not beholden to the party's southern wing. So here, Republicans set the most fringe southern proslavery theory—that slavery might benefit poor whites in the South—alongside an exceedingly rare northern Democratic position—that white immigrants should be enslaved—to claim that northern and southern Democrats supported white slavery and opposed white men's independence. This was, of course, not true. In the South, ideologues such as George Fitzhugh supported white slavery as a way of arguing that slavery was correct in principle and in practice; more mainstream thinkers, however, believed that enslaving Black people elevated white southerners. And in the North, Democrats in fact welcomed European immigrants into their party. But Republicans latched onto the extremes to paint all Democrats as so radically proslavery that they would put white men in chains.

Finally, Republican outlets urged men to vote Republican by encouraging them to think of their duty to protect their families. One such article, titled "Voters Remember," warned voters "that if you vote for Buchanan you vote to invite *supercilious Southern nabobs with their slaves* to the Northern States, to insult you and to corrupt your children." In a Republican paper in Vermont, the message was much the same: "Working-man, if you do not wish to see your children compelled to do work at starvation prices; if you do not desire to build up an oligarchy which will bleed you to death . . . you *must vote*."[64] Exhortations like these pulled together many of the fears that Republican papers themselves had whipped up—the degradation of competing with slave labor, the notion that southern aristocrats looked down on northern farmers and workers, the suspicion that the Democratic Party would allow slavery to return to the free states—and made them even more potent by connecting them to men's concern for their children. It would be bad enough for a man to have to endure southerners' condescension; he could not allow his son to do the same.

When considered alongside the Democrats' tactics, the way Republicans appealed to white men's masculinity reveals a deep irony in the gender politics of the election of 1856: Republicans and Democrats actually shared a sense of white manhood that was based on personal independence, political self-determination, and a sense of superiority to Black people. The partisan press, therefore, was not playing to two radically different sets of values. Rather, editors were trying to prove that their party, their candidates, and their platform demonstrated the most respect for white men's independence.

Associating abolitionism with women's rights, free love, and the supposedly radical marriage of John and Jessie Frémont was a cagey tactic for uniting the Democrats against Frémont and former president and American (Know-Nothing) Party candidate Millard Fillmore. In the South, lumping together the "multitudinous isms" allowed Democrats to make a cohesive agenda out of mastery. Republican gender radicalism and Republican race radicalism had to be stopped in order to preserve southern men's mastery over their women and their slaves. In the overwhelmingly white North, abolitionism did not threaten white men's status in the same way it did in the South. Women's rights and free love did threaten northern men's power, though, and so depicting abolitionism as part and parcel of those two "isms" helped northern men understand abolition as a threat even if they lived in a free state. It also helped northern conservatives see Republicans as a radical party, thus continuing the long trend of decrying one's political enemies as disunionists. In short, radicalism was radicalism, no matter what conservative institution it threatened; and the unsexing of women threatened the identities of northern and southern men alike. Only a united, conservative Democratic Party could thwart Republicans' attempts to divide the country with their radical beliefs on gender and slavery.

On November 4, 1856, James Buchanan defeated John C. Frémont handily, taking nineteen states to Frémont's eleven. The threat of John and Jessie Frémont occupying the White House, of the onward march of women's rights, of free love, and of abolitionism, and of disunion—all seemed halted by Buchanan's election. The *Democratic Review* predicted that "every scheme of disunion will soon perish from amongst us, and the old sentiment of fraternal amity be reestablished." Democrats felt sure that

Buchanan, an almost clinically cautious man, would pursue a conservative course, and that he would favor neither northern nor southern interests during his time in the White House. A New York Democrat composed a song rejoicing that Buchanan would "never betray / Yankee hearts or their rights / then for Jemmie hurrah!"[65]

Voters had not only chosen Buchanan—they had chosen popular sovereignty. This fact contributed to Democrats' ebullient faith in their country's future. When Stephen Douglas orchestrated the passage of the Kansas-Nebraska Act, he created a firestorm of controversy among free soilers who believed the Missouri Compromise could not or should not be repealed. Buchanan's election on a popular sovereignty platform, however, seemed to show that a silent majority of centrist voters supported the Kansas-Nebraska Act. From where Democrats stood in November 1856, it seemed like an incredible victory: they had organized the western lands for a railroad and forever settled the vexing question of slavery in the territories, and the voters had approved.

It is easy to see why popular sovereignty won voters' support. In principle, it sounded wonderful. Let the voters decide! What could be more American, more democratic, or more practical than that? Yet even in late 1856, worrying news traveled eastward from Kansas about violence between pro- and antislavery settlers there. But Democrats remained certain that popular sovereignty would prevail, and that a fair vote on slavery would bring peace and stability to Kansas and to the Union. The next year and a half would prove them wrong.

Domestic Institutions?

UTAH, KANSAS, AND THE
DEMOCRATIC PARTY

In 1856, American newspapers turned their focus to the contest for the White House. Democratic, Republican, and American Party papers all featured the standard partisan fare. "Michigan for Buchanan!" Ohio's *McArthur Democrat* cried. The *Buffalo Morning Express* praised the young men of Buffalo, who had just created a "Young men's Fremont club." The *South-Western* of Shreveport, Louisiana, headed its news section with the declaration, "FOR PRESIDENT MILLARD FILLMORE, of New York." And after James Buchanan claimed victory, the *Baltimore Sun* reported on California's presidential electors casting their votes for Buchanan and his vice president–elect, John C. Breckinridge.[1]

Next to these articles, however, appeared titillating reports on another topic entirely: Mormon polygamy. Alongside its proclamation of support for Buchanan, the *McArthur Democrat* of Logan, Ohio, printed a news item informing readers that a man from Salt Lake City—and his four wives— had just checked into a local hotel. In addition to carrying the news of the young men's Frémont club, the *Buffalo Morning Express* reported at length on the extrajudicial murder of a prominent Mormon man in Michigan. According to the paper, the man's "five wives, or concubines" had "been given by their parents to the will of the Prophet," and thus wished for their husband's death so they might escape from the polygamous marriage. The *South-Western*, which so proudly declared itself for the American Party, printed on the same page rumors about polygamy in Utah. "One bishop married six wives—all sisters, and his own nieces." The paper then attacked the leader of the Latter-Day Saints: "Brigham Young recently built a stone harem for his ninety wives, but they all revolted and wouldn't go into the cage. Ninety women were too much for one man." In the same edition that reported on California's electors casting their votes for Buchanan, the *Baltimore Sun* published a much longer article calculating the precise number of wives held by Utah's prominent politicians. Tallying the husbands and wives in two columns, the paper concluded, "we have the whole number of females . . . amounting to 420; or, in other words, 40 men have 420 wives."[2]

At first glance, the Mormon issue may seem to have been merely a salacious distraction from the real news: a hotly contested presidential election over the Kansas-Nebraska Act and the extension of slavery. And indeed, this is largely how scholars have treated it. Historians of antebellum politics have written almost nothing on the federal politics of Mormon polygamy. Eric Foner's classic work on the Republican Party makes no mention of polygamy or Utah's Mormons in his discussion of the party's formation, nor does Michael Pierson's more recent work on Republicans' gender-cultural identity. These omissions are surprising, since in 1856, the Republican Party placed the Mormon issue front and center in its first national platform. Works on the Democratic Party are similarly silent on Mormonism and politics. And inexplicably, even scholars of Mormon history and Mormon studies make only passing mentions to federal politics in this period—even though that decade featured a war, a famous massacre, and the Republican Party's politicization of Mormon polygamy. The few histories of Mormonism that do spend time on the 1850s focus on explaining how Utah's relationship with the federal government affected the Latter-Day Saints rather than how that relationship played into national politics.[3]

But the two issues—Mormon polygamy in Utah and slavery in Kansas—were, in fact, closely connected. Republicans' 1856 platform proclaimed, "It is both the right and the imperative duty of Congress to prohibit in the Territories those twin relics of barbarism—Polygamy, and Slavery."[4] Republican nominee John C. Frémont and other down-ballot candidates asserted that the Democratic doctrine of popular sovereignty had created chaos and social immorality not only in Kansas, with its "domestic institution" of slavery, but also in Utah, with its "domestic institution" of polygamy.

Frémont lost the election. But by co-opting the southern description of slavery as a "domestic institution," Republicans had made a provocative argument. Northern and southern Democrats alike squirmed as Republicans demanded to know whether the Democratic doctrine of popular sovereignty meant that Democrats supported Mormon polygamy. Since the age of Andrew Jackson, the Democratic creed had emphasized the right of white men to shape the world as they saw fit, with as little intervention from the state as possible. Ideological consistency would demand that Democrats support polygamy, if that was what the men of Utah wanted. But given Americans' repugnance toward polygamy, such a position would be politically toxic. So northern Democrats threaded the needle by claiming that Mormon lawlessness, not Mormon polygamy, justified sending federal troops to Utah. And southern Democrats, who feared that intervention in Utah's "domestic institutions" could later justify the same in Kansas or even in the South, scrambled to find other reasons that the federal government should stay out of the Utah Territory.

The following year, northern Democrats watched in horror as voter intimidation and voting fraud in Kansas threw election after election to the minority proslavery faction in the territory, ultimately resulting in the fraudulent proslavery government in Kansas requesting admission to the Union under the Lecompton Constitution. Southern Democrats were gleeful at the prospect of another slave state, and they won James Buchanan's support for the constitution's approval. But many northern Democrats, following the lead of Stephen Douglas, were determined to defend their beloved principle of popular sovereignty, so they reached for the same weapon Republicans had used in 1856: analogizing slavery to marriage. Douglas marshalled support for "full submission" of Lecompton back to the people of Kansas by appealing to Democrats' deep-rooted belief in white male independence. White men should be allowed to exercise their franchise on every issue—not just slavery.

Benefiting from the Buchanan administration's support, southern Democrats nonetheless won a compromise that sent the proslavery constitution—attached to significant carrots and sticks—back to the voters of Kansas for final approval. But Kansas voters roundly rejected the measure. Southern Democrats were left spinning. They had failed to add another slave state to the Union. But more than that, they felt betrayed. Northern Democrats had sided with the Republicans to sink Lecompton, and they had turned southerners' argument about the familial, local nature of slavery against them. The whole episode revealed that gendered language had failed to resolve the Democrats' profound disagreements over the purpose and practice of popular sovereignty.

"Twin Barbarisms": The Republican Attack on Popular Sovereignty

During the Thirty-Fourth Congress, Republicans held only 37 seats in the House of Representatives, compared to the Democrats' 158. But northern dissatisfaction with the Kansas-Nebraska Act and the Democratic Party had public opinion trending in the right direction for Republicans. In the 1854 midterms, Republicans had picked up 34 seats, mostly in Illinois, Maine, Michigan, and Wisconsin, while Democrats had lost 75. (Profiting from anti-Democratic sentiment, Whigs, Know-Nothings, and an Anti-Nebraska Opposition party together held most of the remaining seats.)

Democrats supported popular sovereignty because it seemed to them a fair and democratic way to denationalize the question of slavery's expansion into the territories. Republicans opposed popular sovereignty because it might expand slavery and because they believed a small vanguard of settlers could not be trusted to represent the whole interest of the United States in the territories. Events in Kansas provided ample evidence for the Republican view. In 1854, the Kansas-Nebraska Act had granted Kansans the right to "regulate their domestic institutions in their own way." Kansas, which the Missouri Compromise had previously mandated become a free state, was now up for grabs. Chaos ensued. Proslavery Missourians quickly moved across state lines to establish homesteads in Kansas. Organizing under the auspices of the New England Emigrant Aid Company, antislavery Northeasterners followed. Midwesterners went, too; though not abolitionists, they dreamed of a free Kansas where they could farm their own land without competition from slaveholders. The competing factions ultimately established their own governments: the technically legitimate proslavery legislature at Lecompton, which had been elected amid violence and voting fraud, and the antislavery shadow legislature at Topeka. Republicans could not support a theory of government that led to the expansion of slavery by illegitimate minority rule.

In 1856, then, Republicans needed to convince voters that a free-soil policy would bring peace and prosperity to the West, and they needed to counter the Democratic position that slavery there should be decided by popular sovereignty. The Kansas-Nebraska Act had expressly mandated that the people of those territories be "perfectly free to form and regulate their domestic institutions in their own way."[5] Pointing out that both slavery and marriage were domestic institutions, Republicans cast doubt on popular sovereignty by arguing that it prevented the federal government from interfering with slavery in Kansas and polygamy in Utah.

In making this argument, Republicans exploited the ambiguity of the terms "domestic relations" and "domestic institutions," which had evolved throughout the nineteenth century. In common law, slavery fell under the umbrella of domestic relations, which also included the relationships between husband and wife and parents and children. So, although enslaved people lacked legal status, the law saw them as part of the master's family. Since 1787, American jurisprudence recognized the power of the states to regulate these domestic relationships. Slavery was a domestic institution inasmuch as it was, legally, a family relationship. But in popular parlance, the frequency of use and meaning of "domestic relations" and "domestic institutions" changed over time, depending on how prominent the slavery issue was in federal politics. In the early nineteenth century, "domestic institutions" was rarely used, and "domestic relations" usually meant relationships among family members or among the states of the new nation.[6]

By the 1830s, abolitionist societies sprang up, and southerners countered by asserting that slavery was a positive good. Accordingly, Americans spoke about the "domestic institution" of slavery more and more, and when they used the term "domestic relations," they most often were talking about slavery. But the term had connotations that "slavery" did not. Americans seem to have used "domestic relations" to emphasize the familial—and therefore inviolable—character of the master-slave relationship. Arguing against interference with slavery in 1835, one paper editorialized, "It is a domestic relation subsisting between the master and the slave, which ought to be viewed as sacred and inviolable as any of the other domestic relations existing in society." Abolitionists had "no more right to interfere with this subject, than they have with the relations subsisting between husband and wife, or between parents and their children."[7]

In the 1850s, slavery's extension became the central question in federal politics—first with the lands won in the Mexican War, then in the Kansas-Nebraska Territory. As a result, the use of "domestic institutions" and "domestic relations" to mean slavery increased. But even then, people continued to use the terms as a proxy for states' rights: the defense of "domestic" control from federal intervention. They also continued to use it to refer to domestic versus foreign policy, family relationships, and so on. The Kansas-Nebraska Act's mandate that the people of those territories be "perfectly free to form and regulate their domestic institutions in their own way," then, appeared in the context of a long and evolving usage of the term "domestic institutions."[8] By the 1850s, most Americans would have understood the term to mean slavery, unless specified otherwise. But the term retained both the familial connotation derived from its earlier usage, as well as wholly different—though significantly less common—denotations.

When Republicans associated slavery in Kansas with polygamy in Utah, they also took advantage of Americans' deep antipathy toward the Church of Jesus Christ of Latter-Day Saints. The Mormon faith originated in the burned-over district of western New York during the Second Great Awakening. Joseph Smith Jr. reported that beginning in 1820, he received a series of visions from God telling him to reestablish the true Christian church. In 1830, Smith published the *Book of Mormon*, a new body of Christian scripture that he professed to have translated from a set of engraved golden plates given to him by the angel Moroni. Claiming status as a prophet, Smith rapidly amassed followers.

The same year that he published the *Book of Mormon*, Smith settled in Kirtland, Ohio. The number of Mormons in the township grew from 100 in 1833 to 2,000 in 1838. Their growing numbers made local non-Mormons nervous. A local non-Mormon press warned that Mormons planned to seize control of the local government; a mob of anti-Mormon Ohioans tarred and feathered Smith; and a separate mob nearly castrated him. Many Mormons fled for Missouri, but they fared no better there. In 1838, after a series of skirmishes between Mormons and the Missouri State Militia, Governor Lilburn Boggs issued a mandate that one scholar has described as "quasi-genocidal." Executive Order 44 declared that Mormons had "made war upon the people of this state" and "must be exterminated or driven from the state if necessary for the public peace."[9] Mormons left Missouri for Illinois, where legislators initially welcomed the influx of taxpaying immigrants. By 1844, Nauvoo's population had reached 15,000—rivaling that of Chicago—and the Mormon militia there, called the Nauvoo Legion, numbered over 5,000.

In Illinois, a new issue stretched tensions to the breaking point: polygamy. In 1844, Smith confided in other members of the Mormon hierarchy that he had received a revelation that all Mormon men would practice plural marriage. Outraged, a group of Mormons exposed Smith's plans in the *Nauvoo Expositor*. Drawing on a device long used in American captivity narratives, the men described Smith's wives as innocents held in sexual slavery. "The harmless, inoffensive, and unsuspecting creatures," the paper warned, "are so devoted to the Prophet, and the cause of Jesus Christ, that they do not dream of the deep-laid and fatal scheme which prostrates happiness . . . that she should be [Smith's] Spiritual wife; for it was right anciently, and God will tolerate it again."[10] In the imbroglio that ensued, Smith declared martial law, the governor jailed Smith for treason, and an anti-Mormon mob murdered Smith and his brother, Hyram. Their prophet dead, and facing the prospect of further violence, the Mormons fled Illinois. Brigham Young, their new leader, sought "a place on this earth that nobody else wants"—and in the Salt Lake Basin, he found it.[11] Far away from their persecutors and supported by a proexpansionist federal government, the Mormons quickly developed the area. Utah became a U.S. territory in 1850.

But even the 1,300 miles between Illinois and Utah could not prevent lurid stories about Mormon polygamy from trickling back east—which East Coast newspapers eagerly published. In a typical article of this genre, the *New York Times* reprinted long portions of a recently released book on the Mormons in Utah. After claiming that Smith's licentiousness had led to the revelation of polygamy—he "gathered around him a gang of female dupes, he gave full sway to his passions; and to justify his caresses, put forth his new revelation on the subject of marriage"—the author detailed the expansion of polygamy in Utah. This included a description of the houses Mormon men supposedly built for their wives. "A man with half a dozen wives builds, if he can, a long, low dwelling, having six entrances from the outside, and when he takes in a new wife . . . adds another apartment. The object is to keep the women and babies . . . apart, and prevent those terrible cat-fights which sometimes occur." The author went on to explain that this rampant polygamy denigrated women and left children alone and neglected. "A *wife*, in Utah, cannot live out half her days," the author informed readers. "In families where polygamy has not been introduced, she suffers an agony of apprehension on the subject" because "the man, from the moment he makes up his mind to bring one or more concubines into the family, becomes always neglectful, and in most cases abusive to his wife." "The children," meanwhile, "[are] subject to a frightful degree of sickness and mortality. This is the combined result of the gross sensuality of the parents, and want of care toward their offspring."[12]

The contemporary proliferation of illustrated periodicals further spread anti-Mormon stereotypes. These magazines were hugely popular: by the late 1850s, the humorous monthly *Yankee Notions* had a circulation of at least 30,000 per issue; by the beginning of the Civil War, the circulation of both *Harper's Weekly* and *Leslie's Illustrated Weekly Newspaper* exceeded 100,000. In April 1852 the *Old Soldier* published an anti-Mormon cartoon titled "Mormon Breastworks and U.S. Troops." The cartoon portrays a line of Mormon women standing up and holding their babies aloft; the first woman in the row has a very large chest. Behind them crouch members of a Mormon militia. Faced with the choice of harming the women or retreating from the field, an American officer calls for retreat, crying, "Cesar [*sic*] himself would be defeated before such Breastworks."[13] By featuring so many women and babies, the cartoon poked fun at polygamy. And by reversing nineteenth-century gender norms—the women are protecting the men, instead of the other way around—it offered a critique of Mormon society in Utah more broadly. Interestingly, having so many wives made Mormon men less masculine, rather than more so.

Novelists also drew readers in with salacious tales of polygamy in Utah. The 1855 anti-Mormon novel *Boadicea the Mormon Wife: Life Scenes in Utah* describes a Mormon girl trapped in a polygamous marriage in Utah.

MORMON BREASTWORKS AND U. S. TROOPS.

Officer U.S.A. {*Trumpeter! Sound the retreat! we never can carry that Battery in the world. Cæsar himself would be defeated before such Breastworks.*}

"*Mormon Breastworks and U.S. Troops,*" 1852. *priAPC 0099,*
American Political Cartoons, Huntington Library, San Marino, California.

The novel's heroine, Boadicea, falls in love with and marries a dashing young Mormon man, Hubert, who promises to be faithful to his new bride. Soon after their marriage, a church leader tries to convince her to become his "spiritual wife." Boadicea refuses, but soon after, Hubert brings home a woman named Cephysia and announces that she will become his second wife. The novel continues thus: a church leader who is infatuated with Boadicea strangles Hubert, Cephysia poisons Boadicea's child before committing suicide, and, in a scene that eerily foreshadows the 1857 Mountain Meadows Massacre, Mormon men dress up like Native Americans and massacre traveling settlers to steal their money. Ultimately, Boadicea escapes from Utah and moves back east. In 1855, Orvilla S. Belisle's *The Prophets; or, Mormonism Unveiled* portrayed a heroine trapped in a Mormon harem. The reading public in the East devoured the anti-Mormon books: Metta Victor's 1856 *Mormon Wives: A Narrative of Facts Stranger Than Fiction* sold more than 40,000 copies in the 1850s. Though entirely fictional, these portrayals nonetheless had a profound effect on American readers. As Bruce Burgett has noted, anti-Mormon novels "translat[ed] political disputes . . . into narratives of domestic bliss and betrayal, thus bringing home to a wider audience the abstractions of legal and state policy by locating the impact of those policies on the largely middle-class sensibilities and bodies of . . . characters and readers."[14] By domesticating a political issue, the novels mobilized reform.

Utah had become a U.S. territory, and its growing population would soon qualify it for statehood. Anti-Mormon fiction raised questions: Could non-Mormons in the East allow polygamy to continue in an American territory? And could they admit to the Union a state whose people practiced polygamy? In the election of 1856, Republicans argued that the federal government maintained "sovereign powers over the Territories of the United States" and must use those powers to ban polygamy in Utah.[15] Given the rising tide of anti-Mormon sentiment, this position alone might have won votes for Republican candidates. But then Republicans connected the issue of polygamy in Utah to the issue of slavery in Kansas: the federal government should prohibit both polygamy and slavery in the territories. In so doing, they co-opted the public's aversion to polygamy to support the party's crusade against slavery's expansion and its vision of a stronger federal government.

Co-opting the language of women's rights activists and abolitionists, Republican politicians analogized slavery to polygamous marriage—not to abolish slavery or reform marriage laws but to condemn popular sovereignty. Republican politicians warned voters that if they accepted men's right to choose slavery in Kansas, they would also have to accept men's right to choose polygamy in Utah. Republican William Seward said as much in a speech before the Senate on April 9, 1856. "Will you . . . end the debate," he asked, "by binding Kansas with chains . . . ? Even then you must give over Utah to slavery, to make it secure and permanent in Kansas; and you must give over Oregon and Washington to both polygamy and slavery, so as to guaranty [*sic*] equally one and the other of those peculiar domestic institutions in Utah." The Kansas-Nebraska Act had abrogated the Missouri Compromise's ban on slavery north of the 36° 30' parallel, instead allowing voters in the territories "to form and regulate their domestic institutions in their own way."[16] By arguing that both slavery and polygamy were domestic institutions—which was to say familial, and therefore beyond the reach of the federal government—Seward asserted that the

Kansas-Nebraska Act allowed settlers to institute slavery in Kansas and polygamy in Utah.

Republican newspapers echoed this argument, repeatedly attempting to discredit the Democrats' popular sovereignty solution for Kansas by claiming it would result in polygamy's codification in Utah. On March 20, 1856, the *Buffalo Daily Republic* reported on the Utah legislature's preparations to apply for admission to the Union. According to the paper, Brigham Young had issued a message asking for Congress to "recognize the principle of self-government." The *Republic* portrayed this as a request for the federal government to apply popular sovereignty to Utah—and therefore to admit Utah under a constitution that allowed polygamy. Indeed, "nothing else can be understood by it," the *Republic* declared, "and it remains to be seen what ingenious 'dodge' will be resorted to by Senator Douglas." The editor knew that the Democrats—and Douglas, their presumptive nominee for that year's presidential election—were in a bind. If they supported the principle of popular sovereignty, how could they deny Mormons the right to make their own laws regarding polygamy? The *Republic* continued, "The utter absurdity of the doctrine of squatter sovereignty was never so fully exemplified as when its operation is attempted to be applied to the 'domestic institutions' of Mormonism." If Democrats believed popular sovereignty was just, then "there can be no reasonable objection to the universal application of its principles," the *Republic* concluded.[17]

A circular published in April by the Republican National Convention hammered home the failure of popular sovereignty. "Mr. Douglas's act for the Territories, which 'leaves the people perfectly free to form and regulate their domestic institutions in their own way . . . ,' certainly authorizes the Mormon State to come into the Union with the Turkish system full blown, which makes slaves of all colors, and wives without number." The circular expressed a common theme in anti-Mormon criticism: Mormons' practice of polygamy was not merely deviant, it was outright alien. God might have allowed polygamy to exist among the ancient Jews, but no modern civilization could condone a practice that Americans associated with Turkey, Africa, and Asia. Antislavery intellectual Francis Lieber submitted the same critique of Mormonism. Statehood for Utah would infuse "a foreign and disturbing element" into the nation, Lieber argued. Mormon polygamy would diminish "one of the elementary distinctions—historical and actual—between European and Asiatic humanity." Republicans saw polygamy as a foreign import, used to hold white women in servitude. Playing up this description of polygamy—as a foreign system used enslave white women—emphasized what Republicans saw as the danger of popular sovereignty: the ability for a small group of men to establish and codify barbaric social practices in the United States. The circular from the Republican National Convention concluded that if popular sovereignty continued as the law of the land, "we should have Negro Slavery forced on one Territory by a usurpation set up by the sword, and the right of the Mormons recognized in another to hold a multitude of the gentler sex in servitude."[18]

Abolitionists of course shared Republicans' antipathy to slavery in Kansas. Like many Americans, abolitionists had regarded the Missouri Compromise as sacrosanct and its abrogation as a breach of trust. Moreover, no slave states had joined the Union since the admission of Texas in 1845. If Kansas entered as a slave state, it would put the nail in the coffin of the Missouri Compromise and represent a step backward in abolitionists' struggle to end slavery. As a result, abolitionist publications encouraged their readers to vote the Republican ticket in 1856, employing the same analogy between slavery and polygamy that Republicans used. On February 2, in response to a Democrat's speech in favor of popular sovereignty, the *Anti-slavery Bugle* retorted, "If [the people] may establish Slavery, may they not also establish Polygamy, or any other Wrong?" Even after the election, the *National Era* continued to attack popular sovereignty by linking it to the growth of polygamy in Utah, asking, "If a handful of settlers in a large territory have the right to determine their domestic institutions . . . by what power, in what way, can these Utah settlers be reached?" The response? They could not be: popular sovereignty prevented the federal government from exercising power over the Mormons' domestic institutions. "Squatter sovereignty, being supreme . . . may establish the abomination," the newspaper finished.[19] The Western Anti-slavery Society published the *Anti-slavery Bugle*; abolitionist Benjamin Smith Jones and his wife, Jane Elizabeth Jones, herself a protégée of reformer Abby Kelley Foster, edited the paper. Founded by Arthur and Lewis Tappan, the *National Era* was the voice of the American and Foreign Antislavery Society; Gamaliel Bailey served as its editor. These abolitionist editors shared little, politically, with mainstream Republicans. Yet they realized that their readers, like Republicans, uniformly abhorred Mormon polygamy. Abolitionist editors mobilized that revulsion to foment opposition to popular sovereignty and the Democratic Party.

Republicans drew on the work of popular writers and cartoonists to protest the incursion of Mormon polygamy into Utah and slavery into Kansas. Anti-Mormon fiction, in particular, featured storylines that centered on sexual violence against white, Protestant women. In Maria Ward's

Female Life among the Mormons: A Narrative of Many Years' Personal Experience, by the Wife of a Mormon Elder, Recently from Utah, the narrator marries a Mormon man, though she does not convert to the religion. When the couple moves to Utah, the narrator is horrified by the violence and licentiousness of the Mormon men there. One woman shows the narrator "her arms and bosom black with hideous bruises," describing them as "the marks of beatings that [my husband] has given me." The narrator even describes an attempted assault by a Mormon dignitary. Upon visiting the man's home, the narrator found "his whole countenance glowed with the fervor of an August noon"—an indication of sexual excitement—and then "he attempted to kiss me." Of course, she "shrank from his touch, as from the sting of a serpent." Even after she rejected his initial advance, the man informed her, "My charmer, your home is henceforth with me"; when she spurned that demand, "his countenance grew dark with suppressed passion."[20] This storyline made use of an established device in American reform literature: rape. Writers used rape narratives—about innocent white women, taken in and then assaulted by Shakers, Oneidans, Mormons, and especially Catholics—to warn readers about the threat these communities' sexual practices posed to monogamy, the nuclear family, and natalism. But the rape narratives also demonstrate white Protestants' broader concern about an increasingly heterogenous America. As Kathleen Kennedy has put it, writers "displaced the violence of the act of rape from the literal bodies of women onto the symbolic bodies of the nation."[21]

The similarities between the lecherous Mormon man and another figure in reform literature, the lustful southern slaveholder, were no coincidence. Many anti-Mormon novelists hailed from New England and had never met a Mormon, much less been to Utah. But New England reformers had long stereotyped southern slaveholders as temperamentally volatile and sexually violent; indeed, abolitionists made the rape of enslaved women and the division of Black families a central part of their critique of slavery. Anti-Mormon writers simply transferred these critiques to Mormon men. *Female Life*'s narrator witnesses physical abuse, experiences sexual assault, and watches men tear apart their families because they cannot resist the temptation of a second wife. With little firsthand knowledge of Mormons or Mormonism, these writers hoped that the sexual depravity that helped turn reform-minded northerners against slavery would prove equally effective in galvanizing anti-Mormon sentiment.[22]

The establishment of polygamy in a federal territory compounded gentiles' concerns about the practice. *Female Life* reflected this concern as well. At one juncture, the narrator's Mormon husband explains to her the supposed political goals of the Latter-Day Saints. "Our policy is to become independent of the heathens in civil as well as social matters. We will have our own laws, institutions and government," he says. "But you do not mediate treason against the United States Government, do you?" his wife asks. Her husband responds, "What is the United States to me, that I should remain in obedience to a form of laws and state of society that my soul abhors?" This exchange was designed to shock readers, who could not fathom such a blithe disregard for their beloved Union.[23] It also foreshadowed the federal government's battles with Brigham Young for control over the Utah Territory. And when read along with the novel's anti-polygamy scenes, it demonstrates why Americans were so concerned about Mormon control over the Utah Territory to begin with. To non-Mormons, it seemed that a small group of religious extremists had seized a federal territory — a shared inheritance for all white Americans — and established a social practice that, by its very presence, would result exclude anyone who disagreed with them. For Republicans, this was the problem with popular sovereignty.

Republicans used the same tropes of lecherous men and innocent women to condemn the Kansas-Nebraska Act. In their portrayals of the situation in Kansas, as in their descriptions of Utah, Republicans depicted settlers as a lecherous group of men with a particular social practice — in this case, slavery — that precluded upright free soilers from settling in the territory. A Republican cartoon, "The Cincinnati Platform, or the Way to Make a New State in 1856," dramatized the metaphorical violation of the Kansas Territory by linking it to the sexual threat proslavery men supposedly posed to free-soil women. The cartoon portrays a group of slave owners marching their chattel into a besieged Kansas town. In the foreground lies a white woman, her dress torn off to expose her breasts; she has either fainted or died. To antebellum viewers, her vulnerable, exposed body would have indicated that she had been raped by the slaveholding men marching past her. Democratic presidential and vice presidential nominees James Buchanan and John C. Breckinridge watch over the scene. Breckinridge observes, "Buch, these dam'd poor whites with their Free notions are a curse to any Country and must be removed." Buchanan replies, "You are right Breck, let out some of the democratic blood and work them at 10 Cents a day and you will soon clear them out."[24] The cartoon told readers that that the introduction of slavery would result in the rape of white women and the humiliation of free laboring white men, forced to work for low wages. Inasmuch as white women embodied national virtue, the cartoon also warned readers that popular sovereignty threatened the country's

"The Cincinnati Platform, or the Way to Make a New State in 1856," 1856.
Library Company of Philadelphia.

moral future. Popular sovereignty would replace an honest republic of
small farmers with a bastardized democracy of slaveholders.

Another Republican cartoon, "Liberty, the Fair Maid of Kansas," shows
a feminized Kansas begging to be spared from lecherous northern Democrats, who lick their lips and leer at her. Armed with a tomahawk, knife,
and rifle, a drunk Franklin Pierce, the incumbent president, hovers over
Liberty. He jeers, "Come Sissy, you go along wid me, I'l[l] take Good care
of you." Liberty cries, "O SPARE ME GENTLEMEN, SPARE ME!!" But
her aggressors have no sympathy. With the bloody scalp of a free soiler
hanging from his belt, Senator Lewis Cass of Michigan taunts, "Poor little
Dear, We wouldn't hurt her for the world, would we, Frank? Ha! ha! ha!"
In the background of the cartoon, a proslavery border ruffian threatens a
free-soil woman—whose husband and children he has just killed—with
sexual innuendoes. Like "The Cincinnati Platform," the cartoon portrayed

"Liberty, the Fair Maid of Kansas—in the Hands of the 'Border Ruffians,'" 1856.
Library Company of Philadelphia.

northern Democrats as complicit in the expansion of slavery to Kansas—
and therefore in the sexual assault of free-soil women by proslavery border
ruffians. The images were ridiculous: northern Democrats did not favor
the rape of white women. But as Brie Swenson Arnold has shown, Republican newspapers gave credence to these lithographs by printing dubious
reports of the rapes of free-state women in Kansas.[25] And more broadly,
these Republican gender tactics simply represented the flip side of the
Democratic campaign. To call attention to abolitionism, Democrats had
exploited fears about race mixing in the North and the sexual assault of
white women by enslaved men in the South. To underscore the danger of
popular sovereignty, Republicans fabricated a threat to white women by
slaveholding men. Both sides assured voters that they would protect white
women's morality and, more abstractly, the nation's virtue.

In 1856, then, Republicans used Mormon polygamy to criticize popular
sovereignty. They blamed the doctrine, and its Democratic supporters,
for the federal government's inaction in Utah. Given Americans' voracious appetite for anti-Mormon, antipolygamy literature, that criticism
alone would have been incisive. It also bolstered the Republican Party's
bona fides as the party that elevated white women by promoting a kind of

domestic feminism. But most powerfully, the critique of popular sovereignty in Utah underlined the Republican critique of popular sovereignty in Kansas. In Utah, as in Kansas, Democrats had territories determine their domestic institutions; in Utah, as in Kansas, this policy had supposedly resulted in the abuse of white women. This gendered attack on popular sovereignty strengthened the Republican's broader condemnation of popular sovereignty as a failed policy that had produced nothing but chaos and immorality in the western territories. Popular sovereignty had given control over the territories to men who were morally unfit to exercise that power.

"What Ingenious 'Dodge'": Democratic Obfuscation on Polygamy and Slavery

Despite the violence in Kansas, Democrats still believed in popular sovereignty. Their platform declared it "the only sound and safe solution of the 'slavery question.'"[26] But the doctrine also happened to be a political necessity—especially for northern Democrats. To northern Democrats, popular sovereignty seemed like the only way to appease southern slaveholders without sacrificing the party's increasingly tenuous hold on northern voters. When Republicans blamed polygamy in Utah on popular sovereignty, then, northern Democrats found themselves in a predicament. Should they betray popular sovereignty in Kansas by supporting intervention in Utah? Or should they protect popular sovereignty by allowing polygamy to continue, despite its deep unpopularity among their voters?

During the 1856 campaign, Democrats never mounted a meaningful counteroffensive against the Republican claim that popular sovereignty promoted polygamy. Part of the problem lay in the fact that Democrats themselves had used the term "domestic institutions" to refer to both slavery and other social institutions. In his 1855 State of the Union address, Franklin Pierce blamed northerners for meddling with the South's domestic institutions, while the South left the institutions of the North unmolested. Pierce declared that northerners "engage in the offensive and hopeless undertaking of reforming the domestic institutions of other states, wholly beyond their control and authority." Here, Pierce was referring to abolitionists and their crusade against southern slavery. Pierce continued, however, to call on "the people of the southern states [to] confine their attention to their own affairs, not presuming officiously to intermeddle with the social institutions of the northern states."[27] Pierce's reference to the "social institutions" of the North reveals that even before Republicans raised the issue in reference to polygamy, Democrats understood that term to encompass social practices beyond slavery.

As a result, it was difficult for Democrats to argue that Mormon polyg-amy fell beyond the purview of the Kansas-Nebraska Act—even though regulating marriage was far from the legislation's intent. Instead, they tried to distract from the issue with a hodge-podge of arguments and accusa-tions. On June 12, 1856, the *Brooklyn Daily Eagle* tried to at once turn the issue into a question of religious freedom and to discredit Mormonism as a religion. The constitution "should undoubtedly secure impunity for every form of faith and worship," the paper reasoned, "but whether it should cover Mormon polygamy, or Chinese idolatry and the worship of sticks and stones, is not so clear." At another point, an Illinois congressman tried to turn the polygamy-slavery analogy back on the Republicans, asking whether they thought that since "Washington, Jefferson, and Madison . . . were slaveholders," Republicans meant to "denounc[e] them as no better than Mohammedans."[28]

Democrat James Buchanan won the White House, but Democrats' troubles with Mormon polygamy and popular sovereignty continued well past Election Day. The 1854–55 Steptoe Expedition, sent west for rea-sons unrelated to the Mormons, had wreaked havoc on the relationship between the Latter-Day Saints and the federal government, as U.S. troops socialized—and slept with—Mormon women. U.S. troops skirmished with Mormon militias. Rumors circulated that Mormons were conspiring with the Pahvant Indians against federal agents. Non-Mormon federal officials found it nearly impossible to exercise power due to local resistance. In May 1857, the Buchanan administration responded to the unrest by declaring Utah "in a state of substantial rebellion" and ordering 2,500 troops to the territory to replace Young with a new governor.[29]

Coupled with the Republican discourse analogizing polygamy to slavery in the election of 1856, the deployment of troops to Utah left Illinois sena-tor Stephen Douglas scrambling to explain why the federal government's intervention there did not create a precedent for intervening in Kansas. On June 12, in a major speech in Springfield, Illinois, Douglas explained that the federal government was sending troops to Utah to quell unrest among aliens, not to interfere with polygamy. "The Territory of Utah was organized under . . . the compromise measures of 1850, on the supposition that the inhabitants were American citizens," Douglas began. "It was conceded on all hands, and by all parties, that the peculiarities of their religious faith and ceremonies imposed no valid and constitutional objection to their reception into the Union, in conformity with the federal constitution." But over the past seven years, Douglas argued, "rumors and reports" had surfaced other issues with the inhabitants of the territory. "Nine-tenths of the inhabitants are aliens by birth, who have refused to become natural-ized," Douglas averred. Moreover, "all the inhabitants, whether native or alien born, known as Mormons . . . are bound by horrid oaths and terrible penalties to recognize and maintain the authority of Brigham Young, and the government of which he is the head, as paramount to that of the United States." Finally, Douglas claimed, "The Mormon government, with Brigham Young at its head, is now forming alliances with the Indian tribes of Utah . . . to prosecute a system of robbery and murder upon American citizens." "Under this view of the subject," Douglas concluded, "I think it is the duty of the President . . . to remove Brigham Young and all his followers from office"—"to apply the knife and cut out this loathsome, disgusting ulcer."[30]

U.S. troops left Fort Leavenworth, Kansas, in July 1857, and began marching west toward Utah. Receiving word of the troops' movements, Brigham Young reactivated the Nauvoo Legion and ordered them to harass and delay the progress of the American troops. Rather than esca-lating, however, the Utah War ultimately fizzled out. The onset of winter offered the two sides a chance to negotiate, resulting in pardons for most Mormons involved in the conflict, the transfer of Utah's governorship from Brigham Young to non-Mormon Alfred Cumming, and the peaceful entrance of the U.S. Army into Utah. The war's only major clash occurred in September 1857, when the Mormon militia slaughtered 120 members of a non-Mormon immigrant party in an event known as the Mountain Meadows Massacre. Yet even after the Utah War had ended, Douglas continued to justify the intervention by arguing that it was necessary to quell a rebellion against the federal government. "Did . . . I propose to intervene . . . because of polygamy or Mormonism?" he asked a colleague on the Senate floor in 1859. No: "I showed that the information before us led us to believe that they were in a state of rebellion, denying the authority of the United States."[31]

As usual with Douglas, it is difficult to parse whether conscience or convenience moved him to take this position. As David Smith has noted, in the early 1850s, Mormons practiced polygamy in Utah and nonetheless enjoyed good relations with the federal government; only when Mormons began to harass federal officials and non-Mormon settlers did the feder-al government step in. Smith argues that the Buchanan administration intervened to protect the state's power, not to stamp out polygamy. As we saw, anti-Mormon literature bears this thesis out: amid the scenes of polygamy and violence, authors inserted breathless exclamations of their own support for the U.S. government and for the Union. So Douglas may have told the truth when he claimed he supported sending troops to Utah to enforce the federal government's power. But that argument happened to offer Douglas a very convenient escape from a tricky situation: he needed to protect the principle of popular sovereignty—on which he had staked his political career—but he could not be seen as supporting Mormon polygamy. If readers of the *Buffalo Daily Republic* had been keeping an eye out for "what ingenious 'dodge' will be resorted to by Senator Douglas" on the Utah issue, they might have found it here.[32]

While northern Democrats worried about protecting the principle of popular sovereignty, southern Democrats cared about protecting slavery—both in the Kansas Territory, where they hoped to establish the institution, and in the South. Their constituents disliked Mormons and their polygamous practices just as much as northerners did: one scholar has described polygamy as one of the "dominant moral issue[s]" of the nineteenth century. And indeed, Americans' intense disgust for Mormon polygamy has led some historians to assume that Democrats leaped at the chance to send troops to Utah.[33]

But southern Democrats realized that forbidding polygamy in Utah might be used to justify banning slavery in Kansas. They knew this because southern defenders of slavery had been among the first to analogize slavery to marriage. Whereas women's rights activists used the comparison to criticize both institutions, proslavery southerners deployed it to naturalize them. Initially, southern slaveholders had likened the relationship between master and slave to the relationship between father and child. But childhood was temporary. Slavery was permanent. So by the late 1830s, southern polemicists supplemented the parental analogy with a marital one. Just as women were naturally suited to become wives, they argued, so too were African Americans suited to become slaves; just as a woman's position as a wife came with duties and obligations, so too did that of the slave. The comparison "lent slavery a beneficent patina without changing its power relations," Nancy Cott writes. But the argument had the potential to cut both ways. If marriage and slavery were parallel institutions, then criticizing one could easily lead to criticizing the other.[34] Southern Democrats wagered that their constituents cared more about protecting slavery than they did about suppressing Mormon polygamy, and so they vehemently opposed military intervention in Utah.

As part of their efforts, southern Democrats tried to explain why the domestic institution of polygamy did not fall under the purview of the Kansas-Nebraska Act. These arguments were often weak and jumbled. A reader of the *Baltimore Sun*, for instance, granted that the inhabitants of the territories could regulate their domestic institutions and that like slavery, polygamy was a domestic institution. But the man made the spurious claim that when the Kansas-Nebraska Act became law, Congress did not know that Mormons practiced polygamy. As a result, he argued, the law did not cover Mormon polygamy, and thus "it will be for Congress to determine whether they will tolerate the establishment of the domestic institution of polygamy." Even the relatively moderate, ostensibly nonpartisan *New Orleans Times-Picayune* tried to explain away the connection between polygamy and slavery. The paper's correspondent in Salt Lake City argued that the Founders implicitly gave Congress the power to reject a state from applying for admission to the Union if the state did not have a social organization "in harmony with that existing at the time of the adoption of the Constitution."[35] Apparently, Congress could reject Utah's application to the Union on the grounds that the Founders would have been shocked by Mormon polygamy. Utahans could "regulate their domestic institutions in their own way," but Congress reserved the power to deny the state admission to the Union.

Occasionally, southern Democrats argued outright that the federal government did not have the right to intervene in men's marriages. On June 10, 1857, the *Washington Union*, a pro-Buchanan paper, asserted that the executive branch had no authority "for interfering to regulate the marriage relation." A month later, an editorial from the *Weekly Mississippian* echoed that principle. "The Government of the United States was not established, nor is it within the scope of its authority, to interfere with the . . . social and domestic institutions of the States or territories. It has no more right to interfere with the marital relations in Utah, than it has to suppress gambling or Sabbath breaking in Mississippi." The fire-eating *Charleston Mercury*, a leading defender of slavery, characterized Mormon polygamy as prostitution to prevent the federal government from getting involved. "Brigham calls all who are sealed to him wives, but they are only concubines. Now, is there any law of the United States making concubinage a crime?"[36]

In part, the papers' arguments against federal interference with marriage, gambling, or prostitution reflect Democrats' long-standing inclination to keep the federal government out of white men's private affairs. Democrats were not alone in this. Nancy Cott has shown that "the federal principles of the United States allowed each state to make its own rules on marriage and divorce." Indeed, the Mormons themselves drew on these same traditions of federalism and negative liberties to argue for noninterference in polygamy. On August 30, 1857, Utah state representative and Mormon apostle John Taylor delivered a speech in Salt Lake City on the relationship of the Latter-Day Saints to the federal government. "We have turned this desert into a flourishing field, and the desert has blossomed as the rose, and God has blessed our labours. And whom have we interfered with? Have we gone over to the States and interfered with them?" Taylor asked.[37]

But the southern newspaper editors were not concerned with safeguarding federalism for federalism's sake. Their arguments reveal that southern Democrats worried more about protecting slavery. Southern Democrats could not accept federal intervention in Mormon polygamy without opening the door to interference with slavery in Kansas or the South. A correspondent of the *Richmond South* said as much after Buchanan sent troops to Utah. "I do not approve of [the Mormons'] domestic institutions," the writer maintained. But "it is their business, not mine. . . . As a Southern man, my sympathies are with the Mormons . . . Let the Mormons be crushed for their religion, for that is the real difficulty—and it may not be long before our negro masters, our traders in human chattels . . . may be crushed out to vindicate the glory of God."[38]

The arrival of American troops in the territory and the removal of Brigham Young as governor placed Utah firmly under federal control. But even as the two sides negotiated a peace, the Tennessee newspaper editor George Poindexter warned that southerners should not rejoice over the federal government's renewed control over Utah. "The war against Utah, and the ardor with which it is clamoured for by the mass of the country, is to the South an admonition of the danger attending the maintenance of their own domestic institutions," Poindexter warned. "Slavery is denounced with more fury at the North than polygamy, and slaveholders are held in greater abhorrence than Mormons. The arms of the Government can be turned . . . against one as well as against the other institution." For Poindexter, a Democrat and a supporter of slavery, the Utah War had come at too high a cost: it had set the precedent of sending troops into a U.S. territory to interfere with a "domestic institution."[39] Poindexter worried that southern slavery would be the next target.

During the election of 1856 and the Utah War, northern Democrats needed to protect the principle of popular sovereignty against Republicans' attacks. Southern Democrats, meanwhile, wanted to protect slavery from future federal intervention. Northern and southern Democrats offered diverse responses to the conflict in Utah, ranging from disclaiming a desire to interfere to justifying interference on grounds unrelated to polygamy.[40] All of their responses, however, show that they accepted the Republican argument that "domestic institutions" could include both marriage and slavery. If Democrats wished to style themselves as the party that respected white men's rights as voters and as patriarchs, it seemed they needed to at least tacitly accept Mormon men's right to practice polygamy.

"Regulate Their Domestic Institutions": Northern Democrats and the Lecompton Constitution

Republicans took Democrats by surprise when they linked marriage to slavery to condemn popular sovereignty. In 1857, however, northern Democrats made their own connection between marriage and slavery to defend popular sovereignty against a new enemy: the Lecompton Constitution.

In February 1857, shortly before James Buchanan took the oath of office, the territorial legislature in Lecompton, Kansas, scheduled a June election for representatives to a constitutional convention. The proslavery legislature rigged the election in favor of a proslavery constitutional convention. Legislators forbade voting by immigrants who arrived after March 15, making it more difficult for free-state supporters to arrive in time to vote. (Proslavery settlers from neighboring Missouri could make the move in plenty of time.) In light of this and other proslavery machinations, free staters largely boycotted the election of delegates, resulting in the election of a large majority of extreme proslavery men to the convention. Predictably, these men produced a proslavery constitution. When a later, fair election indicated that Kansas voters would reject this Lecompton Constitution, the delegates offered Kansans a false choice. Voters could ratify the constitution "with slavery" or "with no" slavery—but the latter option only banned the importation of slaves into Kansas, leaving the slavery that already existed intact. As David Potter put it, "[Lecompton] delegates, acting in the name of popular sovereignty, had offered the voters a 'choice' which affirmed the inviolability of slavery no matter what option was taken."[41] When Lecompton delegates submitted their constitution to Congress to apply for admission to the Union, it forced congressmen and the president to take sides on slavery in Kansas—exactly the outcome the Kansas-Nebraska Act had been designed to avoid.

Southerners quickly made the Lecompton Constitution a test of northern Democrats' commitment to southern rights. Virginia Democrat R. M. T. Hunter issued a public letter declaring that his support of Buchanan was contingent on the president's acceptance of Lecompton. Some southern militants even threatened to secede if Congress denied Kansas admission as a slave state. Buchanan—a Pennsylvanian who took pride in his strong personal and political relationships with southerners—took southerners' demands into consideration. Moreover, Buchanan believed that the referendum on "with" or "with no" slavery offered voters plenty of choice. And he had previously defended the legality of the Lecompton convention, desperately wanting to devolve the slavery issue back to the states. So, in his annual message on December 8, Buchanan declared, "Whether Kansas shall be a free or a slave State must eventually . . . be decided by an election; and the question can never be more clearly or distinctly presented to the people than it is at the present moment."[42] Buchanan had decided to support the admission of Kansas under the proslavery Lecompton Constitution. Worse, he turned the issue into a test of party loyalty, making it known that if Democrats wished to enjoy the administration's good favor, they must support Lecompton.

Many northern Democrats balked at this demand. They refused to accept that the Lecompton Constitution—the product of fraud and subterfuge—reflected Stephen Douglas's "great principle" of popular sovereignty. Though agnostic about the existence of slavery in Kansas, northern Democrats could not accept the suppression of white men's free choice at the ballot box, which they saw as their masculine prerogative and essential to republican liberty. They also worried about their political futures. Supporting Lecompton would make northern Democrats seem like southerners' lackeys—a real handicap in the upcoming 1858 midterms, since many northern voters already worried that southerners were coming to control northern Democrats with the same brute force they exerted over their enslaved workers. And more concretely, recent election results had demonstrated the clear anti-Lecompton mood among northern voters.[43] So in the winter of 1857–58, northern Democrats resuscitated the Republicans' analogy between slavery and marriage for their own ends: to force popular sovereignty to be carried out fairly by resubmitting the full Lecompton Constitution to the voters of Kansas. If southern Democrats accepted men's right to control one domestic institution—marriage—why would they not allow Kansans a fair vote on the other domestic institution—slavery?

Before the Lecompton Constitutional Convention submitted its constitution to the U.S. Congress, Douglas did not elaborate on what he meant by "domestic institutions." In his June 1857 speech in Springfield, he used the term without defining it. "Give fair play to that principle of self-government which recognizes the right of the people of each State and Territory to form and regulate their own domestic institutions," Douglas promised, "and sectional strife will be forced to give way to . . . fraternal feeling."[44] Listeners would have assumed that when Douglas said "domestic institutions," he meant slavery. After all, that was the issue that divided Kansans.

But then the Lecompton Constitution arrived in Congress, and Douglas needed to justify his break from the Buchanan administration. On December 12, Douglas arose before the Senate to give his first major speech opposing the Lecompton Constitution. "Did we not," Douglas asked, "come before the country and say that we repealed the Missouri restriction for the purpose of . . . carrying out . . . the great principle of self-government, which left the people . . . free to form and regulate their domestic institutions in their own way?" No Democrat could disagree with Douglas there. That point conceded, Douglas continued, "We agree that [the people] may decide for themselves the relations between husband and wife, parent and child, guardian and ward; why should we not, then, allow them to decide for themselves the relations between master and servant? Why make an exception of the slavery question by taking it out of that great rule of self-government which applies to all the other relations of life?"[45]

Douglas had pulled off a logical coup against southern Democrats. He accepted their argument that slavery was a family relation. But he then he used their ideas about other family relations—husband and wife, parent and child—to dispute their politics on the slavery question. Southern Democrats and their doughface allies believed that men should retain undisputed control over laws regarding family relations. Douglas pointed out that by refusing to resubmit Lecompton for a full up or down vote, southern Democrats were denying men in Kansas the right to control the family relation of slavery as they saw fit. This put southern Democrats in an awkward position. Either they would change their position to allow a fair vote on Lecompton, or they would be exposed as hypocrites who supported white men's authority over their families and their government only as long as those principles resulted in the expansion of slavery. As the Kansas debates continued, other anti-Lecompton Democrats seized on Douglas's argument. "There was not a man who would dare to say that domestic institutions did not include the relations of husband and wife, parent and child, as well as master and servant," declared anti-Lecompton Pennsylvania congressman William Montgomery in March 1858.[46]

The tactic also served Douglas's presidential aspirations. Looking toward 1860, Douglas wanted to shore up his credentials for the nomination. Douglas thought that allowing a legitimate vote in Kansas would bring peace and stability to Kansas, defang the slavery issue, undermine Republican support for federal intervention, and ultimately strengthen the Democratic Party. It would also bolster Douglas's bona fides as a reliable defender of white men's prerogatives.

On December 8, 1857, in his first State of the Union Address, Buchanan had acknowledged that "'domestic institutions' are limited to the family. The relation between master and slave and a few others are 'domestic institutions.'" But Buchanan believed the Kansas-Nebraska Act had only ever meant to give men the right to a direct vote on the slavery question. "There was no question . . . before the people of Kansas or the country, except that which relates to the 'domestic institution' of slavery," Buchanan asserted.[47] It was a fair point: the fight over the Kansas-Nebraska Act had been a fight over slavery, not marriage or children. But four days later, Douglas counterattacked, charging that Democrats had always meant for the "domestic institutions" language of the Kansas-Nebraska Act to be interpreted broadly. Recalling the presidential election of 1856, Douglas asked his fellow senators,

> Do you think we could have . . . carried the Presidential election last year . . . on the principle of extending the right of self-government to the negro question, but denying it as to all the relations affecting white men? No sir. We . . . carried the election in defense of that great principle, which allowed all white men to form and regulate their domestic institutions to suit themselves—institutions applicable to white men as well as black men . . . concerning all the relations of life, and not the mere paltry exception of the slavery question.[48]

By 1854, "domestic institutions" most commonly meant slavery. But the term's historical diversity of uses allowed Douglas to claim an expansive definition. That interpretation, moreover, dovetailed nicely with Democratic doctrine, which had long emphasized white men's prerogative to exercise power over the world around them, with minimal intervention from the federal government.

Other anti-Lecompton Democrats carried forward Douglas's claim that the "domestic institutions" of the Kansas-Nebraska Act meant all domestic institutions—not just slavery. The *Press*, a pro-Douglas paper published in Philadelphia, reported, "Alluding to the President's message, [Pennsylvania Democrat John Hickman] said . . . this doctrine of popular sovereignty is not as popular as it was. It was formerly supposed to mean something giving the people power over all domestic institutions. But now, as thought by the President, it is to be sweated down to the contemptible dimensions as to whether they shall hold a negro in bonds or not."[49] On December 31, the *Press* published a letter purported to be from "one of the purest, most consistent, and most devoted Democrats in this State—a man who has *always been* Mr. Buchanan's *friend*, and has occupied many important public positions." Referencing the debates over the Kansas-Nebraska Act, the anonymous writer willingly admitted "that, in the controversy between the Democratic party and those opposed to them in regard to popular sovereignty, slavery was the question most prominently discussed." But the writer claimed that he believed nobody discussed other institutions "for the obvious reason that no one questioned the right of the people of the Territories to regulate every other 'domestic institution.'" He finished, "The very fact that the right to regulate every other institution was, by common consent, lodged with the people of each Territory (and therefore, not discussed,) is a strong argument in favor of the position that the whole Constitution ought to have been submitted to the people of Kansas."[50] This former friend of Buchanan's sided with the anti-Lecompton Democrats because he believed that if popular sovereignty did not allow white men to vote on everything, it was not popular sovereignty at all. He, Douglas, and Pennsylvania Democrat Hickman cast Buchanan's vision of popular sovereignty as an insult to white manhood.

Douglas and other anti-Lecompton Democrats expanded the definition of "domestic institutions" even beyond family relations. They argued that the term also encompassed the institutions of the state—from banks, to courts, to the legislature—on which white men had the right to vote as well. In his same December 12 speech in the Senate, Douglas asked why Kansans should not have a fair vote on slavery, when "we agree that the people may decide for themselves what shall be the elective franchise . . . what shall be the rule of taxation."[51] Pennsylvania congressman William Montgomery echoed this call, contending that "a bank was as much an institution as slavery itself." Because it failed to allow men to vote on all domestic institutions—banks as well as slavery—the Lecompton Constitution was "illegal."[52]

A subscriber to Philadelphia's Democratic paper, the *Press*, agreed with Douglas and Montgomery's expansive definition of "domestic institutions." "Has it come to this, that there are no institutions in Kansas but freedom and slavery?" the writer asked. "If the people's agents could not speak authoritatively for them on the question of freedom or slavery, is not the presumption irresistible that there were other questions of constitutional law wherein they would fail to give satisfaction?"[53] This Democrat agreed with Douglas that "domestic institutions" covered all the institutions of state, not just the laws regarding slavery. But the private citizen went further than Douglas—a politician trying to win over moderate southerners— ever could. Pointing to Kansas politicians' failure to deal evenhandedly with the slavery issue, the man questioned whether those same men could be trusted to regulate any of the state's institutions.

In 1854, northern and southern Democrats had united to repeal the Missouri Compromise and place slavery in the territories under local control. Northern Democrats had promised their constituents that the Kansas-Nebraska Act would restore true democracy to the territories. The Lecompton Constitution, however, did not represent the will of the majority. Northern Democrats thus rejected the constitution on principle—it was not democratic—and for practical reasons: it was unpopular among their constituents. Northern Democrats prevailed on their southern counterparts to allow Kansans a full up or down vote. Southern Democrats had long described slavery as a patriarchal, familial, and local institution. If slavery was domestic in the sense of familial, northern Democrats countered, should not Kansans control the institution, along with all other family relations? And if slavery was domestic in the sense of being a state institution, rather than a federal one, should not Kansans have the final say on the issue? Ultimately, northern Democrats believed that only a real vote would stand up under scrutiny and bring about a final settlement of the slavery issue.

"In Their Own Way": Southern Democrats and Lecompton

As late as June 1857, most southern Democrats believed that Kansas would be admitted as a free state. But the submission of the Lecompton Constitution to Congress had put a new slave state suddenly—surprisingly—within their reach. Southern Democrats could not allow Congress to send the constitution back to Kansans for a full ratification vote because recent election results in the state had demonstrated that a clear majority of Kansans—10,226 to 6,226—favored a free Kansas.[54] And with California's recent admission to the Union, if Kansas entered as a free state, southerners would be outvoted on any measure relating to slavery. Southerners stood to either gain a slave state or lose control of the Senate.

When northern Democrats turned the proslavery argument about the domestic, local nature of slavery against their southern counterparts, southern Democrats struggled to mount a cohesive response. Most often, they simply called on the original meaning of the Kansas-Nebraska Act, arguing that when legislators had written "domestic institutions," they meant slavery. Given the term's increasing use in the late antebellum era to denote slavery, it was a fair argument. Tennessean Aaron V. Brown, Buchanan's postmaster general, penned a letter to the editor of the proadministration *Washington Union*. He wrote, "Nobody had ever doubted or questioned the right of the people of [Kansas] to decide the relations of husband and wife, guardian and ward, &c., in their own way. . . . *The only matter in dispute* has been about the question of admitting or excluding *slavery* from the Territories." Douglas had accused southern Democrats of not trusting white men to legislate on family relationships. Brown assured readers that was not the case. He contended that the Kansas-Nebraska Act simply applied to slavery, not marriage, and therefore a vote on the constitution with or without slavery fulfilled the original purpose of the act. Henry Fitch, an Illinois district attorney and supporter of the Buchanan administration on the Lecompton question, agreed. "The right conferred of regulating their domestic institutions in their own way could scarcely be interpreted to suit the convenience of Judge Douglas, into a prohibition to manage their domestic institutions," he remarked in a July 1858 speech in Chicago.[55]

In response to Douglas's December 12 speech, the pro-Lecompton *Washington Union* made a similar argument. Again referring to the original meaning of the Kansas-Nebraska Act, the *Union* claimed that "this term 'domestic institutions,' if judged technically, does not include the organization of legislative, executive, and judicial departments." Rather, the writer continued, "If we judge it by the popular standard, we find that, though not strictly accurate, it has been adopted into the political vocabulary with most expressive emphasis as referring to domestic slavery. . . . That this was the idea prominent with those who passed the bill will hardly be denied by anyone conversant with the action of Congress on that occasion."[56] The *Union* acknowledged that "domestic institutions" sometimes meant the institutions of state, but the writer claimed that legislators held the popular meaning of the term—slavery—foremost in their minds when they wrote the act. Therefore, proper execution of the act only required a vote on slavery, not on the Lecompton Constitution as a whole.

The Kansas-Nebraska Act made the people of the territories free to "regulate their domestic institutions in their own way." While Douglas and his followers harped on the meaning of "domestic institutions," pro-Lecompton Democrats focused on the words "in their own way." Democratic senator James Green of Missouri argued that Kansans had indeed regulated their domestic institutions in their own way—by delegating that power to the constitutional convention at Lecompton. Ignoring the rigged election of delegates to that convention, Green said, "The way they, the people, chose, was to leave it to the action of the Convention, which body was under no obligation to submit the Constitution, or any part of it, to the popular vote."[57] If Congress rejected Lecompton, it would demonstrate a lack of trust in Kansans' ability to govern themselves.

Other Democrats piled on to this argument by characterizing the conflict in Kansas over the Lecompton Constitution as a domestic dispute. Indiana senator Graham Fitch addressed the ongoing political conflict in Kansas in a speech on December 22, 1857. "If any domestic differences occur between [Kansans] and their servants, their representatives or delegates, the same doctrine of non-intervention" that formed the basis of the Kansas-Nebraska Act "prohibits us from interfering. Their domestic differences, like their 'domestic institutions,' must be settled by them 'in their own way.'" On March 2, 1858, at a meeting of proadministration Democrats in New York City, Representative James Hughes of Indiana used similar language to push for acceptance of the Lecompton Constitution. "Let Kansas become a State of the Union at once," he demanded, "and let her regulate her domestic institutions and settle her family quarrels in her own way, 'subject only to the constitution of the United States.'"[58] By equating the divide over Lecompton among Kansans to a mere family dispute, Fitch and Hughes tacitly acknowledged the voting fraud and bloodshed that had convulsed Kansas, while at the same time disclaiming the federal government's responsibility to demand a fair vote. Requiring Lecompton's ratification would be akin to one man inserting himself into another's family troubles.

Pro-Lecompton Democrats had never denied men's right to manage their families and their local governments as they saw fit. Nor did they contest Douglas Democrats' claim that "domestic institutions" could, in some other context, encompass the family or the institutions of state and local governance. But for various reasons—supporting slavery for the southerners, and quickly settling the slavery question for northerners—they also wanted to pass Lecompton, which meant forbidding men in Kansas from voting on the full constitution. To reconcile respecting white men's autonomy with denying them a vote, they held that the Kansas-Nebraska Act referred only to slavery and that requiring a full referendum would disrespect Kansans by implying they could not govern themselves.

The debate over Kansas's admission to the Union lasted from the late fall of 1857 through the spring of 1858. In both houses of Congress, Stephen Douglas helped form a coalition of Republicans and anti-Lecompton northern Democrats. In the Senate, that coalition could not stop the pro-Lecompton forces. But in the House, the anti-Lecompton coalition had the strength to at least force a compromise. Representatives William Hayden English of

Indiana and Alexander Stephens of Georgia developed a bill that offered a referendum: Kansans could accept or reject the whole Lecompton Constitution. But the English Bill attached carrots and sticks to Lecompton's passage. If Kansans accepted Lecompton, Kansas would immediately join the Union and be granted additional land (though less than the Lecompton convention had requested). If they rejected Lecompton, Kansas would have to wait for a few years before reapplying to the Union. Despite the incentives, Kansans rejected the proslavery Lecompton Constitution by a ratio of six to one. Kansas would not become a state until January 1861.

Incensed at the loss of a potential slave state, southern Democrats blamed northern Democrats for Lecompton's failure. Northern Democrats rejected Lecompton because they saw that it did not represent the will of the people. Yet southern Democrats believed that their northern counterparts had sunk Lecompton because they did not want Kansas admitted as a slave state. They grumbled that northern Democrats had betrayed them, convincing them to support popular sovereignty while secretly plotting to bar any new slave states from entering the Union. When Douglas collaborated with Republicans in the battle over Lecompton, he contributed to southerners' impression that far from being reliable allies, northern Democrats might in fact be closeted Republicans.

In 1856, Democrats had agreed, at least in principle, on popular sovereignty and white patriarchy. The Lecompton debate destroyed their consensus on popular sovereignty: northern Democrats wanted a fair vote, while southern Democrats wanted only slavery. Yet they still agreed, a least in principle, on white patriarchy—on white men's right to govern their states and their families as they saw fit. In an attempt to force the other side to concede on Lecompton, then, northern and southern Democrats seized on their shared vision of patriarchy and weaponized it against each other. The debacle thus not only bred ill-feeling between northern and southern Democrats—it also revealed that their gender tactics could divide as easily as they could unite.

3

Butchery for Our Mothers

NATIONALISM, SEPARATISM, AND GENDER IN THE WAKE OF JOHN BROWN'S RAID

On the morning of October 18, Baltimoreans awoke to a startling head-line in their local paper. "SLAVE INSURRECTION AT HARPERS FERRY. HEADED BY 250 ABOLITIONISTS. The Citizens in a State of Terror—White Persons Imprisoned—Slaves Set Free."[1] On October 16, under the cover of night, abolitionist John Brown had led twenty-one men southwest across the Potomac from Maryland into Harpers Ferry, Virginia. The men hoped to free enslaved workers by inciting a rebellion against white slave-holders. The raiders easily executed the first part of their plan: cutting telegraph lines, arming a few dozen local Black men, taking white hostages, and seizing control of the federal arsenal in Harpers Ferry.

Brown had planned to take the weapons and retreat westward into to the Allegheny Mountains; from there, he would launch raids deeper into the South. But after having seized the arsenal, Brown changed course. Abandoning his plans for guerrilla warfare, Brown and his men hunkered down in the arsenal, hoping that local yeomen and enslaved people would rush to join them. They did not. Instead, on October 17, the local militia surrounded the would-be liberators, who had barricaded themselves in a nearby firehouse. A day later, ninety U.S. Marines arrived from Washing-ton. Brown realized his desperate position, but he refused to capitulate. The Marines stormed the building, rapidly overwhelming Brown and his men. On October 19, Brown was taken into custody; on October 25, he was tried for treason against the Commonwealth of Virginia, multiple first-degree murders, and inciting a slave insurrection. On November 2, Brown was convicted, and on December 2, 1859, he was executed by hanging in Charles Town, Virginia.[2]

Overnight, the raid on Harpers Ferry became a flashpoint in American politics. Contemporary responses to the event exhibit how Americans of all political stripes found their hopes and fears for slavery and the Union brought to life by John Brown and his men. But a gendered reading of Democratic responses, in particular, helps us understand two critical outcomes of the raid: why Republicans struggled to distance themselves from Brown, and how Deep South Democrats' separatism started to gain currency over northern Democrats' nationalism in the Border and Upper South. Northern Democrats, in condemning the raid, flooded their newspapers with descriptions of the gender and antislavery radicalism of both Republicans and Brown's supporters. But even as they did that, they also retooled the message that the center could hold: that northern Democrats, together with border state moderates and the last remaining Deep South Unionists, could shore up the party's nationalist core and constitute a bulwark against further radical incursions, turning the tide against abolitionism.

In the wake of the raid, northern Democrats' mixed messaging no longer worked. Though ultimately ineffective, Brown's raid represented a literal and physical threat to white families that activated the defensiveness of white southern masculinity. As a result, secessionists' relentless fearmongering—featuring gendered rhetoric about the dangers of slave rebellion to southern women and homes—gained traction in the Border South. Deep South Democrats claimed that a radical, disordered northern society—epitomized by Lydia Maria Child and other abolitionist women—had seeded John Brown's raid. And they held up white southern women, by contrast, as both symbols of a conservative, racially hierarchical society and as real wives and daughters who needed to be protected against the supposed sexual threat posed by Black men. Goaded on by southern fire-eaters, Border and Upper South Democrats began to seriously wonder if the Union could protect them from northern radicalism.

"A Representative Man": Northern Democrats on the Attack

Between 1856 and 1859, Republicans won midterm elections in state after state—including in former Democratic strongholds like Pennsylvania and New York. Smarting from these losses, northern Democrats seized on John Brown's raid to prime northerners for the 1860 elections. They claimed that all Republicans were abolitionists and that all abolitionists were gender radicals. Tainting Republicans and John Brown's supporters with images of gender radicalism blurred the lines between the two groups, putting Republicans on the defensive in the weeks and months following the raid.

Most Republicans unequivocally denounced Brown and his tactics; many called him a madman. Abraham Lincoln boasted that Democrats could not "implicate a single Republican" in the "Harpers' Ferry enterprise." In Lincoln's home state, the *Chicago Press and Tribune* claimed its "opposition to slavery [was] based upon moral and economic considerations," but it "depreciate[d] . . . everything looking towards violent measures for the enfranchisement of the slaves of the South." David Davis, the future Supreme Court justice and a friend of Lincoln, wrote his son, "What a mad affair that was at Harper's Ferry!" The *New York Tribune* told readers that John Brown's family had a history of insanity. Benjamin Wade, a radical Republican who supported abolition and women's rights, tried to convince his Senate colleagues that even abolitionists repudiated Brown's violent tactics: "Do not jump to the conclusion that the people who hold meetings in admiration of the personal qualities of John Brown, one single man of them, stand forth to justify his nefarious and unwarrantable act," Wade begged.[3] According to Wade, these Republicans admired the strength of Brown's convictions but not his tactics. Republicans had begun to convince northern voters that forbidding slavery in the western states would save those lands for free white farmers and, eventually, lead to slavery's peaceful decline. They did not want the albatross of a violent abolitionist raid hung around their necks.

But Democrats worked to link Republicans to Brown just as strenuously as Republicans tried to distance themselves from him. Northern Democrats alleged that Republican midterm victories had emboldened Brown. As a Democratic paper in Cincinnati editorialized, "[Brown] must have taken courage from the late elections in Ohio and Pennsylvania, and supposed that he would have not only the moral, but the physical backing of these two great states." And even though the midterms had barely passed, another election was coming up: the raid had taken place less than a year before voters would cast their ballots in the presidential election of 1860. Democrats warned voters that the election of a Republican president would lead to further violence. "Such a President, having his sympathies with the insurrectionists, would be slow to move in arresting their outrages," the paper claimed. Additionally, "the very fact that there was a President with such sympathies would encourage insurrection all through the slave states." Democrats still believed that the Lower North and Upper South could act as a bulwark against sectional tensions—if only they continued to vote Democratic. By linking Republican victories to slave insurrections, the *Cincinnati Enquirer* hoped to shore up Democrats' chances in the upcoming election.[4]

Democrats alleged that John Brown's raid was the natural result of Republican antislaveryism—or as they called it, fanaticism. On October

22, a Democratic paper in Portsmouth, Ohio—located in the conservative Butternut area just across the Ohio River from Kentucky—told readers there was no such thing as moderate antislavery. "Sober, discreet, prudent, order-loving citizens—conservative 'republicans' in politics . . . hope to fetter and finally extinguish [slavery] by gradual and peaceful means," the paper began. "Yet . . . do they not know that the main-spring of the political anti-slavery movement is FANATICISM?" The paper claimed that the only difference between Republican politicians and John Brown was that the former were "men of speculation," while the latter was a "m[a]n of action." By this formulation, the mere limiting of slavery's expansion inspired abolitionist insurrection. Another Democratic paper portrayed John Wentworth, an Illinois Republican and former mayor of Chicago, as a closeted abolitionist. Wentworth was no radical: he had served in the House as a Democrat until just four years prior. Though Wentworth had praised Brown's intentions—"His object was freedom; freedom to every person"—he had repudiated Brown's violence. Nonetheless, the *Illinois State Register* claimed that the disavowal was mere "pious horror" that masked Wentworth's support for abolitionist-led insurrections.[5] Northern Democrats hoped that by holding Republicans responsible for Brown's raid, they could stem the tide of voters fleeing their party in favor of Republican candidates.

In addition to accusing all Republicans of being abolitionists, Democrats charged all abolitionists with cowardice—a distinctly unmanly trait. In an article titled "The Cowardly Desertion of Capt. Brown by His Former Patrons," the southern-sympathizing *Brooklyn Daily Eagle* called out Brown's supporters for disavowing him after his arrest. "The Republican leaders," the paper opined, "now that their . . . agent . . . is likely to pay the forfeit of his crimes by his life, with unparalleled and cowardly treachery turn upon him and denounce him to the authorities." In a similar article the *Eagle* denounced Frederick Douglass as a "skulking and cowardly negro . . . who promised to stand by [Brown] . . . but now pronounce[s] him insane." The *Eagle*'s reporting stretched the truth: the so-called Secret Six, a group of northern men that included one Republican politician, had not denounced Brown, they simply claimed not to have known about his plans. (Douglass had refused to support the raid entirely.) Yet the *Eagle* hit on a core truth: that as Brown martyred himself for the cause, his supporters denied him, fled to Canada, or went into hiding. The *Eagle* emphasized their cowardice to conflate and undermine abolitionists and Republicans. If the men who supported Brown were not real men, then their political views must not be worthy of respect, either.[6]

Northern Democrats used the same tactic against the women who supported Brown's raid, denigrating them as opinionated and manly. On December 2, the day of Brown's execution, men and women in New York, Boston, and Philadelphia gathered to mourn his death. Of these assemblies, the *Brooklyn Daily Eagle* spat, "[The meetings] were chiefly confined to negroes, strong-minded women, and weak-minded females of the masculine gender." The *Eagle* article implied that since only free Blacks, mannish women, and feminine men supported abolition, abolition was not worth supporting. When Brown coconspirator Edwin Coppock was hanged two weeks later and sent to be buried in Salem, Ohio, the local Democratic newspaper even attacked the mourners at his funeral. "These sympathizers held a grand pow-wow over the corpse," the *Daily Empire* sneered, "exposing it to admiring throngs of strong-minded women and their weak-minded husbands."[7] The gendered insults revived and strengthened the accusations that Democrats had made against Republicans in 1856. Then Democrats had decried Republicans as agents of women's rights, free love, and abolitionism. Now, according to Democrats, their jeremiads had come true: with the support of the Republican Party, weak men and strong-minded women were gathering in public, cheering a slave insurrection.

The former congressman Charles Jared Ingersoll piled on, penning a screed against Brown's supporters. Commercial and social ties linked Ingersoll's native Philadelphia to the South: southerners purchased a large portion of the goods manufactured in Philadelphia, and they sent their sons to be educated in the city. Ingersoll's son even married the daughter of a Tennessee senator. Like many northern Democrats, Ingersoll believed it was the duty of Lower North states like Pennsylvania to broker compromise between the slaveholding South and what he called "the slave-hating northeast." Ingersoll's letter, which he mailed to the Republican *New York Times* for broad circulation, defamed all abolitionists as cowards. Other than Brown, Ingersoll wrote, the abolitionists were not willing to die for their cause. He proposed a solution: "a few clergymen hanged in their canonicals, with strong-minded women in short petticoats, would be spectacles, not indeed to be desired, but which might at least vouch for the[ir] sincerity."[8] In other words: at minimum, hanging abolitionists would render their panegyrics to Brown less hypocritical. But one senses that Ingersoll hoped that hanging the abolitionists would also silence them for good.

In the months after the raid, then, Democrats claimed that both Republicans and abolitionists supported Brown, and both Republicans and abolitionists supported gender radicalism. And they alleged that all Republicans were abolitionists, and all abolitionists were gender radicals. These allegations—logical fallacies though they were—set Republicans back on their heels, forcing the party's papers and politicians to disavow Brown repeatedly. By conjuring a vague but menacing connection between Republicans, abolitionists, gender radicals, and John Brown, Democrats succeeded in putting Republicans on the defensive through the fall of 1859.

Conciliating the Border and Upper South

In addition to priming the pump for the 1860 presidential and congressional elections, northern Democrats also needed to calm and conciliate their counterparts in the Border South. Nationalists to a fault, northern Democrats persisted in believing that voters in the Border South states of Kentucky, Maryland, Delaware, Missouri, and Virginia—and even the Upper South states of North Carolina and Tennessee—could act as a bulwark against sectional division. Historians have not been so sure. Some, like Edward Ayers, Christopher Phillips, and William Freehling, agree that white people in the Border and Upper South had a great deal in common with white people in the Lower North, up until and indeed even after the South's secession. Others, by contrast, emphasize the long-simmering conflict between slave and free states in the region. And still other scholars focus on the internal politics of the Border South states. Michael Robinson, for instance, argues that the aggressive tactics of secessionists in Kentucky, Maryland, Delaware, and Missouri sparked a vigorous Unionist response that ultimately kept these states out of the Confederacy.[9] These historians' debates about the Border South—about its loyalties and its geographical boundaries—mirror those of the people they study. Secessionists and unionists cared less about whether a slave state shared a border with a free state than they did about the state's commitment to slavery and to the Union. Delaware, Maryland, Virginia, Kentucky, Missouri, North Carolina, Tennessee: in 1859, all of these states seemed up for grabs, and northern Democrats needed to reassure them of slavery's safety in the Union.

One way northern Democrats did this was by trying to rekindle a sense of the Union as a national family, tied together by mutual respect and affection. Michael Woods has shown how in the antebellum era, Americans often imagined the Union as a confederacy bound not by force or interest but by affection and love. In the months following John Brown's raid, northern Democrats used the idea of brotherly harmony to plea for calm and reconciliation. In November, Joseph Lovejoy held forth at the National Hotel in Washington, D.C. Lovejoy was the brother of abolitionists Elijah and Owen, but he had come to believe that preserving the Union mattered more than abolishing slavery. Lovejoy reminded his listeners that Brown had "dragged five men, the heads of families, from their beds and murdered them, as he would dogs." This assault had come "from [Virginia's] sister States," Lovejoy lamented, "from whom it ought to expect kindly salutations and the most friendly relations." New York Democrat James Thayer used the same language in a speech in Manhattan. Thayer declared that following the "bloodshed and domestic disturbance" of John Brown's raid, northern Democrats must "meet with scrupulous fidelity the engagements entered into with our sister States"—"the obligations the constitution imposes upon us." In the Democratic stronghold of Philadelphia, the crowd at a Union rally adopted a series of resolutions expressing sympathy with the citizens of Virginia, including one "disavowing any right or wish to interfere with the domestic institutions of sister States." And New York businessman W. R. Stark assured a friend in Asheville, North Carolina, that "the Harpers Ferry affair . . . is looked on here as a great piece of rascality—but of no more general importance than would be the murderous attack of a lunatic on his best friends." He went on to promise that "the national heart is sound to the core" and that its "life blood . . . is the entire independence of the states in all domestic matters."[10]

Yet even among these reassurances, we can see the bonds of the affective Union beginning to fray. In November, Democratic senators William Bigler of Pennsylvania and Alfred Iverson of Georgia had a particularly testy exchange. Iverson had recently charged that northern Democrats were as unsound on the slavery question as Republicans. Bigler, a doughface who had supported the proslavery Lecompton Constitution, could not tolerate this accusation. "No portion of the democratic party sympathized with Brown in his atrocious outrage on the sovereign state of Virginia," Bigler reminded Iverson. Then he demanded that Iverson "say of the northern democracy . . . what you cannot say for yourself, that is, that we have labored day after day, in season and out of season, in defense of the rights and interests of our sister states."[11] Bigler still believed in an affective Union of "sister states" bound by affection rather than force. But he charged that Iverson did not: Iverson did not advocate for northerners as Bigler advocated for southerners—revealing the limits of a polity bound by familial affection rather than laws and force.

Northern Democrats tried to sympathize with their Border South counterparts by describing Brown as a criminal, emboldened and supported by the Republican Party to wage war on white men's property and white women's honor. John Brown had disrupted the peace of southern homes;

his success would have unleashed rape and murder on white southern women and children. Caleb Cushing, a Massachusetts Democrat with strong southern sympathies, deployed this language in a December 8 speech at a "Union Meeting" in Boston. Cushing had started his career as an antislavery Whig, but by 1859 he had thrown himself into saving the Union—at the expense of his former antislavery beliefs. At Faneuil Hall, Cushing asked listeners to imagine, "in the dead of the night, the husband reposing in the beloved arms of his wife, with their dear little children around them." Into this domestic scene—"the fancied repose of their common security under the laws of their country"—"they are aroused from their slumbers by the treacherous approach of armed murderers."[12] The speech seems intended to serve a dual purpose. Delivered in Boston, it would have moved northern Democrats to sympathy; though they did not live in a slave society, they could understand a man's desire to protect his wife and children. And reprinted in Border South papers like the *Baltimore Sun* and *Richmond Dispatch*, it would have told anxious readers that their northern allies understood their fears, lamented the breakdown in law and order, and were committed to protecting white southern families.

Northern Democrats also exploited white men's self-conception as protectors to attack both abolitionist and proslavery extremism. Philadelphia's *Public Ledger* warned, "The conflict at Harpers ferry is a foretaste of what may be expected when the contest becomes general between two sections of the country, a point to which extreme opinions would rapidly drive us." If, the paper told readers, "the good, sober sense of the people does not interpose in time . . . the reality will be . . . smoking houses and fields bathed in blood."[13] The language about burning homes and violated women would have shocked northern readers as much as southern ones. The *Ledger* wielded that power to claim the political middle ground between northern abolitionists and southern fire-eaters, whom northern Democrats considered equally dangerous.

The novelist and writer Ann Stephens also exploited the specter of rape to appeal for political moderation. On December 2, Victor Hugo had penned a letter to the editor of the *London Star* praising John Brown as "heroic" and his sons, who were killed in the raid, as "sacred martyrs." On December 27, Stephens, a New Yorker, responded in a public letter to the editors of her local paper. She spent the first two pages apologizing for writing the letter at all, claiming she had "hop[e]d that some more able person—some statesman or author of his own strength—would answer Victor Hugo . . . but so far . . . our statesmen are too busy, and our authors remain silent." The excuse was typical for women writers at the time, who were expected to justify their foray into the public sphere. But since "the honor of our country belongs alike to its men and its women . . . when that is assailed, its defence [*sic*] is proper to either." Then, she combined gendered appeals with the typical Democratic denunciations of John Brown. She decried Brown as a "great criminal." She described Republicans as a "small party" of "extremists." She called on readers to think of white southerners, "thousands of my own countrywomen, gentle, good, and lovely, given up a prey to wild insurrection." And she lauded the "hol[y] work" of "soften[ing] the bitterness of sectional strife . . . into one great national brotherhood."[14] Stephens's gender lent this argument extra weight: John Brown had attempted something so unthinkable that a woman had to speak up on behalf of her white southern sisters, and sectional tensions had risen to such a level as to justify the extreme measure of a woman's intervention.

Yet whether used to encourage northerners to sympathize with southern patriarchs or condemn radical politics, the rhetoric of rapine was fairly rare in the North. On the one hand, this is unsurprising. Language about rape and murder simply played better in the South, where it exploited the deep fears of whites living among those they oppressed and reflected years of proslavery propaganda. On the other hand, it indicates that northern Democrats were not as focused on shoring up their support in the Border South as they were on holding the political middle in the North.[15]

"Strong-Minded Women Who Sanctify Murder": A Shift in the Border and Upper South

Northern Democrats had miscalculated. The Border South was not the nationalist bulwark that northern Democrats imagined it to be. It was true that travel, commerce, demography, and culture made the Lower North and the Border South more similar than regions further afield. But as Stanley Harrold has explained, the proximity of slave to free society generated conflict, as white southerners demanded northern assistance in returning runaway slaves. And unlike their northern counterparts, Border South Democrats worried about the enemies within, including nonslaveholding whites, whose commitment to slavery they questioned, and free Blacks, whom one historian has described as "a conspicuous anomaly in the heart of the slave order."[16] Following as it did the Democrats' gendered campaign tactics of 1856, the perceived Lecompton betrayal of 1857, and Republican victories in the 1858–59 midterms, John Brown's raid touched off a pronounced shift in Border South Democrats' thought. By tapping into fears of northern gender and abolitionist fanaticism, John Brown's raid moved them away from northern Democrats' nationalism and toward the separatism more commonly espoused in the Deep South.

In the fall and winter of 1859, a few southern Democrats reprised the line from 1856, continuing to blame Republicans, rather than northerners in general, for the raid and for abolitionist radicalism. A Marylander and a Democrat who had moved to San Francisco, Jefferson Martenet wrote to his mother about the raid. "I fear this Harpers Ferry business will end in Civil war yet," he wrote. "The prominent Black Republican papers indirectly sanction Brown's cause. Only last week their organ in this city . . . said 'No matter how *good the cause*, Brown was wrong in periling human life *without* a *reasonable chance of success.*' What more could they say in defense of insurrection and bloodshed?" he asked. Almost a full year after the raid, Granville Torbett, the editor of the *Nashville Union and American*, still blamed Republicans—and Republicans alone—for supporting John Brown's raid. "The Republicans," he editorialized, "are no longer entitled to their old party designation. They . . . proclaim themselves JOHN BROWN Abolitionists, which is equivalent to saying that pikes and firebrands are better than votes for the purposes of government."[17]

Fiery though this language was, it still represented a moderate position among Border South Democrats—and a minority one. Most blamed the raid on northern fanaticism more broadly. Virginia governor Henry A. Wise was not a secessionist, yet he held northern society as a whole accountable for John Brown's raid. Wise harbored ambitions for the 1860 presidential race, so he could not be too extreme: in the winter of 1859–60, Wise still claimed to be a Unionist, but he expressed concerns about a government that could not protect slaveholders from abolitionist meddling and now abolitionist invasion. On December 5, 1859, in his message to a joint session of Virginia's House and Senate, Wise observed, "For a series of years social and sectional differences have been growing up, unhappily, between the States of our Union and their people." "Abolition has seemed to madden whole masses of one entire section of the country. It enters into their religion, into their education, into their politics and prayers . . . into all classes of people, the most respectable and most lawless, into their pulpits and into their presses and school-houses, into their men, women and children of all ages, everywhere." That fanaticism, he said, "has raised contribution in churches to furnish arms and money to such criminals as [John Brown] to make a war for empire of settlement."[18] According to Wise, fanaticism had led northerners to support a race war in the South.

Wise did not just blame Republicans for Harpers Ferry—he blamed all northerners. Nothing in Wise's papers reveals whether these remarks represented Wise's genuine beliefs or a crass political calculation. But they are important either way. If Wise truly thought that most northerners supported Brown's raid, then we have an example of a prominent Virginian and lifelong public servant turning against the North. And if Wise called out northern society to relieve political pressure from the more radically proslavery politicians in his state, then that indicates the growing power of proslavery conditional unionism in Virginia.

Brown's raid even moved Arunah Shepherdson Abell's *Baltimore Sun*—which one historian has described as "the soul of border-state moderation"—to antinorthern hysteria. In an article titled "Is John Brown a Representative Man?," Abell set out to prove that the majority of northerners supported Brown. "Day after day . . . week after week, we have the cumulative evidence, furnished voluntarily by the press and the pulpit, that John Brown is in fact the representative man of a very large class of the people of the North," Abell warned readers. Though Abell paid lip service to party politics, asserting that Brown's spirit "actuate[d] the whole republican party," he primarily described the raid in sectional terms: he blamed "this numerous class" at the North, claimed "it is no party question," and called for unity in the South regardless of party affiliation. Also published in Baltimore, a tell-all account claimed that Brown's raid was but the tip of a vast northern conspiracy—a harbinger of future insurrections.[19]

Private letters reveal the polarizing effect of this kind of reporting. On the day John Brown was hanged, Virginian Patrick Cabell Massie wrote to his uncle William, a plantation owner. "I have been greatly surprised at the sympathy manifested for him at the North," Massie wrote. "With but few exceptions both pulpit and press have united in expressions of praise and sympathy and in denunciation of the South." This was categorically untrue. Nonpartisan northern outlets criticized the raid. The publishers of *Harper's Weekly*, which enjoyed a national readership, wanted to "unite rather than to separate the views and feelings of the different sections of our common country"; as a result, the magazine derided Harpers Ferry as "the work of a half-crazed white." Even most Republican papers denounced Brown as insane. The Republican *New York Tribune* dismissed the whole raid as having "never appeared to us, from the first, as consistent with soundness of mind." Republican politicians Abraham Lincoln and William Seward joined the papers in disavowing Brown.[20] Regardless, Border South Democrats were increasingly inclined to see the raid as the result of northern—rather than just Republican—fanaticism.

Despite the violence, and despite their belief that more and more northerners supported abolition, many Democrats in the Border and Upper

South still believed that northerners simply misunderstood the institution of slavery—that if they knew it as southerners did, they would not support its abolition. In a November 11 letter to her son, Catherine Martenet Richardson of Baltimore reported that she had just finished reading Caroline Lee Hentz's *The Planter's Northern Bride*. Hentz wrote the book in response to Harriet Beecher Stowe's *Uncle Tom's Cabin*. The novel's protagonist, Eulalia, is the daughter of a New England abolitionist. When she marries a southern slaveholder, she initially condemns his slaveholding. After she sees how well her husband treats his enslaved laborers, however, she warms to the institution, and indeed even intervenes to stop a plot by a group of local abolitionists to incite a slave rebellion. The plot gives life to all the themes common in "anti-Tom" literature: Eulalia and her husband make great sacrifices for their enslaved workers' happiness, and when a northern abolitionist convinces one enslaved woman to run away, she finds herself unhappy and uncared for in the North. The book spoke to Richardson, who had immigrated from Germany but taken on the prejudices of her adopted home and political party. She wrote to her son, "All those crazy people who are against the South ought to read it. If it had been written for the Harpers Ferry affairs it could not be more like it. Tis excellent—you would be delighted with it."[21] Richardson believed that if all the northerners who thought slavery immoral could live with the institution as Eulalia had, they would experience the same change of heart.

In a letter to Virginia governor Henry Wise, Portia Baldwin of Winchester, Virginia, expressed a similar sentiment. Baldwin sighed, "Now if the North will but come to their senses, and be quiet we may yet be a happy people." For Baldwin as for Richardson, slavery was not the problem—northern agitation was. If slavery was a positive good, the only reason enslaved people might dream of freedom was because abolitionists had convinced them they should.[22] Brown's raid provided southerners with another example of northern intervention in the southern institution. Nonetheless, these women saw an easy fix: if northerners accepted slavery as a positive good, or even simply minded their own business, the Union could continue on in peace.

The Democratic paper in Charlotte, North Carolina, affirmed this point. The Union could recover from the blow of Brown's raid if northern Democrats could recapture power in the northern states. In an article titled "Action Wanted, and Not Sympathy," the *Evening Bulletin* called on these "dormant voters" in the North to act. "Let their voice penetrate the villages, the inland towns, and the ignorant masses there, who are influenced by fanatical priests, demagogues, and strong-minded women, who sanctify murder and canonize Brown." And at the ballot box, "let their deeds, also, be felt in such reaction as will give future security to the South"—that is, by voting Democratic.[23] This article, along with the letters from Richardson and Baldwin, represents the views of Democrats in the Border and Upper South following Brown's raid. They believed that the majority of northerners had gone Republican, and, therefore, radical, supporting a program of abolition and women's rights. This view resembled that of Deep South Democrats far more than it did that of Democrats in the North. But many Border and Upper South Democrats still hoped that northerners had gone only temporarily insane. If northern Democrats regained power and influence, white southerners imagined, abolitionist agitation would subside.

In decrying northern radicalism, Border South Democrats had come to echo the language and concerns of their counterparts in the Deep South. The *New Orleans Times Picayune*, a Democratic paper whose editors nonetheless typically supported sectional compromise, denounced the raiders as "victims of that social and political error [with] which a large proportion of the northern mind is indoctrinated and imbued." Brown's men did not choose this path of their own free will. Rather, the radicalism that prevailed in the North had spread like an illness. This metaphor made radicalism seem all the more dangerous: once one form of radicalism gained a toehold, all of the others would soon follow. The other article, titled "Where Is the Responsibility?," made the same point. The raid was "but the legitimate growth of the ultraisms which have been permitted to gain such an ascendancy over the minds of the Northern people," the editor opined.[24] Democrats typically used "ultraisms," in the plural, to refer to abolitionism, women's rights, free love, Fourierism, and other radical social movements as a group. In this particular case, the use of "ultraisms" indicates that the editor saw John Brown's raid as the result of northern abolitionism yet also as inextricable from northerners' broader desire for women's and economic freedom.

To prove that fanaticism had consumed the North, southern Democrats pointed to the public memorials and speeches northern abolitionists dedicated to Brown. In the October 28 issue of the *Liberator*, William Lloyd Garrison claimed that "Capt. Brown had many to sympathize with him." This would have struck fear in southern hearts: how many northerners sympathized with Brown? How many more plots were afoot? In a similar vein, on November 8, transcendentalist writer Ralph Waldo Emerson gave a lecture at Tremont Temple in downtown Boston. Emerson asked his audience to "look nearer . . . at that new saint, than whom none purer or more brave was ever led by love of man into conflict and death—a new saint, waiting yet his martyrdom and who . . . will make the gallows glorious, like the cross." Emerson—a man who spent his life writing on the importance of nonconformity—did not represent the mean of northern thought. Nonetheless, the Democratic *Semi-weekly Mississippian* pointed to Emerson's speech as evidence that most northerners supported Brown—so many as to make the North feel foreign to southerners. "Such declarations as these from northern oracles, and the known complicity of so many leading men in the non-slaveholding States, in the movement of Brown, suggest the idea that the two sections are already arrayed as two hostile nations."[25] The specter of a radical North arrayed against a conservative South paralleled the rhetoric in secessionist papers like the *Charleston Mercury* much more closely than it did the nationalist message of papers like the *Brooklyn Daily Eagle*.

Border South Democrats viewed northern women, in particular, as metonymic of the social disorder that they believed pervaded the North and had led to John Brown's raid. Lydia Maria Child epitomized everything southerners hated. Child was a Bostonian, a women's rights activist, and an abolitionist—serving as a member of the executive board of the American Anti-slavery Society in the 1840s and 1850s. All of these things gave southerners plenty of reason to despise Child, but when she wrote a public letter to Virginia governor Henry Wise, requesting permission to minister to Brown in prison, she became a special target of their ire. In October, following Brown's capture and imprisonment, Child wrote to Wise what she called a "plea of sisterly sympathy with a brave and suffering man," that she may travel to Virginia "for the purpose of nursing your prisoner." Though she believed that Christianity "justified men in fighting for freedom," she promised that she would not "seek to advance these opinions in any way . . . after your permission to visit Virginia has been obtained." On October 29, Wise acquiesced, albeit in a backhanded manner. "I could not permit an insult even to woman in her walk of charity among us, though it be to one who whetted knives of butchery for our mothers, sisters, daughters, and babes," he wrote.[26] That is: Wise would be sure to protect this innocent white woman, even if Brown had not.

Unbeknown to Child, Wise provided his correspondence with her to the *New York Tribune*, which promptly published the letters. When southern Democrats read Child's request to minister to Brown, they unleashed a torrent of invective against her that continued for months after Brown's execution. Eliza Margaretta Chew Mason, the wife of Virginia Democratic senator James Murray Mason, led the charge. "Do you read your Bible, Mrs. Child?" Mason asked in a public letter to Child. "If you do, read there,

'Woe unto you, hypocrites,' and take to yourself with two-fold damnation that terrible sentence." According to Mason, Child's support for Brown was hypocritical first because Brown's "aim and intention was to incite the horrors of a servile war—to condemn women of your own race . . . to see their husbands and fathers murdered, their children butchered, the ground strewed with the brains of their babes."[27] Mason charged that by supporting an abolitionist, Child had betrayed both her race and her sex.

Next, Mason accused Child of a second hypocrisy: that Child supported abolition but did not love the enslaved. "Now, compare yourself with those your 'sympathy' would devote to such ruthless ruin," Mason seethed, "and say . . . would YOU stand by the bedside of an old negro, dying of a hopeless disease, to alleviate his sufferings as far as human aid could?" Mason reported that southern women did all of this and more, demonstrating their true sympathy for these supposed members of their extended family. Unlike Child, who incited violence and grasped for public recognition, "we"—that is, wives of slaveholders—"endeavor to do our duty in that state of life it has pleased God to place us."[28]

Of course, this was untrue. For one, Mason provided her correspondence with Child to the Virginia newspapers, a sign she—the wife of a Democratic senator—knew how to play politics just as well as Child did. Her claim that white women cared for the people they enslaved was also false. As Thavolia Glymph and Stephanie Jones-Rogers have shown, white plantation mistresses perpetrated violence as readily as white plantation masters.[29] But Mason nonetheless drew a sharp contrast between abolitionist women and slaveholding women—and by connection, between northern and southern women and indeed northern and southern society. Child did charity because she wanted recognition; Mason did charity because it was her Christian duty. To Mason, this difference represented the difference between northern and southern women in general: northern women sought roles outside the home, while southern women were content with their role inside the home, one that, if carried out, strengthened the bonds among races and stabilized society.

If Child's intentions were less than pure, why had she gone to Virginia? Democratic newspapers in the region concocted a variety of explanations for the trip—all of them unflattering to Child. One claimed the move was a publicity stunt to drum up sales for a forthcoming book. "Will this philanthropic lady care for, or do any thing for the families of John Brown and his victims?" asked Edgar Snowden, the editor of the *Alexandria Gazette*. "It seems that when the State is to be invaded . . . no consent is asked or cared for; but for the privilege of coming to the State . . . why then consent must be asked that capital may be made and a book perhaps may be sold." Similarly, in a letter to the editor reprinted in newspapers across North Carolina, one woman attributed Child's behavior to "a thirst for notoriety" that was "driving the sex insane . . . the fountain is the insatiate vanity which nothing but the lightning of the press or the clamors of a multitude can appease." And another paper insinuated that Child may want to do more than just minister to Brown: "Mrs. L. Maria Child . . . asks to be allowed to 'nurse' and 'soothe' the insurrectionist, Brown," the *Richmond Enquirer* wrote.[30] The thought of a woman and a man alone together in a prison cell raised the prospect of extramarital sexual activity. By claiming that Child sought money, fame, or sex—all things that, according to prescriptive morality, women should not care for—the papers impugned Child's femininity, her motives, and northern women as a whole.

The Child episode allowed Democratic papers across the South to recapitulate a long-standing defense of slavery: northerners in general, and northern women in particular, should take care of social problems in the North before they meddled with slavery in the South. Joseph Clisby at the *Macon (Ga.) Telegraph* claimed that when Child's daughter fell ill while traveling in the South, Child would not respond to her letters or send money to pay for her care—even though Child had rushed to Virginia to minister to Brown. (Naturally, Clisby claimed that local southern gentlemen ultimately came to the daughter's aid.) As a result, the Clisby concluded, "Mrs. Child wanted to fly to the bedside of the wounded assassin, John Brown . . . not in truth to do a work of mercy, but to gain the notoriety of identifying her name with the Brown raid. But when true humanity . . . appeal to her on behalf of a sick daughter, they appealed in vain—because there was no eclat in nursing an afflicted child." Though relatively even-handed in his coverage of sectional issues, Clisby could not resist scolding Child for forsaking her own family in favor of meddling in southerners' private affairs.[31] A similar article in Virginia reported that a number of women lay sick and in need of care in Lawrence, Massachusetts. "Where, oh where is Mrs. Lydia Maria Child?" the paper asked. "Can only murderers, horse thieves, and traitors stir her sympathies? Why is she not at the bedsides of these ill-fated sufferers? Is it because they are of her own sex? Or because it is their misfortune to be white instead of black?"[32]

Both newspaper articles follow the same storyline: white northern women needed help, and Child neglected them. This trope conveyed a few ideas about Child in particular and abolitionism in general. For one, it unsexed—and therefore discredited—Child. The *New Orleans Picayune* said as much, calling Child an "unsexed termagant" and claiming that she lacked a woman's "soft touch and . . . eyes that beam with gentlest sympathy"; her "shrewish treble" spouted only "hyena hatreds." Barbara Welter has explained that in antebellum America, women judged themselves and were judged by others on four principal virtues: piety, purity, submissiveness, and domesticity.[33] Women exploited the perception of their piety and purity, in particular, to justify their involvement in politics, claiming that the public sphere could benefit from their superior morality. By claiming that Child had abandoned other white women, southern Democrats were making the case that Child lacked virtue. This meant that Child was not womanly, and that she had no right to interfere in politics. Further, it implied that a desire for fame, rather than a charitable impulse, motivated Child's attempts to help Brown.

Second, Child's alleged abandonment of her daughter painted her as a woman who preferred public life to motherhood—thereby failing to embody romantic notions of female domesticity. Here, Child had fallen short of another tenet of "true womanhood": that women should relish their roles as daughters, wives, and mothers. Nancy Cott has argued that this ideology was indigenous to New England and differed from the southern ideal of the "lady." Yet the judgment southerners heaped on Child reveals the basic similarity between the northern and southern ideals: women should remain within the home and obey their husbands. By neglecting her daughter, Child had shown southerners that she was no lady—a conclusion which tarnished Child and her politics.

Third, both stories make Child seem like a traitor to her race and her sex. Child chose to care for an abolitionist man instead of her own daughter or the ailing white women in Massachusetts. To southern Democrats, that decision echoed the problem with Child's support for Brown. Her sympathy for an abolitionist made her a race traitor. It also made her a gender traitor: she supported a man who tried to unleash a slave insurrection on the white women of Virginia. Southern Democrats would have seen Child's supposed preference to help Black men rather than white women as unnatural, which, again, would unsex and discredit her.

Finally, the stories added a gendered twist to the southern argument that abolitionists should help impoverished northerners before they tried to free enslaved southerners. Defenders of slavery had long maintained that forcibly enslaved people were in fact part of idyllic extended families. They hoped this characterization would make slavery seem benevolent. But they also used it to justify their hostility to any interference with the institution. No man should intrude on another man's family, and therefore northern men should not impinge on southern men's enslaved families. But now Child, a woman, had expressed a desire to minister to John Brown—the man who had hoped to violate all southern families—yet she was unwilling or unable to take care of her own family and her own section.[34] The affair continued to provide political fodder for both sides through 1860: southern women wrote into newspapers to criticize Child, while the American Anti-slavery Society—seeking to publicize Child's devotion to the cause—published and sold 300,000 copies of her correspondence with Wise and Mason.[35]

Child was not alone in backing John Brown. A number of other abolitionist women had met Brown, had advance knowledge of his raid, or came out in support of Brown after Harpers Ferry. Julia Ward Howe, whose husband, Samuel Gridley Howe, was a member of the Secret Six, met Brown in the 1850s; she later remembered the meeting with "great gratification." Quaker activist Abigail Hopper Gibbons knew about the insurrection in advance because Brown spent an evening at her home several weeks before the raid. Though she abhorred his violent tactics, she nonetheless kept a John Brown pike in her parlor for years after the raid. Harriet Tubman helped plan the raid and is thought to have helped raise money for the venture. After Harpers Ferry, abolitionist and women's rights activist Abby Kelley Foster joined members of a Worcester, Massachusetts, antislavery society in passing a resolution declaring "that, as Abolitionists, we have no disclaimers to make, no apologies to offer." Susan B. Anthony arranged a meeting in Corinthian Hall in Rochester for the evening of Brown's execution. Rebecca Spring was the daughter of abolitionist Arnold Buffum, the wife of a wealthy philanthropist, and a part of the same reform community in New Jersey that counted Sarah and Angelina Grimké as members. She visited Brown in prison twice. (When Spring was initially denied access to Brown, one southern newspaper commented that "all Yankees, of either sex . . . should be at once driven from our midst.") Mary Ellen Russell, the wife of Massachusetts judge Thomas Russell and a long-time friend of Brown's, also went to see Brown in prison.[36]

To women in this Border and Upper South, Child represented a broader problem with northern women: they yearned to be involved in public life. In the wake of Child's public intervention in the Brown affair, southern women wrote to friends, politicians, and Democratic newspapers to criticize northern women's supposed desire for political power. In a January 26, 1860, letter to her local paper, a North Carolina woman who only identified herself as "Lilian" asserted that women should not be involved in politics. But first, apparently aware of the irony of writing to a public outlet to decry women who inserted themselves in public life, she began, "I once thought

I would never again contribute a line to a newspaper, or write one thought that should have birth in a mind deemed inferior (I mean in comparison with the others [*sic*] sex)." She continued, "I would not have you infer . . . that I have anything to do with politics . . . or that I am a champion of women's rights!" But she claimed that the number of women in politics had become too large to ignore—she had to speak up. The rest of her letter despaired that "some women of our land"—undoubtedly northern women—were active in politics. "I would not have her voice which should ever be attuned to sweetness, heard in the tumult of angry debate and the fanatical wrangling of the day. I should grieve to see that gentleness which should ever be her crowning grace sullied by being brought into contact with such rude elements," the woman wrote.[37]

Portia Baldwin of Winchester followed a similar formula when she picked up her pen on December 17, 1859, to write to Virginia governor Henry Wise. Though later a strong proponent of secession and the Confederacy, Baldwin still felt sympathy for the widow of Heywood Shepherd, a free Black man shot at the beginning of Brown's raid. Baldwin taught Shepherd's children in Sunday school. After assuring Wise that Shepherd had been "a worthy and industrious man," she asked whether Wise could arrange financial assistance for Shepherd's widow and children. Like Lilian, Baldwin thought her cause merited her intervention. Also like Lilian, Baldwin did not want to be perceived as involving herself in public matters—even though she was. So she pleaded with Wise to keep her role private. "As I do not covet the reputation of the strong-minded women of the North, yet I hope I have some of the good sense of the South, I must request that my name may not appear in any form in this matter," Baldwin wrote.[38]

Though they hailed from the Border South—Baldwin less than fifty miles from Pennsylvania—Lilian and Baldwin believed they were very different from women in the free states. Both thought Child represented a profound flaw in northern society: that too many northern women were dissatisfied with their roles as wives and mothers. How did they come to this conclusion? Southern domestic novelists had long described differences between northern and southern society and even northern and southern women. Elizabeth Moss has shown that as early as the 1830s, southern women presented through their fiction a vision of the "true" South. Novelists like Caroline Gilman, Caroline Hentz, and Maria McIntosh wrote about an ordered and stable South, governed by noblesse oblige, and contrasted it with a competitive and individualistic North. Moss writes that these novels both "buil[t] on existing stereotypes" yet "unconsciously widened the chasm they had intended to bridge."[39] Yet those early novels did not bear the same sharp edge as these barbs against Child and her northern sisters.

Perhaps, then, we should look to the Democratic Party. In 1856, Democrats had lambasted Republican women as too eager for public influence. After Brown's raid and Child's letter, southern women put these two things together, combining the long-standing tropes about sectional difference with Democrats' harsh criticism of Republican women. The mixture southern women created was potent. As male Democrats had done, the southern women decried northern women as strong-minded and radical—demonstrating that all the free states had come under the sway of the most radical Upper North elements. They also elevated southern women as the pure, feminine mirror image of northern women. Where Child nursed Brown to gain fame, southern women nursed the people they enslaved because they were good Christians. Where northern women advocated loudly for abolition, southern women worked quietly to help the victims of Brown's raid. These conservative southern women raised the stakes for southern Democrats. They brought into focus an image of the enemy, and they elevated themselves as a cause worth fighting to protect.[40]

The apotheosis of white southern women mixed with hackneyed stereotypes of enslaved men to breed panic about slave rebellion. In the Border South, white men worked themselves into a frenzy imagining the rape of white women that—they believed—would have ensued had Brown's raid been successful. Indeed, the prosecution played to these fears during Brown's trial, describing the "disheveled tresses of a frightened beauty" scared by the raid. Democratic politicians and editors seized on this fear to mobilize support for their party, linking the rape of white women to abiding concerns about abolitionist incursions, slave flight, and the Republican Party. Indeed, the fear of slave flight was well-founded. As William Link has explained, "slaves' rejection of their bondage helped to create a particular sectional dynamic: it was their resistance that fueled slaveholder anxiety, and slaveholder anxieties fostered the political crisis." But politicians fanned the flames of these fears. Henry Wise claimed to have received intelligence of "organized conspiracies . . . to commit rapine and burning along [Virginia's] borders on Maryland, Pennsylvania, Ohio, and Indiana, proceeding from these States and from New York, Massachusetts, and Canada." Tellingly, Wise here lumped together the moderate states bordering Virginia with the more solidly antislavery states of the Upper North and even Canada, avowing that they posed an equal threat to slavery and to white women's sexual purity. James Fulton, editor of North Carolina's *Wilmington Journal*, used similar language, describing how "the . . . negro has again been instigated to murder and rapine by the devilish machinations of white men," and warning that "Maryland, Delaware, and the northern part of Virginia swarm with the emissaries of the Abolitionists." Like Wise, Fulton rolled together whites' fears—of slave flight and insurrection, of abolitionist incursions, of secret internal enemies—and amplified them with the specter of white women's sexual violation. A sensationalist account of Brown's raid, published in Baltimore in the waning months of 1859, used the same language. "The late and tragical occurrences at Harpers Ferry," the book began, "startled many firesides from the feelings of security in which they have heretofore tranquilly reposed." Brown had hoped to "invade and violate the rights of the Southern States, kindle a servile war, and spread rapine, pillage, and bloodshed among their people."[41]

Northern Democrats imagined that moderation reigned in the Border South. But in harping on fears of northern incursions, slave flight, and rapine, Border South Democrats far more closely resembled their Lower South counterparts. Unsurprisingly, James D. B. DeBow contended that northerners supported slave rebellion, property theft, and the carrying off of white women. In his magazine's April 1860 issue, DeBow published a long letter from the former president John Tyler. The Virginian alleged that "citizens of the North in close correspondence with many of the most prominent and influential political leaders of that section . . . in September, 1859 unfurled the black banner of abolition . . . and invited the slaves throughout the South to rebellion and a feast of blood and rapine." Similarly, the *New Orleans Times-Picayune* claimed that Brown's raid had aimed for "the desecration of households, robbery, murder, and arson, and a horrid concourse of kindred crimes." A few weeks later, on December 1, the *Times-Picayune* reprised this point, emphasizing the horrific consequences for white southern women had Brown been successful. "Not content with running off a few negroes from their masters, John Brown and his party of marauders were willing to cause a general insurrection," the paper reported. Such an insurrection would "overturn the whole social compact, which protects life [and] guards female innocence"—that is, white women's bodies from Black men's supposed hypersexuality.[42] Taken together, publications like these turned the isolated incident of Brown's raid into a broader threat against white southern women, white southern homes, and white southern men's wealth and property in slaves.

If the rape and murder of white southern families came to pass, whom should southerners blame? Even moderate southern Democrats contended that northern Democrats would be somehow responsible. John Polhill, the editor of Georgia's *Federal Union* declared, "Honest and conscientious men at the north" must "now see the necessity of putting down a party whose principles, if carried out, can lead only to civil war, murder, and rapine." The editor of a relatively moderate paper that supported states' rights but not secession, Polhill did not yet claim that the majority of northerners supported Brown.[43] Yet he nonetheless placed responsibility for stopping future incursions—future "rapine"—squarely on the shoulders of northern men, including northern Democrats. If northern Democrats could not quash the Republican Party, and if an abolitionist then incited an insurrection, then northern Democrats would have failed to protect southern men's property and southern women's honor.

Democratic appeals to protect white women were powerful for two reasons. First, contemporary mores and laws dictated that a woman's body belonged to her husband. She owed him sexual access, and he owed her financial support and physical protection. If a man's wife was raped, the man had not held up his end of the contract—which in turn represented a failure of his authority and his honor. Second, the appeal to protect white women related back, as most things did in the South, to slavery. The condition of slavery followed the mother: if the mother was free, the child was free; if the mother was enslaved, the child was enslaved. The rape of a white woman by a Black man therefore threatened the institution of slavery, because the union might beget a free Black child.[44] This is why white men issued and responded to calls to protect white womanhood.

Far from mere idols, white southern women spewed invective of their own against Brown and his men. Twenty-year-old Amanda Edmonds lived less than forty miles south of Harpers Ferry, on her family's plantation in Fauquier County, Virginia. She claimed in her diary a month after the raid that she had passed the whole night of the raid—of which she at that point had no knowledge—consumed by a "feeling of utter dread," only to awake and find out about the violence. Edmonds inveighed against Brown and his accomplices. "Rascals!" she exclaimed. "To free the slaves of the South, that our dear old State should be made a free State O! The idea is overbearing." Against the enslaved men who set fire to a neighbor's wheat weeks after the raid, she spat, "I could see the fire kindled and [the enslaved people] shringed and burnt untill [*sic*] the last drop of blood was dried within them and every bone moulder to ashes." When Brown dropped to his death on December 2, Edmonds was elated, writing in her diary, "This day will long, long be remembered, as the one that witnessed Old Ossawattamie the villain—murderer, robber, and destroyer of our Virgin peace, swinging from the gallows." She later added, "What an awfully sublime, a glorious, a charmed scene. I almost wish I was a man so I could have been there to look upon it." Many other women felt similarly. In a letter to Andrew Hunter, the district attorney for Charles Town who prosecuted Brown's case, one man confided that his wife "has had several hearty crying spells because she cannot be there, to lend a helping hand, in her way, such as I hear the ladies have so cheerfully done . . . to the comfort of the soldiers."[45]

Threats real and imagined haunted white women in the South. Slave rebellion represented a genuine threat to slaveholding women's economic well-being and social status, which depended on the oppression of enslaved men and women. Though southerners had instituted ever-more draconian measures to stymie unrest, fear of a Haitian-style rebellion still loomed over the white South. The imagined threat was of rape by enslaved Black men. As Elizabeth Fox-Genovese has explained, white proslavery propaganda characterized enslaved men as either "Bucks" or "Sambos." According to this propaganda, Sambos were naturally docile and subservient, but Bucks were virile and sexually aggressive—an implicit threat to white women on the plantation. Fox-Genovese notes the irony in this fear, since "the main interracial sexual threat was that of white predators against black women"—of slaveholders raping the women they enslaved.[46] However baseless, the fear of Black men's sexuality amplified the fear of rebellion: once liberated, some enslaved men may not pose a threat, but others, white southerners feared, would assault white women. Edmonds's fear of insurrection and desire for revenge indicates that white southern women were not mere symbols for southern men to wield in political arguments: they also desired revenge against abolitionists and the continuation of slavery. Edmonds could not burn alive the people who were resisting their enslavement, nor could she attend Brown's hanging. But like many white southern women, Edmonds became more militant in her critique of northern society and her support for southern secession in the months following the raid. A group of women in Virginia even formed their own southern rights association the day after Brown's hanging. For white southern women, John Brown's raid raised fears about the demise of slavery and its attendant horrors—including the real threat to their social and economic status and the imagined threat of sexual assault. In response, these women became some of the most impassioned critics of abolitionism and defenders of southern nationalism.[47]

"Patriarchal Tenure": Secessionists React

Ultimately, Brown's raid shook Border South Democrats' faith in the Union's ability to protect southern women and southern property from northern women, men, and ideas. If the Union's laws had not protected the South from renegades like Brown and sympathizers like Child, why should southerners expect anything different in the future? On December 5, in his final message as governor to the Virginia state legislature, Henry Wise reported on a recent exchange with James Buchanan. Wise had written Buchanan to ask what the federal government could do to protect Virginia from future abolitionist attacks. Both men were Democrats. Yet Wise was disgusted with Buchanan's response. "He seems to think that the constitution and laws of the United States do not provide authority for the President to interpose to '*repel invasion*,'" Wise told Virginia's legislators. "I differ from this opinion. Neither the framers of the constitution nor the Congress of 1795 were guilty of so gross an omission in their provisions for the national safety." After quoting extensively from the Constitution to prove his point, Wise reasoned, "If I am right in my views of our guarantee of protection" and "he, the executive of the United States, does not concur with me, [he] will not enforce the protection we need." "On the other hand," Wise continued, "if he is right . . . we cannot legally claim that the United States shall keep the peace." He finished, "In either case . . . We must rely on ourselves, and fight for peace!"[48]

Wise and his fellow Democrats believed that Virginia should mobilize to protect slavery from abolitionism and from the possible treachery of nonslaveholding whites—even if that meant preparing to secede. Patrick Cabell Massie, a slaveholder in Nelson County, sided with Wise and the Democrats. Because northerners had sympathized with Brown, Massie wrote to his uncle, "it is clear that our reliance must not be on their sense of justice but upon our own ability to resist." Like Wise, Massie had begun to wonder whether the Union could protect white southerners from slave insurrections and believed that southerners must be ready to use force to protect their interests. A strong Unionist opposition, however, opposed this plan. These former Whigs tried to pave a third way between the fanatics of Massachusetts and the fanatics of South Carolina in the hope that Virginia could hold the Union together. John Brown raided Harpers Ferry in the middle of this ongoing political battle; Virginia's Democrats capitalized on the fear and drama to sway public opinion in their favor.[49]

And at this, fire-eaters rejoiced. John Brown's raid gave life and visceral power to what they had argued for decades: that the Union did not and would not protect slavery, and that the South should therefore secede.[50] Most southern Democrats had previously dismissed the fire-eaters as fringe radicals; now, even in the Border South, many Democrats were concluding that the fire-eaters may not be so radical after all. The *Charleston Mercury*, a radical paper in a radical state, happily encouraged Virginians' concerns about the Union. Virginia had once been a stronghold of Unionism, the paper wrote. But "the Harpers Ferry *emeute*, like a slap in the face, appears to have wakened her up to some consciousness of her rights and dignity." Then the *Mercury* played to Virginians' masculine pride: "The contempt in which she was held, implied by such an invasion—the scorn heaped on her by the whole northern press—the imputations of cowardice and weakness . . . have shown Virginia . . . she ought to be with the South."[51]

In the months following Brown's raid, fire-eaters seized on Border South Democrats turn away from northern nationalism to encourage them to mobilize for secession—and even war. The raid was "a prelude to what must and will recur again and again, as the progress of sectional hate . . . advances," the *Charleston Mercury* warned. Southerners needed to put an end to their "tame and passive policy," which the paper argued had "allow[ed] slavery to be carried out of the border states." If they were to be men—to protect their property and their honor—southern men would have to become more aggressive in their political demands. That might mean, the *Mercury* told readers in another article, that southerners should demand to rule themselves. The "ignominious toleration and concession by the South, with the lights of the present"—that is, of Brown's raid—"reflected on them, show to the most bigoted Unionist that there is no peace for the South in the Union. . . . The South must control her own destinies or perish." And upon seeing a Richmond, Virginia, editorial that finally countenanced secession, the *Mercury* huffed, "Well! It is better late than never."[52]

The secessionist *DeBow's Review* agreed. John Brown's raid—the attack of a "notorious horse-thief and murderer"—had demonstrated one inescapable fact: meddling, modernizing northerners would not let the South alone until they established "a government without . . . a principle of conservatism, and . . . a society without a patriarchal institution, or an element of subordination." By "patriarchal institution," *DeBow's* meant slavery. And indeed, conservatism, slavery, and subordination were the building blocks of southern slave society. Without slavery and subordination (of Black to white and women to men), southern society would crumble. "For these results," the author averred, "there is but one mode of escape . . . *Secession and a new Confederation*."[53]

Like northern Democrats, southern radicals called on the idea of a national family in the months following the raid. Unlike northern Democrats, these radicals conceptualized the national family as one that only included the southern states. In the South Carolina State Senate, Thomas

Wagner of Christ Church Parish offered a resolution speaking of the "increasing violence, and in new and more alarming forms," against the institution of slavery—a reference to the events at Harpers Ferry. The resolution continued, "South Carolina . . . earnestly invited and urges her sister States of the South to originate the movement of Southern separation." And following Mississippi's adoption of a series of resolutions threatening secession, the *Semi-weekly Mississippian* editorialized, "we have every reason to hope that South Carolina, Georgia and Alabama will . . . meet Mississippi in Convention. . . . And this step will, doubtless, precipitate other States (which are but waiting the example of their sister States,) into the movement."[54] These radicals proposed a new national family: one that included only southern states, among which there existed the fraternity they imagined had marked the original Union.

One Mississippian, Richard Thompson Archer, followed these calls for secession to their logical conclusion. Archer, a cotton planter, owned more than 13,000 acres of land and enslaved over 500 people, making him one of the wealthiest men in the South. On December 8, he drafted a letter to the editors of a newspaper. "'The irrepressible conflict' has begun, the South is invaded," Archer wrote. "It is time for all patriots to be united, to be under military organization, to be advancing to the conflict determined to . . . die in defense of the God given right to own the African. If young men are slow to prepare for the conflict, to volunteer in the service of the South, it is time for old men to set them an example." Archer then called for volunteers for a cavalry troop that he planned to raise. Archer's land and the enslaved people who cultivated it were in Mississippi—far from the free states and their abolitionists. Yet Brown's raid, and the southern Democratic press's response to the raid, had worked in tandem to convince Democrats across the South that their land, their property in slaves, their wives, and their "patriarchal tenure," as Governor Wise once put it, were all now at stake.[55] Archer believed that southern men must be willing to secede and to fight to protect a patriarchal slave society.

Democrats' 1856 campaign tactics had sowed the seeds of conflict within the party. The divergence in Democratic responses to John Brown's raid demonstrate that those seeds had taken root. Pulling straight from the 1856 playbook, northern Democrats blamed the raid on Republicans, linking John Brown to the broader spirit of gender and abolitionist radicalism that they claimed pervaded the Republican Party. This made it difficult for Republicans to distance themselves from Brown and his tactics. With their energies focused on drawing voters away from the Republican Party, however, northern Democrats failed to attend to the racialized and sexualized anxieties of Democrats in the Border and Upper South, paying only cursory attention to white fears of rape, murder, and insurrection. Yet to Democrats in that border region, the raid proved what the rhetoric from 1856 and the Republicans' midterm victories had made them suspect: all Republicans were radicals, most northerners were Republicans, and therefore most northerners were radicals—radicals who now clearly wished to threaten southern slavery and southern homes with their violent abolitionist raids. With the party's presidential nominating convention set to meet in the spring, southern Democrats' deepening sense of alienation made compromise on a candidate and a platform truly ambitious goals—ones that would ultimately prove to be out of reach.

4

A Social and Moral Contest

THE DEMOCRATIC SPLIT AND THE
1860 CAMPAIGN

By early 1860, the Lecompton debacle and John Brown's raid had left the Democratic Party unsettled indeed. As Democratic partisans began preparing for the party's national convention in Charleston, South Carolina, one Democratic editor brooded over "the troubles that are seething and boiling in the political cauldron."[1] He was right to be concerned. Northern politicians were determined to push ahead with popular sovereignty and stave off a Republican insurgency. Southern men worried the national party could not protect southern slavery and southern homes from northern radicalism. Infighting even appeared in state organizations, as partisans divided over whether to send proslavery or pro–popular sovereignty delegates to Charleston. In January, Alabama's Democratic convention instructed delegates to bolt the national convention if the platform did not include a federal slave code. Georgia's Democrats sent delegates to Charleston with no platform statement on slavery at all. And both Illinois and New York sent rival pro- and anti–Stephen Douglas delegations to Charleston.

With delegates like these—and in light of the events of the preceding four years—the die was cast for a fractious campaign season. At their national conventions in Charleston and Baltimore, northern and southern Democrats nominated and ran separate candidates. By splitting the vote, Democrats upset the electoral calculus and contributed to the election of Republican Abraham Lincoln. The Democratic Party collapsed over slavery, as the party's discourse descended into a welter of accusations and counteraccusations in an atmosphere of suspicion and betrayal. Democrats expressed alienation from each other in highly gendered political language. Emphasizing as it did the social and cultural incompatibility of North and South, that language made Democrats' disagreements seem more profound and compromise seem dangerous. Between April and November 1860, gender politics solidified the split between the northern and southern wings of the party, united the Upper and Lower South, and primed the pump for secession.

Northern Democrats wanted a popular sovereignty platform and a northern nominee, and they needed to fend off the rising Republican Party. So northern Democrats condemned Republicans as dangerous radicals on gender and slavery alike, emphasizing especially Republicans' supposed support for interracial sex. In the South—the Upper South, in particular—northern Democrats tried to pick off moderate votes by decrying fire-eaters as gender radicals of a different sort. According to northern Democrats, extreme southerners had become intoxicated with the power of ruling their plantations, and now planned to subjugate nonslaveholding whites as they had subjugated their slaves. For northern Democrats, whose manhood centered on total autonomy over home and government, this was deeply disturbing. They avowed that compromise with any extremist party—Republican or fire-eater—would be an affront to their honor and manhood, and that popular sovereignty was the only manly solution to the slavery question.

Southern Democrats, however, wanted a proslavery platform and a southern nominee. To consolidate southern members behind these goals, they articulated a vision of two different societies. Using the line that they had deployed against Republicans in 1856, southern Democrats claimed that northerners supported women's rights, free love, miscegenation, and abolition. They attributed the popularity of these heresies to the general penchant for freedom in the North. Southerners, on the other hand, did not support those "isms." They enjoyed a stable, patriarchal society, which southern politicians and writers attributed to the presence of slavery. To hold partisans in line—especially reluctant Upper South Democrats— southern Democratic newspapers equated a refusal to compromise with masculine strength and equivocation with cowardice. And while northern Democrats claimed Republican rule would result in miscegenation, southern Democrats alleged that the real threat was a northern victory, whether by Abraham Lincoln or Stephen Douglas.

Fatefully, secession-minded fire-eaters took this argument one step further. They believed that if Lincoln were elected president (a likely outcome after northern and southern Democrats nominated separate candidates in June), the South should secede immediately. Reviving fears raised by John Brown's raid, these Democrats claimed that a Republican presidency would lead to slave insurrection, racial equality, and the rape of southern white women.

Intransigence and Masculinity
in Charleston and Baltimore

Opening their convention at Charleston's Institute Hall on April 23, Democrats were the first party to hold a national presidential nominating convention in 1860. Tellingly, they would be the last to choose their candidate. Chosen by the fractious state conventions, northern and southern delegates arrived with diametrically opposed goals. Northern Democrats fretted over the party's electoral viability—and with good reason. Over the previous five years, northern voters had left the party in droves, sick of what they saw as their representatives' capitulation to southern slaveholders' interests. Aware of his precarious position, one Illinois congressman wrote to Stephen Douglas warning, "We are not in a condition to carry another ounce of Southern weight."[2] Heading into Charleston, then, northern Democrats knew they would insist on a popular sovereignty platform and a northern nominee. A proslavery southerner would have no chance at beating the rising Republicans, whoever their nominee may be. But following the rejection of the Lecompton Constitution and the shock of John Brown's raid, Deep South Democrats were no longer willing to accept popular sovereignty or the northern nominee—presumably Stephen Douglas—who would be its standard-bearer.

The first salvo in in the Democrats' intraparty battle came in the fight over the platform. On the first night of the convention, a caucus of southern delegates from Alabama, Mississippi, Florida, Arkansas, Texas, and Louisiana set out their demands. Their platform would force a slave code—a set of restrictions on the movement, education, and personal lives of enslaved people, enforced by local white residents—on the territories. Residents of the territories would also be prevented from outlawing slavery until they applied for statehood. The caucus of southern delegates declared that unless the convention adopted their platform, they would quit the convention. They hoped the threat would force northern Democrats to concede to their demands. But denying as it did the masculine prerogative of a free vote, the proslavery platform would be political suicide for northern Democrats. They responded by putting forward a platform that effectively reiterated the popular sovereignty platform of 1856. Unable to compromise, the convention's Committee on Resolutions submitted the two platforms to the general convention. The popular sovereignty platform won 165 to 138 on an almost straight sectional vote. Immediately, LeRoy Pope Walker—a keen secessionist—took the floor and called on his fellow Alabamians to walk out of the convention. They did, and forty-nine delegates from Mississippi, South Carolina, Florida, Texas, Delaware, Georgia, and Arkansas followed. As secessionist as any white Charlestonians, women spectators descended from the galleries and placed roses on the departing delegates' empty seats in a gesture of support.[3]

Yet even the mostly northern contingent that stayed in the Institution Hall could not settle on the convention's second question: the choice of a nominee. Two days and fifty-seven ballots later, the convention was deadlocked. The remaining delegates voted to reconvene in Baltimore on June 18, hoping, in part, that the states whose delegates had seceded from the convention might send different, more moderate delegates to Baltimore. The choice of location was also significant: Democrats hoped that the Border South city would foster an atmosphere more amenable to compromise than the secessionist hotbed of Charleston.

In the period between the Charleston and Baltimore conventions, Democratic papers in the Deep South praised the courage and manliness of the Charleston bolters, hoping to prevent any compromise with the northern wing of the party. On May 12, the fire-eating New Orleans *Daily Delta* wrote, "The delegates of the South to the Charleston Convention proudly and nobly sustained the manhood of our section by refusing to recognize the right of a dominant section to exclude them from equal enjoyment of the common territory of the Union." The *Macon Daily Telegraph* offered similar support to Georgia's delegation, describing the bolters as "most honorable men."[4]

This language ratcheted up around the end of May, when southern Democrats wrangled over whether to attend at the next national convention in Baltimore or depart for a separate, southern convention in Richmond. The *Macon Daily Telegraph* warned that southern men "would stultify themselves by a return to Baltimore. It would be a wound upon their honor. . . . We know some of them well, and hesitate not to say their manhood and chivalry revolt at such condescending obsequiousness." South Carolina state senator John Townsend echoed this sentiment. On June 7, Townsend delivered a speech decrying the push to compromise as an "insult to our *manhood*," as if it "could be driven from its propriety, by *fear of consequences* and the power of numbers." With the Baltimore convention about to begin, Townsend urged southern Democrats to quit the national party. "How . . . absurd is it, for the South, to be placing her dependence upon 'Presidents' and 'parties' when she can work out her own deliverance," Townsend cried. Townsend blamed "womanly fears of 'Disunion'" for preventing southern Democrats from taking "manly and resolute ACTION."[5]

Moderate southerners felt the heat from these attacks. A moderate who supported the Baltimore convention, *Mobile Register* editor John Forsyth Jr. fumed that "these boasters . . . presume to call other people 'submissionists'!" Then Forsyth engaged in a bit of gender-baiting of his own, claiming that most secessionists were too cowardly to follow through on their program. "We have tried by every appeal and taunt that could touch their manhood and pride to induce them to do it . . . yet no sooner do we find an opportunity to pick up their gage of battle . . . than they begin to whimper like spanked children, and to back square out of the issue."[6] An astute political operator, Forsyth realized that the secessionists' gendered attacks had put moderate southern Democrats in an uncomfortable position. By equating intransigence with masculinity, politicians like Townsend pressured moderates like Forsyth to forsake the Baltimore convention and support the nomination of a separate, southern candidate.

Northern newspapers also spent the spring of 1860 urging against compromise. During the Charleston convention, one correspondent spat that proslavery Oregon senator Joseph Lane had "managed Oregon as though he held it politically as his own property." But with Lane in the running for the presidential nomination, the correspondent declared that "a body of sturdy democrats . . . cannot be managed like a plantation of Southern laborers."[7] Northerners—Democrats included—resented elite southern slaveholders and their stranglehold over national politics. This feeling had grown especially acute in the years following the caning of Charles Sumner. Northerners saw the attack on the Senate floor as evidence that slaveholders planned to exercise mastery over white men in the same way they did their slaves. The newspaperman's comments about Lane speaks to northerners' determination that they must stand up to southerners at the Charleston convention, lest they forfeit their political power and their manhood.

Northern Democrats kept up their gendered threats on the eve of the Baltimore convention. Set to convene at Baltimore's Front Street Theater on June 18, this convention seemed even less likely to succeed than the one in Charleston. Republicans had selected Abraham Lincoln as their standard-bearer in mid-May, providing ammunition for Douglas supporters to insist that only a fellow Illinoisan would be able to hold onto the Midwest. Then there was the question of whether to seat the delegates who bolted at Charleston, which one Wisconsin paper cautioned would be akin to sacrificing the convention's manhood. "The convention owes it to its dignity and self-respect never to open its doors to the factious set, who defied its authority," the paper warned. "There will be back-bone enough to rebuke and put down all such insolence, or the convention will surrender both honor and manhood."[8] Northern Democrats had compromised with southerners for years, but by the spring of 1860, some among them had begun to see that compromise as capitulation and subservience. That shift limited the political options for any northerners who may have wanted to seat the delegates and nominate a national candidate. For two full days, the convention's credential committee debated whether to seat the bolted delegates. Finally, on June 22, delegates voted to exclude Florida and Alabama's delegations from the convention. The rest of the southern delegates walked out of the Front Street Theater in protest. The Democratic Party had officially split in two.

Reconvening in Baltimore's Institute Hall the next day, the southerners—plus some New York, Minnesota, Vermont, Pennsylvania, and Massachusetts men and all of the Oregon and California delegations—readopted the proslavery platform from Charleston. That platform called for absolute protection of slavery in the territories. To represent this platform, southern Democrats nominated the Kentuckian and sitting vice president of the United States, John C. Breckinridge. Jefferson Davis had convinced Breckinridge that accepting the nomination would reunite the Democratic Party and ensure Lincoln's defeat in November. But Breckinridge's more radical supporters hoped his nomination would split the party, secure Lincoln's victory, and justify southern secession.[9]

For their part, the northern delegates who remained at the Institute Hall in Baltimore approved a platform that reaffirmed their position from 1856: slavery in the territories would be decided by popular sovereignty. Unsurprisingly, they chose Stephen A. Douglas, the architect of the Kansas-Nebraska Act and the country's preeminent champion of popular sovereignty, as their nominee. With the newly formed Constitutional Union Party having nominated former senator John Bell of Tennessee on May 10, Douglas was set to wage three campaigns: against Lincoln, against Bell, and against Breckinridge.

"Manliness and Independence": The Contest in the North

Douglas's foremost challenge was to vanquish Lincoln in the northern states, where Republicans had made serious inroads over the previous five years. In 1856, John Frémont had come within two states of winning the election, and in the ensuing midterms, Republicans had flipped a number of House seats.[10] They had done this by selling a message of free soil and manly independence. Republicans believed that if a man could not find honest work in the East, he should be free to move west to work the land there—without having to compete with slave labor. At their mid-May convention in Chicago, Republicans chose a platform and a nominee that reflected this faith in antislavery, free labor, and masculine self-reliance. Republicans conceded "the right of each state to order and control its own domestic institutions." But insisting that "the normal condition of all the territory of the United States is that of freedom," Republicans called for slavery to be banned from federal territories. The platform also deplored John Brown's raid and expressed support for government funding of public works projects. To represent this platform, they nominated Abraham Lincoln, a former congressman from Illinois and relative moderate in his party. Republicans' portrayals of Lincoln emphasized his strength, independence, and hard work, making him the embodiment of Republican manhood. The Kentucky politician Cassius Clay, recounting Lincoln's early life of manual labor, asked, "Does it not inspire manliness and confidence in the bosom of any man to know that really a man can have an open field and a fair fight, and the devil take the hindermost? If you want this equal manliness for yourselves go for ABRAHAM LINCOLN in 1860." And Republican cartoons, such as one published in the *Wide-Awake Pictorial*, often depicted Lincoln as a muscular, hard-working backwoodsman, ready to take on the Democratic Party.[11]

Republicans contended that free labor would ennoble the common man—just as it had done for Lincoln. In a debate with his colleague Jefferson Davis, Republican senator William Fessenden of Maine contended that "free labor is in its character independent, and tends to promote the wealth and manliness of the laborer; while slave labor tends to degrade and impoverish the laborer." The celebrated lawyer William M. Evarts made a similar point in a speech in Auburn, New York. "Free labor," Evarts declared, "is the application of the whole man by himself—the master of his own limbs." An article in a Wisconsin paper even encouraged women to marry brave, hardworking men. Titled "Labor—Degrading!" the article went on, "Is it? So says the slaveholder. So says the proud and scornful young miss . . . and so says that haughty young dandy who can't black his own boots." These characters were, of course, all standard stereotypes of southern slaveholders. "Well girls," the article counseled. "You had better let him learn to take care of himself . . . before you think of taking him for a companion." Young women should instead look for a man "that has strong arms, a courageous will," "who is not afraid of manly toil."[12]

When southern newspapers or politicians belittled white northern farmers or laborers, Republican papers reprinted the jibes, hoping to pique

The Last Rail Split by "Honest Old Abe."

"The Last Rail Split by 'Honest Old Abe,'" 1860.
Image published with permission of ProQuest LLC.
Further reproduction is prohibited without permission.

readers' pride and move votes. In 1858, South Carolina senator James Henry Hammond had given a speech describing northern men as a "whole hireling class of manual laborers" who were "essentially slaves." With its comparison between free white northerners and enslaved African Americans, the speech infuriated northern men. In June 1860, a New Jersey reporter evoked the speech when he forecast that the state would go for Lincoln. "Having a large population . . . all being working men, we don't believe we are—in the classic language of Senator Hammond—the 'mudsills of society,' but free men."[13] Race was everything in antebellum America: it determined whether a man could be enslaved, whether he could vote, whom he could marry—even whether or not he was seen as a man. By resurrecting the Mudsill Speech, the *Tribune* reminded readers that northern Democrats were connected to southern Democrats, and southern Democrats thought northern white men were no better than slaves. It was a powerful play to white masculinity.

A Republican paper in Ohio published a similar piece. The article began by citing quotes allegedly drawn from Democratic papers, such as "Slavery, White or Black, is the natural and normal condition of the laboring man," and "Mechanics and laborers are a servile class unfit for self government," "born with saddles on their backs" so that slaveholders may "ride them." Replete with that language of submissiveness, rape, and bestiality, these selections were sure to offend northern workers, whose manhood was founded in their whiteness and independence. "How do the mechanics and laboring men of the North relish such doctrines?" the Republican paper asked. "Are they ready to be white slaves? . . . Do they wish to bend their backs and be bestridden by [Henry] Wise, [Robert] Toombs, [and Lawrence] Keitt?" "Are they debased enough for the 'whip, the reins, and the spur?'"[14] White northern men could not tolerate the imputation that they were no better than enslavers' animals, women, and laborers.

In a similar play to pick off moderate northern voters, Republican papers charged that northern Democrats had been degraded by their supposed subservience to southerners. In response to each of the recent political imbroglios—the Utah War, the Lecompton Constitution, John Brown's raid—northern Democrats had tried to walk an ever-finer line between the demands of their nonslaveholding constituents and those of their slaveholding southern colleagues. Using gendered language, Republican papers pilloried northern Democrats for caving to southern demands. A paper from southern Ohio called northern Democrats "the despisers of free labors—the dough-faced demagogues . . . servile tools, who, like well-fed negroes, are willing slaves." And in Iowa, a paper rallied its readers to the polls by exhorting, "Freemen . . . if you have in your bosoms a spark of manliness and independence, you will go to the polls next Tuesday and pass . . . a verdict upon these servile tools of the slaveholding oligarchy."[15] Republican papers held up northern Democrats' repeated compromises as proof that southern Democrats controlled their northern colleagues as thoroughly as they did their slaves. This gendered and racialized accusation implied that northern Democrats were weak, degraded, and unfit to lead.

Consolidating their moderate image, Republicans even walked back their appeal to women supporters. In 1856 Republicans were hardly revolutionaries, scoffing at women's rights and free love. But more progressive Republicans had emphasized that Jessie Frémont would advise her husband John on political matters, garnering support from Republican women. By 1860, even these small gestures toward women's inclusion had disappeared. Mary Todd Lincoln was as well-connected as Jessie, yet Republican papers emphasized her role as wife and mother, not as a political adviser. Upon visiting the Lincoln household, a *New York Daily Times* correspondent only reported that Mary Todd took "honorable pride in the distinction which had fallen upon her husband." Campaign biographies, meanwhile, took care to note that she excelled at housework. One biographer noted that visitors to the Lincoln home were greeted by Mary "the hostess," whom he described as "the pattern of lady-like courtesy and polish," who "converses with freedom and grace, and is thoroughly *au fait* in all the little amenities of society." Such a hostess, the author promised, "will do the honors of the White House with appropriate grace."[16] By portraying Mary Todd as a conventional, respectable upper-middle-class wife and Abraham as a manly rail-splitter, the Republicans pitched their party as an advocate of hard-working white men.

Though Lincoln and the Republicans ran a fairly conservative campaign, one would not have known it from Democratic propaganda. To beat back the Republican threat, northern Democrats reprised their argument from 1856: a Republican president would use the federal government to institute a radical social program of abolition, women's rights, free love, and miscegenation. The Republican Party was not the protector of free white masculinity: it was the ultimate threat to it. The printing company Currier and Ives published a political cartoon by Louis Maurer that made exactly this point. Titled "The Republican Party Going to the Right House," the cartoon depicts a motley crew of social radicals following Abraham Lincoln into an insane asylum. Lincoln sits astride a rail borne by Horace Greeley, the reformist editor of the *New York Tribune*, and is followed by his supposed supporters, including a free love advocate, a women's rights

"The Republican Party Going to the Right House," 1860.
Library of Congress, Prints and Photographs Division, LC-DIG-pga-04994.

activist, a free Black abolitionist, and a socialist. Affordable and widely available, the cartoon encapsulated the Democratic argument for a broad audience: Republicans wanted to free everyone from the social norms that made for a stable society and country.[17]

In the cartoon, a women's rights activist declares, "I want woman['s] rights enforced, and man reduced in subjection to her authority." Give control to Lincoln, the cartoon implied, and he would impose a radical women's rights agenda on the country. Maurer drew the woman as short and thin, with a long, pointy nose. In so doing, Maurer dismisses her message: only shrews supported women's rights.

This unflattering depiction of the women's rights activist echoed Democrats' campaign rhetoric about the movement and its supposed connection to the Republican Party. *New York Herald* editor James Gordon Bennett frequently used his organ to convince northern voters that the Republican Party supported women's rights. One article smeared the Republican Party as the "Woman's Rights Party." Another charged that "the whole structure of the black republican party . . . is that 'slavery is an evil and a crime,'" and that around that belief "have been gathered other ideas belonging to the same school, and inculcating the same exaggerated notion of individual rights, such as Fourierism, [and] woman's rights."[18] In the late eighteenth century, French thinker François Marie Charles Fourier had proposed founding utopian collectives that would eliminate gender roles. To Democrats, who saw power as a zero-sum game, that proposition represented an existential threat to white men's near-absolute authority over public and private life. Bennett was intensely racist and unscrupulous—prone to publishing personal conversations, breaking promises, and switching allegiances. But his *New York Herald* had the largest subscription of any American newspaper of its time, so when it claimed that Republicans would enforce women's rights and antislavery, there was a good chance that many northerners would believe it.

In the Maurer cartoon, two free love advocates—a short, ugly woman and a man with long, feminine hair—march behind Lincoln. The woman looks at Lincoln and exclaims, "Oh! what a beautiful man he is. I feel a 'passional attraction' every time I see his lovely face." Next to her, the man announces, "I represent the free love element, and expect to have free license to carry out its principles." Together, the activists' appearance, their message, and their support for Lincoln—a white man whom Maurer drew with apelike features—made a mockery of the free love movement and underlined the Democrats' point that gender and racial disorder marched hand in hand.

Northern Democratic newspapers picked up this line of attack. One Wisconsin correspondent reported that the Republican National Convention in Chicago had been full of "the same gaunt philosophers who suggest bran bread and free love." Sylvester Graham, the advocate for bran bread and vegetarianism, actually supported a strict chastity, but accuracy mattered less than shock value. The *New York Herald* printed a sensational letter allegedly written by a woman who abandoned her family to be with her lover. The woman had long felt a "passionate desire to be freed from all restraint, moral or physical." Once she became infatuated with another man, the "chaste name of wife" seemed to her a mere "social fiction." Democrats claimed that this letter represented "a free love manifesto" for the Republican campaign. Never mind that the writer had no connection to the Republican Party, or that the Republican *New York Times* described free love as an "ulcerous abomination of unrestrained lust."[19] Democrats expected that the false association between Republicans and free love would be effective because they knew that men feared free love as a threat to their mastery over their wives, their families, and their homes.

To northern Democrats, then, free love was troubling by its very nature. But it also symbolized what they saw as a broader Republican tendency toward lawlessness. The *Herald* had mocked the free love letter as a "Higher Law for Discontented Wives." The editor was referring to an 1850 speech in which Republican William Seward had claimed divine moral law—a higher law than the Constitution—bound him to oppose slavery's expansion.[20] "Higher law" had become a catchphrase among Seward's Democratic detractors, symbolizing what seemed to them an irrational, lawless, and un-American attack not just on slavery but on the American system of law and government: if someone did not like a law, they did not have to obey it. The notion of a higher law was especially threatening to Democratic men, since American laws—on marriage, property, and franchise—upheld their status as patriarchs. When the *Herald* described free love literature as higher law, then, it was marshalling this fear of Republican lawlessness. Republicans would apply the higher-law logic to marriages, inviting wives to leave their husbands.

In the Maurer cartoon, the next person in line after the free love couple is a free Black man. Maurer drew him using common anti-Black caricatures, including large lips and ostentatious clothing. The man proclaims, "'De white man hab no rights dat cullud pussons am bound to spect.' I want dat understood." It was a reprisal of the Democrats' standard claim: Republicans would abolish slavery and grant freedmen social and political equality with white men. This related to a second claim: that abolition and equality would lead to interracial sex. Indeed, Democrats linked recent Republican victories in Ohio to an increase in interracial relationships. A typical article claimed that the town of Madison, Ohio, had been "thrown into great excitement by the elopement of a white woman and a full blooded negro." The elopement was especially scandalous because she left her young child behind with her husband, and because she was "of more than ordinary intelligence and very fair appearance." The paper's white readership would have been shocked that a beautiful white woman left her family to be with a Black man—a choice that, to them, threatened to both harm the white child and beget interracial children. But rather than blaming the woman for the elopement, the paper pointed a finger at her husband's support for abolitionism, claiming it led to her departure.

"An abolition sentiment and an abolition literature has prevailed in the farmer's house for years. This elopement," the paper concluded, "is the legitimate result." This storyline—a white woman leaves her white, Republican husband for a Black man—appeared in numerous northern Democratic papers during this election.[21] It told voters that Republican leadership of the country would have the same effect as Republican leadership of families, resulting in race mixing, chaos, and disunion.

In sum, the Maurer cartoon—with its women's rights activist, its free love advocates, and its free Black man—perfectly encapsulated northern Democrats' case against the Republicans: that they would use the power of the state to embolden radical social movements that posed a grave threat to white men's status as patriarchs.

Nothing encapsulates northern Democrats' and Republicans' divergent views of gender, slavery, and state power better than their recriminations over Stephen Douglas's southern plantation. In 1847, Douglas had married Martha Martin, the daughter of a prominent North Carolina political and slaveholding family. Martin's father, Colonel Robert Martin, owned an 800-acre plantation on North Carolina's Dan River and a large cotton plantation on the Pearl River in Mississippi. Martha died in 1853, and Douglas married Adele Cutts in 1860. But one aspect of his previous marriage continued to haunt him: his ownership of the Martins' Pearl River plantation. Robert Martin had offered Douglas the plantation as a wedding present. Triangulating between his northern constituents and his southern allies, Douglas rejected the offer but claimed that he did so "not because I had any sympathy with abolitionists or the abolition movement, but for the reason that, being a northern man by birth . . . it was impossible for me to know, understand, and provide for the wants, comforts and happiness of those people."[22] Upon his father-in-law's death, however, Douglas nonetheless found it in himself to accept Pearl River as an inheritance.

Throughout the 1850s, Douglas's Republican opponents made the personal political, charging that Douglas owned and profited from his late wife's plantation. In 1855, Senator Benjamin Wade, a Republican and an abolitionist, stood on the Senate floor and accused Douglas of mercenary motives in supporting the Kansas-Nebraska Act. "Where a man's treasure is, there will his heart be also," Wade warned. Douglas shot back, "I implore my enemies, who so ruthlessly invade the domestic sanctuary, to do me the favor to believe that I have no wish, no aspiration, to be considered purer or better than [Martha] who was, or they who are, slaveholders." In 1860 Douglas's authorized campaign biography claimed that the plantation issue had totally blown over, yet the author took the time to recount and dispel the previous accusations. And in a dig at holier-than-thou Republicans, the biographer asked readers, "How many of those who have denounced him as a slaveholder, as being the 'owner of human beings' . . . would have resisted the offer that he declined"?[23]

The Republican denunciation of Douglas's plantation elucidates how the Republican Party saw public life as a manifestation of private morality. Like the Whigs who came before them, many Republicans believed that the government should encourage moral behavior. This impulse linked Republican crusades as disparate as temperance, antipolygamy, and antislavery. Douglas's slaveholding troubled Republicans because it belied a personal immorality that they worried would seep into public life. An inherently violent undertaking, slaveholding also violated many Republican men's masculine values, which included promoting reform movements and supporting women and households as the moral centers of the world.[24] To Republicans, Douglas's slave ownership made him less of a man, not more of one.

Conversely, Douglas's appeal for privacy speaks to the Democratic belief that men's personal lives should not be subjected to public criticism or moral reform.[25] The same spirit that led Democrats to oppose women's rights and abolitionism thus also led them to resist questions about Douglas's slaveholding and to support popular sovereignty. Northern Democrats frequently referred to the doctrine of popular sovereignty as "non-intervention," harkening to their partisans' desire for complete control over all domestic institutions. At a Douglas rally, Herschel Johnson, Douglas's pick for vice president, praised the "doctrine of non-intervention, as it was in 1856"—that is, as in the Kansas-Nebraska Act. The chorus of another Douglas campaign song went, "Our favorite choice are Douglas and Johnson / Our principles, popular sovereignty, non-intervention." Republicans wished to impose their radical ideas about gender and slavery on the rest of the country. Southern Democrats wanted to impose their ideas about slavery on the territories. By promising not to intervene in the territories, only Douglas Democrats stayed true to the Jacksonian vision of negative liberties—of allowing white men to rule themselves. A campaign song in 1860 described America under a Douglas presidency, in which there would be "boys, high hymning through the air / Hosannas unto manhood's independence everywhere!"[26] For Douglas Democrats, the ability to vote on slavery was a white, masculine prerogative. In their eyes, if that principle had been right in 1856, when they won the presidency, and right in 1857, when they rejected Lecompton, then it should still be right in 1860.

Beyond his natural constituency in the North, Douglas also hoped to win the votes of southern moderates—especially in the Border South states of Kentucky, Maryland, Delaware, Missouri, and Virginia, and the Upper South states of North Carolina and Tennessee. In these states, he would have to compete against fellow Democrat John Breckinridge and Constitutional Unionist John Bell.

Constitutional Unionists hoped their newly formed party could sidestep the slavery question and avert disunion. At their national convention in

Baltimore on May 9, delegates adopted a platform that condemned "geo-graphical and sectional parties" and proclaimed "no political principle other than the Constitution of the country, the union of the states, and the enforcement of the laws." For their ticket, the Constitutional Unionists selected the Tennessean John Bell, age sixty-three, and Massachusetts man Edward Everett, sixty-seven. In the words of one historian, it was a platform of "intentional brevity and platitudinous vapidity," represented by two political relics.[27] Constitutional Unionists nonetheless hoped that their men could win enough states—whether on their own or in some joint ticket with the Democrats—to throw the election to the House of Representatives, where Bell might emerge as a compromise candidate.

But their plan ran aground on the political realities and gender politics of the day. To Republicans and Democrats alike, the Constitutional Union Party and its standard-bearers represented an antiquated, weak, and even feminine approach to slavery and politics. A Maine Republican paper derided the Constitutional Union Party as composed of "Granny-dears." And northern and southern Democrats alike sneered at the "fogies" and "old fossils" at the head of the Constitutional Union ticket.[28] Wire-pullers like Democrat August Belmont and Constitutional Unionist Washington Hunt did manage to organize "fusion" tickets in New York, Rhode Island, New Jersey, and Pennsylvania. But most such plans failed, largely because the candidates' platforms were fundamentally incompatible—though the scorn heaped on those who considered the schemes did not help. When Douglasites in Georgia offered to fuse with the Constitutional Unionists, one paper called the proposal "shameless, unprincipled, [and] insulting," showing "contempt for our honor [and] honesty." A Republican paper derided attempts at fusion in Ohio as "utter hypocrisy" that would deprive northern Democrats of "self-respect and manly independence." When told of the fusion plans, Douglas himself spat that "fusion with seceders merely added dishonor to defeat."[29] For Douglas supporters, Breckinridge Dem-ocrats, and Constitutional Unionists alike, going it alone seemed manlier than finding common ground with their opponents.

Without any successful fusion tickets to help them, Douglas Democrats attempted to peel off Upper South voters on their own. They did this by describing southern fire-eaters and northern Republicans as two sides of the same extremist coin. Both would empower the federal government to rule over men's public and private lives, instead of allowing them to rule themselves. According to one paper, "[Douglas] says to both these fire-eaters and the fanatical Abolitionists, stand off, and let the *people* make their own laws. These factional isms both agree on one point, and that is, that Congress should determine law for the Territories." Though the article does not mention women's rights or free love specifically, historian Michael Conlin has explained that Democrats used the term "isms" to describe any movement, from free love to abolition to temperance to women's rights, that threatened established hierarchies.[30] According to northern Democrats, Lincoln would use the federal government to impose this modernizing social program on the people. Breckinridge would use the federal government to impose slavery on the territories. Douglas represented a conservative middle ground: men would be free to decide how to live and what to do about slavery.

"Our Homes and Our Firesides": The Contest in the South

Douglas Democrats, however, misunderstood the political feeling among moderate southerners, which had shifted significantly since 1856. After many northern Democrats—led by Stephen Douglas—refused to support the proslavery Lecompton Constitution for Kansas, moderate southerners' support for popular sovereignty evaporated. John Brown's raid further diminished their faith in their northern allies. Senator Jefferson Davis of Mississippi lamented that popular sovereignty had proven "a siren's song . . . a thing shadowy and fleeting, changing its color as often as the chameleon"; James Mason of Virginia described it as "the most evanescent shadow and delusion."[31] Moderate southerners concluded that Douglas and the northern Democrats would not protect slavery and the Union. During the campaign, then, they deployed the same gender language and strategies as their Deep South colleagues. Both groups alleged that northerners supported women's rights, free love, and interracial relationships. These ideas were anathema to white southerners. Southern Democrats constructed a vision of two profoundly different societies: a chaotic northern one filled with liberated women, emasculated men, and free Blacks; and a stable southern one built of orderly families and obedient slaves. The similarity between Upper and Deep South Democrats' gender tactics and their growing difference from northern Democrats' strategy speaks to the increasing sectional divide in the Democratic Party.

Throughout the election campaign, pro-Breckinridge newspapers warned readers that northerners supported women's rights. A correspondent for the *Weekly Houston Telegraph* reported on a women's rights convention he had recently attended at the Cooper Institute in New York City. He insulted at length the men and women in attendance. He described the "ugly old women" who entered the convention hall, and he sneered that even if the women succeeded in liberalizing divorce laws, "there are very few of those I saw who will ever be blessed with any one having an 'affinity' for them. Ugly is a very mild term to apply to all their countenances." He reserved his deepest disgust for the men who supported these women. "It was humiliating," he wrote, "to see *men* upon the stage with those poor deluded, antiquated dilapidated females, taking part with them in abusing and ridiculing the male sex."[32]

In 1856, Democrats had leveled similar insults at Republican men. But now, in 1860, southern Democrats claimed that most northerners—not just Republicans, and not just New Englanders—had fallen victim to women's rights mania. The *Telegraph*'s correspondent told readers that "the Hall in the Cooper Institute is a very large one, capable of holding several thousand people, and I had not been in it more than half an hour before it was filled." Reading this, Houstonians might have concluded that thousands of New Yorkers supported women's equality—likely the outcome that *Telegraph*'s editor, secessionist Edward Hopkins Cushing, would have wanted. Breckinridge papers in New Orleans and Stockton, California, published similar hysterical descriptions of the women's rights movement in the North, exaggerating the women's demands and the extent of the support they received.[33] These stories resonated with southern Democrats in part because they heard a version of them four years earlier, but also because they contained a kernel of truth. Mary Beth Norton has explained that before the Revolution, northern and southern women alike lived in strictly patriarchal societies. But by the beginning of the nineteenth century, "the long-term trends were moving in opposite directions. In the North, the props of patriarchal power were gradually crumbling; in the South, those same props were in the process of being constructed." Slavery, she notes, made patriarchy "the norm."[34] So, although the *Telegraph*'s correspondent at the Cooper Institute had grossly exaggerated northern support for women's rights, the story reflected real and growing differences between the North and South.

Observing Stephen Douglas's relationship with his wife, one southern Democratic senator saw a prime example of northern gender disorder. Adele supported her husband's career wholeheartedly, entertaining the political elite in their Washington home. Admittedly, the practice of hosting parties for politician husbands blurred the lines between public and private life. But as Catherine Allgor has shown, Washington wives had for decades used these events to form networks, lobby associates, and build power. In a letter to his wife, the senator described "Mrs D's arts to win favour for her husband," including "what crowds of people were entertained at their grand house amid . . . the fumes of whiskey." But to the senator, Adele's hospitality only barely concealed an unfeminine appetite for power. "She carries in her pocket," he wrote, "a little social guillotine which takes off unhesitatingly all stubborn heads. I do not believe that Sallust in describing . . . Cataline . . . contains anything more audacious than the machinations of the demagogue Douglas assisted by his haughty and imperious wife." Eleven days later, the man relayed an even more shocking story: Adele had gone to observe the Senate in session when Stephen was absent from the chamber. Louisiana Democrat Judah P. Benjamin had given a speech criticizing Douglas and popular sovereignty. "So overwhelming was it," the senator wrote, that "it drove [Adele] out of the hall, who in defiance of all rule [had] persisted in remaining to hear the speech when her husband was lying drunk at home being unable to meet the issue with Benjamin."[35]

To the southern senator, Adele and Stephen's relationship was troublesome in multiple respects. For one, it signaled that Adele was far more interested in politics than the senator considered ladylike. Second, her involvement in public life spoke ill of Stephen. Either he could not control his wife—which would be emasculating—or he did not wish to, which would indicate that he did not consider her behavior immoral. Most concerning, the couple's partnership exemplified the gender disorder that southerners assumed prevailed in the North. With her keen interest in politics, Adele corroborated what southerners had been reading about northern women: that they sought political power. In 1856, Democrats took Republican candidate John and Jessie Frémont's relatively egalitarian relationship as an example of gender disorder in the Republican Party. In 1860, this southern Democrat could take Stephen and Adele's relationship as evidence of gender disorder throughout the North.

In addition to decrying women's rights and criticizing Adele and Stephen Douglas's relationship, southern Democratic papers also made the patently false claim that all northerners—not just Republicans—tolerated miscegenation. By slipping back and forth between the words "northern" and "Republican," southern Democrats associated all northerners with the most radical Republicans. A June 30 article in Washington, D.C.,'s pro-Breckinridge *Constitution* provides a good example of this technique. The article begins by nothing that "we do not remember to have seen any condemnation by . . . the republican party organs of the disgusting amalgamation cases which have been continually occurring." But then the article tells readers about the rights granted to free Blacks "in various parts of the North" in general. "It is certainly not against the laws of many of the States for negroes to hold office, vote, or marry white wives; and in such

States, theoretically speaking, negro equality is already established."[36] Whether intentional or not, using "Republican" and "North" interchangeably conflated the two, making it seem that the (caricatured) position of the Republican Party reflected northerners' attitudes as a whole.

Breckinridge newspapers also claimed that northerners traveled south to preach miscegenation to enslaved workers. One such letter appeared in John Marshall's *Texas State Gazette*. The article recounted how a family had hired a white laborer—"an immigrant" from the North—to work alongside the enslaved workers on the family's farm. Soon after his arrival, "the negroes with whom he communed were becoming insolent and insubordinate." Suspicious, the family eavesdropped on the northerner's conversations with the enslaved men. One family member heard the white man "lecturing them on their rights to freedom, and the happiness of the negro in the free States,—their honorable position in society by amalgamation,—that the negro could marry pretty white women, and that white women—ladies—loved negro gents." This article was but one of many that the Marshall published in the spring and summer of 1860, all describing northerners who had snuck into Texas to peddle their dangerous ideas about racial equality.[37] The stories made the North seem like a different and dangerous place, bent on abolition and miscegenation. A staunchly proslavery Breckinridge Democrat and conditional unionist, Marshall saw that these stories could both turn out voters for Breckinridge and bolster the case for secession in case of Lincoln's election.

In reality, northern Democrats feared "amalgamation" just as much as southern Democrats did. Indeed, during the 1858 Senate race in Illinois, Douglas alleged that Lincoln supported miscegenation. "Vote for Mr. Lincoln," he told a crowd in Freeport, "if you . . . think that the negro ought to be on a social equality with your wives and daughters, and ride in a carriage with your wife."[38] For northern and southern Democrats, exclusive sexual access to white women was a key masculine prerogative and a central tenet of white patriarchy. Sexual segregation sustained racial segregation and ensured that white property remained in white hands. But by 1860, some southern Democrats wondered if the northern members of their party really shared this value. Were these "immigrants" to the South outliers, or, as the *Constitution* suggested, did they represent northern public opinion as a whole? If the latter, southern Democrats could not accept any northerner—even a northern Democrat—as their leader. Better to split the party in two and vote for a southern man who shared their values.

Women's rights, free love, Adele Douglas's politicking, interracial sex—all of these accusations connected back to the critical issue for southern

Democrats: slavery. Again and again, southern Democrats warned that popular sovereignty and northern rule threatened the expansion of slavery. North Carolina Democratic congressman Thomas L. Clingman articulated this position in a speech in the Senate. If a man "enters the Territory with his wife, child, horse, and slave," Clingman ventured, "these are taken away from him by force, and he is himself imprisoned." Popular sovereignty would have deprived him of his wife and his slaves—and therefore of his manhood. Thus, Clingman argued, the federal government must protect slavery in the territories. "It is obvious that there should be laws to protect his own liberty and also his right to the possession of his wife, child, horse, and slave. Hence, it follows that there must be power in Congress to legislate on the subject of slavery."[39] A man's mastery over his wife and slaves was central to Clingman's vision of patriarchy, demanding the expansion of slavery into the territories. But a man's control over his private life and his local government was central to northern Democrats' vision of patriarchy, demanding popular sovereignty. To Clingman, the two visions of patriarchy were incompatible, requiring southerners to cast their ballots for a southern candidate.

To stoke their constituents' fear of northern rule, southern Democrats added that abolishing slavery would initiate women's rights, free love, and the end of patriarchy. During the campaign, Nashville pamphleteer James Williams told readers that "the free States of New England have been overrun by fanatics who display their absurd and pernicious principles under the forms of . . . 'abolitionism,' 'atheism,' 'free love-ism,' 'womans' rights-ism,' and many others equally detestable," while those doctrines were "absolutely unknown in the slave States." According to Williams, slavery had prevented radicalism from taking root in the South by elevating white men off the bottom rung of the social ladder. The poorest white man in the South had less reason to be discontent than did the poorest white men in the North. As a result, "The populations from which proselytes to such doctrines are usually obtained, do not there exist, and there are no materials out of which the . . . fanatical leaders can construct a party." According to Williams, northern rule would inaugurate abolition, and once the enslaved were free, women's rights and free love were sure to follow.[40] This argument would have generated enthusiasm for Breckinridge's candidacy—and laid the groundwork for secession in case of his defeat.

In a September speech in Norfolk, former Virginia governor Henry A. Wise reminded voters that southern slavery and southern families hung in the balance in this election. A month earlier, Stephen Douglas had insisted in his own Norfolk speech that Lincoln's election alone would not justify southern secession, and that the president should resist any attempts to secede. In front of 3,000 people, Wise charged that if Douglas was willing to maintain the Union by force, then "we are no longer divided on mere questions of administrative policy." Rather, "the issue goes to the vitals of society and concerns our homes and our firesides. The contest is not political; it is a social and a moral contest."[41] If the federal government could force a sovereign state to remain in the Union, Wise intimated, why could it not also compel that state to abolish slavery—and in so doing, take away a man's right to order his family as he saw fit? If northern politicians were determined to destroy southern culture, then only Breckinridge's election would guarantee the survival of both slavery and the patriarchal order it supported.

Wise's argument about cultural difference had deep roots in southern domestic literature. For years, women novelists had been writing stories that emphasized the fundamental differences between northern free society and southern slave society. With their monolithic portrayals of the North and South, these novels erased intrasectional distinctions and forced readers to think of themselves as either northern or southern—foreshadowing the divide in the Democratic Party.

In particular, authors focused on the role of women in the structure of the family in the North versus the South—and usually found the southern system superior. A native Bostonian living in Charleston, novelist Caroline Gilman took up the theme of sectional difference in her 1834 novel, *Recollections of a New England Housekeeper*. The daughter of a middle-class Boston family, protagonist Clarissa Grey Packard marries a rising lawyer but then struggles to keep house as her servants argue among themselves, quit on short notice, and steal from the family. By contrast, Clarissa Wilton, the protagonist of 1838's *Recollections of a Southern Matron*, lives with her husband on the family plantation, where they take good care of the people they enslave and the local poor whites.[42] Whereas in Boston, Packard feels harried and overwhelmed, in the South, Wilton enjoys a quiet life. Gilman claimed to be neutral in the sectional debate, but her novels belie her belief in the superiority of the South's strict racial and social hierarchy.

In her 1857 novel *Moss-Side*, Virginian Mary Virginia Terhune depicted abolitionism and women's rights as part of a comprehensive program of reform that northerners had aimed at the South. The plot centers around Grace Leigh, an aristocratic young woman in Virginia. Leigh goes to New York to attend the wedding of school friend Louise Wynne. Wynne reveals that she does not love her fiancé; she is marrying him to gain the freedom to pursue a career as a women's rights writer. Leigh is shocked but intrigued.

Later, back in Virginia, Leigh reads Wynne's book, which equates marriage with slavery. Leigh wonders, Is her own husband oppressing her? Should she run away? Only when her sister-in-law counsels her, "I am not a slave, nor are you, and no sophistry should mislead us into making such a concession," does Leigh realize that she is indeed happy with her life on the plantation, and that she should avoid books such as her friend's in the future.[43]

Gilman and Terhune's novels conveyed two themes that Democratic politicians adapted for the stump. The first was the notion that plantations functioned as well-ordered extended households. The clear, interdependent roles for master, wife, and slaves made southern families more stable than northern families. Enslaved people could not survive without their masters, wives could not survive without their husbands, and husbands would be worse off without both. When Henry Wise said that the election "goes to the vitals of society and concerns our homes and our firesides," he meant it literally: abolishing slavery would upend southern plantation homes. That, in turn, would destabilize southern society, since, stripped of their wealth, former slaveholders would no longer be able to care for Blacks and poor whites. This line of reasoning rebuked abolitionists, who had long argued that slavery harmed southern families by breaking up Black marriages and allowing white men to rape Black women.[44]

The second theme southern Democrats adapted from these novels was that women's rights and abolition worked hand in hand. Both epitomized the northern desire for too much freedom, and both were foreign to the South, where enslaved people and wives relished their God-given roles. By complaining about northern "'abolitionism,' 'atheism,' 'free love-ism,' [and] 'womans' rights-ism,'" the James Williams pamphlet echoed the novelists' descriptions of free society. Any unhappiness among slaves or women must be the product of northern meddling, not problems with southern slavery or southern marriages.

In making this argument about sectional difference, southern Democrats revealed that they harbored some concern about voter support for John Breckinridge—particularly in the Upper South, where the race was a true three-way contest. Democratic politicians had already demonstrated their commitment to a southern candidate when they nominated Breckinridge in June. But voters could still cast their ballots for Stephen Douglas or John Bell, the Constitutional Union candidate. To turn out the vote, Breckinridge operatives told voters that popular sovereignty was weak, indirect, and feminine, while slavery's expansion was strong, direct, and masculine. In popular sovereignty, southern Democrats saw only cowardice. The prosouthern Caleb Cushing cried that Douglas Democrats stood "timidly, shrinkingly, and tender-footedly, on the platform." By contrast, Breckinridge stood openly on a proslavery platform, demonstrating the "manly frankness of the true Democrat and patriot." Voters could redeem the Democratic Party and the nation by "frankly, manfully, firmly, and fearlessly planting ourselves on the great fundamental truths of the Constitution"—the protection of slave property everywhere in the Union. Echoing this language, Marylander Robert McClane described Breckinridge's position as "manly and responsive . . . direct, logical, and conclusive," in contrast to the triangulating Douglas and Bell. According to James Henry Hammond, these tactics were working. A month before the election, Hammond wrote to fellow South Carolinian Milledge Luke Bonham, "The true men [were] coming round, as I always expected, [to] Breckinridge."[45] Framing slavery's expansion as manly and honorable proved a powerful argument in the South, where manhood and honor mattered so much.

In a further attempt to solidify support for Breckinridge, southern papers characterized Stephen Douglas as an aggressor who was plotting to dominate a feminized South. A representative article alleged that Douglas secretly wished to make the South endure "outrage on her person, property, or honor," implying that southern white men should defend the South by voting for Breckinridge. And when Douglas announced that he would accept the results if Lincoln were elected, the *Constitution* claimed that Douglas secretly wished for Lincoln's election, so that "the south may be 'subjugated,' 'coerced,' 'whipped into submission' to black-republican rule."[46] According to the *Constitution*, northern Democrats simply wished to control the South. This claim was patently false. But it passed muster because for five years, Democrats had accused Republicans of the exact same thing: promising moderation but secretly plotting to subjugate the South. Southern Democrats split the party by insisting on a southern candidate to fend off this threat. But by using gendered language to impugn Republicans and mollify the South, northern Democrats played no small part in laying the groundwork for their party's collapse.

Breckinridge supporters also tried to move votes by comparing compromise to sexual violation. They hoped this ploy would drive voters away from Douglas and popular sovereignty as well as Bell and his platform, which did not mention slavery at all. In May 1860, Jefferson Davis stood in the Senate and avowed that capitulating on the slavery question "would be to sink in the scale of manhood." It would "make our posterity so degraded that they would curse this generation." According to Davis, compromising on slavery would emasculate southern men for generations. Contemporaries usually reserved the word "degrade" to describe the state of a woman who had been sexually assaulted. That language limited moderate southerners' political options: they could either support Breckinridge and slavery, or they could reveal themselves to be as powerless and pitiful as a woman who had been raped. In November, when Breckinridge's defeat appeared increasingly certain, southern Democrats used similar language to justify having run a separate candidate—a move which by then appeared to guarantee Lincoln's election. The *Constitution* reminded readers that "no craven submission to the dictation of party leaders or wire-pullers has disgraced [Breckinridge's] movement."[47]

All of these claims and accusations—of manliness and courage, of submission and cowardice—tapped into southern men's preoccupation with honor. As Christopher Olsen has explained, southern politicians—especially those from the Deep South—were deeply concerned with vindicating their personal and their society's collective reputation and character. Of course, as we have seen, northern Democrats were not eager to be trampled by their southern counterparts. But living in a slave society made southern Democrats uniquely anxious about proving their honor. This was in part because enforcing slavery required loyalty and reliability on the part of white men. It was also because white men in the South defined themselves in opposition to their slaves. They claimed slaves were cowards and without honor, and therefore white men had to demonstrate that they were courageous and honorable. As Olsen puts it, "The combined effects of honor and slavery sustained a regional obsession with aggressive, competitive masculinity, but also with loyalty to other white men."[48] In this toxic atmosphere, words such as "manly," "fearless," "subjugate," and "submit" were powerful political weapons that demanded a response.

"If Lincoln Be Elected": Fire-Eaters Prime the Pump

Aware that divisions persisted among voters, especially in the Upper South, southern Democrats associated manliness with supporting slavery's expansion and voting for Breckinridge. Fire-eaters, however, used these same tactics to lay the groundwork for secession. Fire-eaters warned that Republicans would abolish slavery and impose racial equality on the South, allegedly leading to the rape of white women by Black men. On October 27, Texas newspaperman Edward Hopkins Cushing editorialized that under Republican rule, "our property is to be despoiled . . . our wives and daughters ravished, and the sanctity of our homes invaded." Better that the "Southern people . . . live independently of the Abolition States . . . enjoying the comforts and security of a truly patriarchal government." Cushing doubled down on this argument less than two weeks later. In an article titled "What Shall the South Do if Lincoln Be Elected?," he warned that Lincoln would "wage a relentless war on the white people of the South, and never to stay aggression till we, the fathers and sons of the South, shall acknowledge the four millions of negroes among us to be our equals and the equals of our mothers, wives, sisters, and daughters." Stephanie McCurry has shown that mastery united slaveholders and yeomen. Both groups of men claimed sexual access to the women on their property and profited from their labor.[49] Cushing warned readers that Lincoln would revoke these privileges. Abolishing slavery would not only abolish a system of labor: it would shatter the system of white patriarchy that allowed white men to control the labor and sexual relations of white women and enslaved workers.

Democrats repeated this narrative in private as well as public discourse. On October 10, the secessionist John Townsend wrote to fellow South Carolinian Milledge Luke Bonham. Bonham already supported Breckinridge. But Townsend wrote to convince him that the South should secede immediately if Lincoln were elected. "Submission to the will of a party who have openly declared themselves our enemies, and that they intend to destroy our property, and (what is worse) that they intend to degrade us and our families to an equality with our slaves—submission, I say . . . is a thought to be entertained not for a moment," Townsend told Bonham.[50] Townsend feared losing his property in slaves, but more than that, he feared racial equality, and he knew Bonham feared likewise. By playing to those fears, he hoped to bring Bonham into the secessionist camp.

A related line of argument called on southerners to vote for Breckinridge but prepare for secession, since only southern rule could protect white southern families from slave rebellion. As Edward Rugemer has shown, antislavery news, people, and ideas had long traveled into the South from places where slavery had been abolished, including Haiti, Great Britain, the West Indies—and now the North. Southerners worried that the election of a Republican would unleash a torrent of abolitionist activism in the South. Fire-eaters seized on this concern, urging white men to consider what would happen to their families if there were a slave rebellion. In April, the pro-secession *DeBow's Review* enjoined readers not to "accept at the hands of the North a civil and servile insurrection, the devastation of their country, the slaughter of their wives and children, the unspeakable horrors of another Santo Domingo." Secessionist William Yancey made a similar appeal in a September speech. While Yancey was speaking, a man shouted, "What will the South do in the event of Lincoln's election?" Yancey reminded the man of John Brown's raid—committed "under the peace of the Constitution that is supposed to protect [Virginia]." What would happen if another John Brown "c[a]me with pike, with musket and bayonet and cannon . . . and our wives and our children, when we are away at our business, [were] found murdered by our hearthstones"? "What would *you* do?" Yancey asked the man. The man responded, "I would stop him before he got that far." This was exactly the answer that Yancey wanted. "Before he got that far" meant seceding before Lincoln could incite a slave insurrection, not after. A letter to the editor of North Carolina's *Semi-weekly Standard* shows how these warnings of insurrection resonated with the average voter. Just a few days before the election, the man pleaded, "Men of the Southern States, protect yourselves, your wives, your children, and everything that is near and dear to you, by voting for John C. Breckinridge and Joseph Lane." Lincoln's rule, according to the writer, "would not so much as protect the lives of our women and children, but leave them to butchery."[51]

Fire-eaters took Democrats' cries about submission a step further, as well, telling voters that submitting to a northern president after the election would be just as degrading as submitting to a northern nominee would have been during the convention. Former Virginia governor Henry Wise wrote to a newspaper in Georgia encouraging men there to vote for Breckinridge, even if that vote helped elect Lincoln and led to secession. According to Wise, southern men needed to show that "there are yet men in the South who can face revolution rather than be degraded in the Union." In Alabama, members of a militia claimed to prefer war to the "alternative of national ruin and degradation."[52] By itself, the repeated public use of this language would tell us that speakers expected it to move their listeners toward secession.

In private, too, secessionists chided each other with this gendered language. Days before the election, Columbia newspaperman A. G. Baskin scolded fellow South Carolinian John Lawrence Manning. "It seems to me your politics are right if you would go far enough," Baskin wrote. Manning, a relative moderate in a state full of ultrasecessionists, hoped to build consensus for secession, rather than supporting South Carolina's immediate withdrawal were Lincoln elected. Baskin did not agree with Manning's approach. "Failing in [cooperation]," Baskin wrote, "rather than submit longer to northern aggression, I would raise the banner of resistance, and if we fall 'let us die with our feet to the foe and our face towards heaven.'"[53]

Submission was a female trait, not a male one. Baskin's use of the word "submit" indicates that he found the prospect of living under a Republican president humiliating, even feminizing—and that he believed Manning might as well.

In a similar vein, fire-eating southerners told Union-minded southern Democrats that fearing disunion was cowardly, while supporting secession was manly. On October 10, William Tennent Jr., a South Carolinian who served as secretary of the secessionist 1860 Association, wrote to South Carolinian Milledge Luke Bonham bemoaning the "slow poison called 'Love of the Union' which seems to have stultified the polity of the Whole South," as well as the "cautious, creeping, cowardly policy" of compromise. He hoped his correspondence committee, which would publish secessionist literature, would "break the chains we have forged for ourselves, lest Lincoln bestow upon us, after his Inauguration, the shackles which we will merit." Fire-eaters thus continued to use the same tactic that they had used before the Charleston and Baltimore conventions: decry compromise of any sort as cowardly retreat. To this, they added a new tactic: decrying love of Union as a feminine sentimentalism. In a June speech, secessionist John Townsend pleaded with his audience, "Let us hear no more of the sophomoric sentimentality about 'the Union.'" Southerners knew their rights. "Were it not for the fatal counsels to procrastination from their political advisers, aided by the womanly fears of 'Disunion,'" that knowledge "would soon ripen into manly and resolute ACTION."[54] Moderate Democrats had taken the manly action of splitting the Democratic Party to secure a proslavery platform. Extremists now asked moderates if they would take the manly action of splitting the Union to secure slavery.

Northern and southern Democrats deployed a variety of gender tactics during the 1860 campaign. Northern Democrats told northern voters that a Republican program of women's rights, free love, and miscegenation threatened their status as white heads of households—southerners leveled the same charges against northern Democrats. Likening compromise to emasculation, northern and southern Democrats refused to set aside their differences to nominate a single Democratic candidate. Picking up on themes from domestic literature, southern Democrats argued that the freedom-loving North was culturally incompatible with the stable, patriarchal South. And secessionist-minded fire-eaters claimed that if Lincoln were elected, only secession could protect white southern men's pride and white southern women's bodies.

These tactics had short- and long-term consequences. They inflamed tensions and ultimately solidified the split between northern and southern Democrats over the nominee and the platform. And they encouraged moderate southern politicians, especially in the Upper South, to side—and indeed identify—with their more radical Deep South colleagues. These outcomes alone were significant. But in vivifying the narrative about northern and southern cultural difference and advancing the case for secession, the gender tactics of the campaign season reverberated well beyond November 6, 1860.

For the Safety of Their Firesides

GENDERING COMPROMISE
AND SECESSION

On November 9, 1860, Americans elected Republican Abraham Lincoln to become the next president of the United States. Lincoln won with 180 electoral votes; ominously, not a single one of those votes came from a slave state. Indeed, ten of the fifteen slave states had refused to place Lincoln on the ballot. Nonetheless, Republican newspaper editors were thrilled. "Let the People Rejoice! LINCOLN ELECTED!" the *Freeport (Ill.) Wide Awake* cried. "SHOUT BOYS SHOUT, VICTORY IS OURS, FREEDOM IS TRIUMPHANT!"[1]

The splintered Democratic Party had suffered a crushing defeat. Despite winning nearly a third of the popular vote, Stephen Douglas claimed only twelve electoral votes from two states. John Breckinridge took seventy-two electoral votes but only 18 percent of the popular vote. John Bell, for his part, did not win enough electoral votes to throw the election to the House. By failing to unite around a single candidate or forge a successful fusion movement, Democrats had paved the way for a Republican victory. Facing these facts, one Democratic paper was led to wonder, "Is the Democratic Party Defunct?"[2]

Though northern and southern Democrats alike abhorred the idea of a "Black Republican" moving into the White House, they responded to Lincoln's election in different ways. In December 1860 and January 1861, as conventions in state after state in the Deep South voted to leave the Union, northern Democrats tried to stem the tide of secession. Their efforts were frenetic—even contradictory. They decried Republicans and fire-eaters alike as extremists and blamed both for fomenting feelings of disunion among moderate southerners. But at the very same time, speaking to southerners, northern Democrats tried to walk back five years of campaign rhetoric that had labeled the Republicans as dangerous radicals, hoping to convince southern moderates to give Lincoln a chance to govern.

Southern Democrats, however, were not convinced. Years of railing against supposed Republican radicalism had caught up with southern Democrats, depriving them of the ability to distinguish rhetoric from reality. They believed Republicans wanted to destroy slave society, they saw that the majority of northerners had voted Republican, and they concluded that the majority of northerners wanted to destroy slave society. Throughout the winter, early supporters of secession justified their position by arguing that the federal government would impose radical social programs—including abolition, women's rights, and free love—that would undermine their place in society and diminish their power over their households. And they began to construct a southern national identity that was based on conservatism and symbolized by an idealized white southern womanhood. Though the Deep South was relatively quick to secede, other regions of the South were not. Warning that northern rule would lead to slave insurrection, secessionists pleaded with men in the Border and Upper South to protect their wives and children from violence by joining the newly founded Confederacy. For a time, these conditional unionists found such an argument unconvincing. But after Lincoln called for 75,000 volunteers in the wake of the attack on Fort Sumter, Upper South Democrats quickly came to see secession and war as the only way to defend southern women and southern homes from an invading northern menace.

"Manly and Unequivocal Measures of Conciliation": Northern Democrats Push for Compromise

On December 20, 1860, South Carolina became the first state to secede from the Union. Emma Holmes, a Charlestonian and the daughter of a wealthy planter, crowed, "Doubly proud am I of my native state, that she should be the first to arise and shake off the hated chain which linked us with Black Republicans and Abolitionists." "Secession," she added, "was born in the hearts of Carolina women."[3] Over the next six weeks, six more Deep South states followed: Mississippi on January 9, Florida on January 10, Alabama on January 11, Georgia on January 19, Louisiana on January 26, and Texas on February 1.

As state after state left the Union, northern Democrats sought someone other than themselves to blame for the secession crisis. Perhaps predictably, given their rhetoric during the campaign, northern Democrats castigated both Republicans and fire-eaters as extremists who were tearing the nation apart. At their state convention in Albany, New York's Democrats held Republicans responsible for southern secession. One Democrat at the convention claimed that "our immediate dangers are . . . not so much the secession from the Union of several dissatisfied States, as that the Republican Party . . . produced the mischief . . . [and] will not yield to the South such constitutional guarantees . . . as will win back to the Union the alarmed states." According to this view, Republican antislaveryism had provoked southern secession, so now it was Republicans' responsibility to bring southern states back into the Union with conciliation and compromise. Other northern Democrats blamed fire-eaters, claiming they had used scare tactics to whip Union-loving southerners into a treasonous frenzy. The *New York Sun*, for instance, lambasted them for appealing "to the baser elements of society" with "the cry of intolerable tyranny and rapine."[4] The claim was not false: as we have seen, secessionists warned fellow southerners that Republican rule would result in the subjugation of white men and the rape of white women—a tactic that they continued to deploy in the winter following Lincoln's election. But in blaming fire-eaters, northern Democrats failed to see secession for what it was: a popular movement to protect against a perceived threat to slavery and the white patriarchy it upheld. They could not abandon the belief that the vast majority of white southerners were conservative, Union-loving men.

If extremists alone were to blame for the secession crisis, northern Democrats reasoned, then surely the reasonable men from the North and South could broker a compromise that would save the Union. From December 1860 through February 1861, several proposals to save the Union came up for debate inside and outside of Congress. For each one, northern Democrats deployed gendered language to generate sympathy for southerners, hoping it would push fellow northern Democrats and conservative Republicans to offer concessions that would draw the Deep South back into the Union and prevent the Border and Upper South from seceding at all.

On December 3, 1860, the Thirty-Sixth Congress convened for its final session. Commentators knew the next three months marked the last, best chance for northern and southern men to find a solution to the brewing secession crisis. Northern editors who had supported Breckinridge in the recent election encouraged northerners to offer concessions to the South. The day the session opened, Isaac Van Anden of the *Brooklyn Daily Eagle* wrote, "An equal responsibility will rest upon the representatives of the North and upon those of the South. Let the former have the manliness to be just and offer to the latter such measures of redress as will be right and proper." Only two months prior, Van Anden had attacked the attempt to join in an anti-Lincoln fusion ticket as "humiliating and degrading," wondering "how any party with a spark of manhood . . . can be influenced to join Douglas for such a *quid pro quo*."[5] In September, compromise would have required northern doughfaces to make meaningful concessions, so Van Anden branded it emasculating. Now that it asked nothing of them, Van Anden praised it as manly.

At central Pennsylvania's *Democrat and Sentinel*, editor C. D. Murray took a similar path. Murray had supported Breckinridge, so even as feelings ran high in the days after South Carolina seceded, he hoped that cooler heads would prevail. "Matters look dark and gloomy, it is true," Murray acknowledged, "but we are still not without a hope that conservative men, both north and south, will soon succeed in obtaining a hearing." To those who would impugn South Carolina's men as "nothing but cowardly braggarts," the *Sentinel* had stern words. "Their history proves exactly the reverse of this. . . . As soldiers in the Revolutionary struggle, in the war of 1812, and in the Mexican War, they were distinguished for bravery and dauntless daring."[6] In describing South Carolinians as war heroes, Murray appealed to northern congressmen to accept whatever measures were required to bring South Carolina back into the Union. Capitulating to "cowardly braggarts" would be emasculating but compromising with gallant brothers-in-arms would not.

It was perhaps unsurprising that doughface editors like Van Anden and Murray pushed for compromise with the South. But during the final session of Congress, even pro-Douglas papers appealed to northern congressmen's masculinity to encourage compromise. In the final two weeks of December, congressmen focused their energy on debating the Crittenden Compromise, a series of constitutional amendments and congressional resolutions designed to appease the South and stem the tide of secession. At the *New York Herald*, James Gordon Bennett pleaded with northern congressmen to adopt the "firm, manly, and unequivocal measures of conciliation" offered by Crittenden "to prevent disaster and loss from becoming total shipwreck."[7] *Herald* reporters had spent the springtime discouraging northern Democrats from capitulating to southern demands at Charleston and Baltimore. Now that compromise seemed to be the only way to save the Union, Bennett sang a different tune. At first glance, describing compromise as emasculating in April and manly in December seems fantastically inconsistent. But all along, northern Democrats' primary goal had been to preserve the Union. In the spring, they believed nominating Stephen Douglas would most likely achieve that end, so they used masculine language to discourage compromise. By December, the Crittenden measures seemed like the best way to save the Union, so they used masculine language to encourage compromise. No core principle of northern manhood mitigated against compromise, as mastery did for southern men. For northern Democrats in both the springtime nominating conventions and the postelection secession crisis, then, gendered language was the tactic and Union was the goal.

After weeks of debate, both the House of Representatives and the Senate rejected the Crittenden Compromise. Republicans refused to sacrifice their core antislavery principles to bring the South back into the fold. They had won the election by promising to restrict slavery's expansion and oppose reopening the slave trade; to abandon these positions would be to abandon their party's first principles. So Stephen Douglas offered another possible solution: an amendment that would enshrine popular sovereignty in the Constitution. On January 3, Douglas stood before the Senate and pleaded with his northern colleagues to put themselves in southerners' shoes. "Apprehension has become wide-spread and deep-seated in the southern people. It has . . . filled them with the conviction that their fire-sides, their family altars, and their domestic institutions, are to be ruthlessly assailed through the machinery of the Federal Government."[8] If northern men believed their families and their social system were under attack, Douglas implied, would not they, too, demand protections? By reminding northern and southern men of their shared status as protectors and patriarchs, Douglas hoped he could revive the Democratic cultural consensus that would, in turn, lead to a political compromise.

As compromise attempts failed and states in the Deep South quit the Union, Americans debated whether the federal government could force a state to remain in the Union. In his December 3 State of the Union address, James Buchanan concluded it could not. "It is manifest upon an inspection of the Constitution," he declared, that "no such power has been delegated to Congress or to any other department of the Federal Government"—an opinion he held even as the secession crisis grew increasingly dire. But while Buchanan was busy constructing constitutional arguments, other northern Democrats were making cultural ones. They framed their opposition to coercion in terms of protecting white southern men's unquestioned power over family and society. On January 11, Isaac Van Anden asked his Brooklyn subscribers to consider the consequences of invading the South. "Suppose an army of northern abolitionists . . . should succeed in devastating and destroying the South. What then? The hostile agitation . . . has gone hand in hand with the other fanaticisms springing from [New England]." By Van Anden's reasoning, a northern invasion of the South would allow northern fanatics to impose their social order on the South. This would be an insult to white southern men's status as patriarchs. "A social despotism is so much more galling than a political one," he argued.

"[A man] may be denied the exercise of his political rights . . . but a despotism that penetrates the sanctities of conscience and social life humiliates him as a man."[9] Northerners had long pushed for popular sovereignty on the grounds that it would allow men to order their families and their society as they saw fit. Here, Van Anden hijacked that argument, applying it to southern men to argue against holding the Union together by force.

This concern with shielding white men from government interference in their personal lives was typically Democratic. As Daniel Walker Howe has explained, "The natural rights philosophy of the Jacksonians asserted the individual's claims to be protected against interference from officious ecumenical reformers." Even forty years after Jackson's presidency, Democrats still claimed the right to be free from meddling reformers. Indeed, this same impulse toward supporting white men's independence had undergirded Democrats' support for the Kansas-Nebraska Act in 1854 and their opposition to mounting a campaign against Mormon polygamy in 1857 and 1858. Southern men established their claim to political power through the governance of wives, children, and slaves. Because a threat to their personal mastery thus constituted a threat to their political power, southern men especially opposed any intervention in men's private affairs.[10] Northern Democrats supported compromise, then, not only because they hoped it would save the Union. They also believed that a peaceful settlement of the issue would respect southern men's need to manage their homes without interference from abolitionists, reformers, or the federal government.

Northern Democrats also bolstered their opposition to the use of force by describing America as a national family. They saw the southern states as akin to the Prodigal Son. Southern states needed to return to the Union of their own volition, because only love could hold families together. On January 18, the *Brooklyn Daily Eagle* published a letter it had received from a reader. The letter read, "The aggressors are our brothers; shall we madly attempt their coercion by force of arms[?] . . . Must we kill thousands of them, to teach the rest to love and respect us?" The writer scorned such a suggestion. "Shame on the man who, in his self-conceit, counsels such treatment in the great American family!" It was neither morally right nor politically feasible to reunite the country by force. Like a family, northerners—Democrats and Republicans—must allow southerners to realize their error and return on their own time. They could facilitate southerners' return by offering concessions. But they could not coerce southerners into loving their northern brethren. Thus, contemporary ideas about men's governance over real families encouraged northern Democrats to spurn coercion within the national family.[11]

When they talked about the Union as a family, northern Democrats were elaborating on an idea that had originated in the early republic: the affective theory of the Union. As Michael Woods has explained, Americans understood the Union as a political body held together by affection, fraternity, and love. They hoped that those positive emotions would bind Americans together as the nation expanded westward. Americans from different parties and different sections subscribed to this view of the Union. Democrat James F. Dowdell of Alabama said, "Sentiments of affection and feelings of fraternal sympathy" constituted "the true bonds of union"; without them, even the Constitution could not hold together the Union. Stephen Douglas argued that the United States ought to be "not only a union of states, but a union of hearts." In 1860, James Buchanan warned that if the Union "cannot live in the affections of the people, it must one day perish." President-Elect Lincoln agreed, describing Americans as "brothers of a common country" who "should dwell together in the bonds of fraternal feeling."[12]

But the secession crisis threw into sharp relief an inherent problem with the affective theory: What would become of the Union if those bonds of affection vanished? If love could not be coerced, then neither could the Union. John Quincy Adams had worried about this possibility decades earlier. "If the day should ever come (may heaven avert it) when the affections of the people of these States shall be alienated from each other," Adams ventured, "far better will it be for the people of the dis-united States to part in friendship with each other, than to be held together by constraint." In the winter of 1860–61, Adams's nightmare vision had come true: the good feelings that had cleaved the South to the Union had vanished. Northern Democrats did not want to coerce southerners to remain in the Union because they respected white southerners' equality in the national family. Forcing southerners to remain in the Union was disrespectful, by this view, and therefore bound to create bad feelings. But neither could northern Democrats countenance the prospect of disunion. That would represent a failure of democratic government that would mark the downfall of the American experiment and, more pressingly, a threat to law and order.[13] Searching, as ever, for a middle ground between Republicans and southern Democrats, northern Democrats concluded that Congress should induce southerners back to the Union with compromise measures, rather than forcing them back in with arms.

Gender and the Construction
of Southern National Identity

As the secession of the Deep South states in December, January, and February made clear, many southern Democrats were not eager to accept northern inducements to keep them in the Union. The electoral tactics of the past five years, combined with the ascension of a Republican to the White House, had persuaded them that the majority of northerners were fanatics who wanted to abolish slavery and force women's rights, free love, and any number of other radical social programs on the South. By the fall and early winter, a significant number of southerners—largely but not exclusively from the Lower South—had already concluded that Republicans would impose this agenda on the South and, in so doing, threaten the system of patriarchy and white supremacy that undergirded their social, economic, and political power.

To secession-minded southern Democrats, Lincoln's election seemed to demonstrate, once and for all, the ascendance of radical social movements in the North. Pro-secession Democratic newspapers strengthened this misconception by publishing overblown accounts of northern radicalism. Take, for instance, two reports that appeared in the *Nashville Union and American*—a paper whose proprietor, J. O. Griffith, one contemporary described as a "pestilent original secessionist." One came from a correspondent who had traveled to Cleveland. "This section as all are no doubt aware, is intensely abolition," he reported. "It is the very Elysium of JOHN BROWNITES; here free-love holds its sway, GREELEYISM, Negroism, or any other ism sufficiently imbrued with fanaticism upon any topic has hordes of ardent supporters." Located in northern Ohio, Cleveland was certainly more Republican than the southern Butternut counties, but it was incorrect to imply that the whole state had turned Republican—let alone fanatical—when Lincoln had taken only 52 percent of the state's vote. Southern Methodist publisher and secessionist John Berry McFerrin presented a similarly distorted view of northern life in a Christmas Eve letter to the *Union and American*. After a cursory acknowledgment that "there are many wise and good men North of Mason and Dixon's line," McFerrin claimed that the vast majority of northerners had lost their way. "The blindness of these fanatics . . . has run many of them to infidelity," McFerrin reported. "Woman's rights, Free-love, [and] spiritualism . . . are some of the legitimate offshoots of the disordered public mind at the North." Readers made the logical leap. If northerners were committed to women's rights and free love, then a federal government populated by northerners could very well impose those ideologies on the South.[14]

Even southerners who were not in the business of trying to sell their fellow Americans on secession fretted to one another about northern fanaticism. Secessionist Richard Thompson Archer, the head of a Mississippi cotton empire that had made him one of the richest men in the country, drafted a letter to a local paper declaring that there was no use in trying to compromise with northern fanatics. "Who believes that concession or reasoning will stay fanaticism? Who believes that it has any stopping place short of the extreme point of its tenets?" In a letter to his mother, Marylander Jefferson Martenet affirmed his belief that "the unwarrantable interference with the affairs of the South by northern fanatics, will never cease. . . . I tell you this generation of Northerners have had abolition bred in their bones, brain, and muscle, and nothing will ever take it out." Martenet believed all northerners had been radicalized. He continued on to warn that these radicals must be forced out of the South. "It would be a pity to force them to live under the despotism of slavery," he wrote. But "probably their fellow humanitarians of New England will invite them to an abode in their land of freedom and philosophy." There, they "would make a splendid pattern of a free-love-free-speech free-everything." On March 2, Theophilus Nash echoed this indictment of northern society in a letter to Margaret Stanly Beckwith, the granddaughter of fire-eater Edmund Ruffin. Writing from New Orleans, Nash expressed the same anxiety about northern fanaticism and the same desire for northerners to quit the South. Nash thought that northern "fanatics," as he twice called them, had taken over the country, which tarnished the Union's honor. "Our country, our nationality is gone!" he exclaimed. "Our proud name, the 'United States' is gone!" Working himself into hysterics, he continued, "Them black-hearted Yankees! All New England can go to Canada . . . with their free-love societies, their spiritualism, and their higher law! . . . I will have none of them!"[15] Archer, a wealthy planter; Martenet, a Marylander on the make in San Francisco; and Theophilus Nash, writing from New Orleans, had little in common. But all believed that Republican rule represented a threat not just to slavery but also to the system of patriarchy and white supremacy that guaranteed their power and position.

Democrats had conjured images of Republican free love colonies to great effect in the elections of 1856 and 1860. Here, four years later, we see southern Democrats deploying the same tropes to divide the Union. The durability of this language demonstrates that the anxiety about free love was not merely a political trope—though it was that, too. Rather, southerners seemed to genuinely fear the advance of free love colonies. To them, free love was part and parcel of a whole program imported from Europe—including free love, women's rights, spiritualism, Fourierism, and abolitionism—that sought to undermine the family, religious, and property structures of the South. Since white men owned their wives' property, led churches, and profited from slavery, a threat to even one of those structures threatened white male dominance. The warnings about free love, therefore, constituted a powerful emotional appeal to white southern manhood on behalf of secession.

The panic about a Republican social revolution did contain a small element of truth: Republican leaders believed free society was superior to slave society. The Republican platform in 1860 had adopted a far less crusading tone than in 1856, when it had decried the "twin barbarisms" of slavery and polygamy. But Republicans' moderated tone did not fool secessionists. For years, leading Republicans had maintained that the canker of slavery had caused southern society to rot from within. In his 1858 "Irrepressible Conflict" speech, for instance, William Seward declared that slavery led to "poverty, imbecility, and anarchy," whereas free labor "secures universal contentment, and brings into the highest possible activity all the physical, moral, and social energies of the whole state." These kinds of speeches—and their printing and reprinting in southern papers—offended southern men's sense of pride in their region and in themselves. As Christopher Olsen has put it, "When Republicans questioned the moral turpitude of the entire region, they also maligned the individuals who lived there." So when a Republican took control of the White House, Olsen explains, men in the Deep South "believed that northern criticism demanded satisfaction for the sake of family and community honor."[16]

Since 1856, southerners had counted on northern Democrats to stem the tide of Republican fanaticism. But the Republican victory in 1860—along with the failure of the Lecompton Constitution and John Brown's raid—convinced them that northern Democrats could not and indeed would not check the advance of the Republican Party and its abolitionist, women's rights, and free love supporters. In early December, a speaker at a meeting of the Southern Rights Association in Jefferson Parish, Louisiana, reminded attendees of northern Democrats' broken promises. "Before this election we were told—and many true and loyal southerners believed the tale—that there were enough conservative men at the North to keep in check that fanatical abolition element, from which materials are gathered to make raids and commit robberies on the South. We were told that . . . with money, influence, and power, they could stay the advancing tide of destructive fanaticism." But, the speaker concluded, "the ballot box has told the tale." Similarly, in a January 15 speech in the North Carolina House of Commons, one representative asked listeners to reflect on the events of the past two years. "Let me remind [you] of the great Union meetings after the John [Brown] raid," he warned. After that show of support for the South, "they elected a miserable, white-livered, black-hearted abolitionist to the highest office in their gift. And yet we are told they are to be trusted."[17] In this telling, northern Democrats were, at best, politically weak. At worst, they were deceptive—tricking southerners into believing slavery was safe within the Union, while secretly working with Republicans to undermine the institution. In short, these secessionists concluded, southerners who feared northern abolitionism and northern free love should not look to northern Democrats for protection. If they wished to protect southern women and southern womanhood, they would have to do it themselves.

By describing the North as a place with fundamentally different social norms, secessionists began to construct a uniquely southern national identity. Historians have long recognized that nations do not arise naturally from similarities in language, religion, culture, or economic interests. Rather, ordinary people have to invent nations; they must decide that certain similarities are significant enough to justify the creation of a new state. Likewise, historians recognize that people construct nations based on perceptions of difference—difference from other peoples or nations. Feminist historians add that people have frequently used gender identities to justify nationalism. As one historian has put it, "Attachments to modern gender and national identities have developed together and reinforced each other."[18] Together, these insights help us understand why southern Democrats harped on the supposedly irredeemable social order in the North. They shared an economic interest in maintaining slavery, and they believed that a Republican government, elected by northerners, threatened that interest. But they also thought they shared a culture. Slavery, they believed, provided the groundwork for a stable society in which white and Black, man and woman, understood their roles, creating a social order that put white men on the top of the ladder. This patriarchal society stood in stark contrast to northern free society. There, abolishing slavery had been but the first step in creating chaos, in which everyone sought to free themselves from the ties—including marriage and gender roles—that southerners believed were essential to a harmonious society.[19]

Southerners reflected on these supposed differences between northern and southern societies in their private letters. In a letter to his mother, Jefferson Martenet praised southern slave society, writing, "Slavery . . .

in the South . . . involves the rights, interests, and prejudices of a whole community." He was right: the presence of slavery affected all of southern society, from economics to social relations to gender relations. Martenet continued, "It is high time that this clap trap cry of 'free speech' 'free press' 'free love etc' was dropped. . . . A healthful state of society demands certain concessions from its individual members, each yields a small portion of his freedom for the welfare of the whole, and upon no other basis can society exist at all." Higher-ups in the Democratic Party agreed. On January 23, after his state seceded, South Carolina governor Francis Pickens wrote to Jefferson Davis about creating a southern government that would pro-tect southern society from fanaticism. "As to who may be selected to fill the highest civil offices," he began, "they should be high-toned gentlemen of exemplary purity, and firmness of character . . . and no demagogism. We must start our government free from the vulgar influences that have debauched and demoralized the government at Washington."[20]

At best, these depictions of the North and South were gross distortions of reality. At worst, they were outright lies. In the South, white plantation owners raped and murdered their enslaved workers with impunity, and they broke up Black families to pay debts or punish enslaved workers. This was not stability. Slavery also forced wealthy white women—who otherwise benefited from the institution—to contend with their husbands' rape of enslaved women and the children those assaults produced. Mean-while, in the North, free love colonies were few, small, and isolated. And membership in the abolitionist group the American Anti-slavery Society peaked at about 200,000–250,000 adherents—meaning that only about 1 percent of the people living in states that would remain in the Union called themselves members.

However unfounded or exaggerated, southerners' concerns about sec-tional difference testify to their broader anxiety about maintaining an orthodox society that would sustain slavery. As historian David Potter has written, "The more speculative a society became in its social thought, the more readily it might challenge the tenets of the established order."[21] So southerners tended toward orthodoxy—in religious practice, which emphasized personal salvation; in its education system, which stressed classical learning; and, I argue, in its gender norms, which emphasized patriarchal control of households. The Democratic campaigns of 1856 and 1860 encouraged southerners to see their slave society as significantly different from, superior to, and under threat from northern free society.

Secessionists conjured an idealized white southern womanhood to embody the supposedly profound differences between the South and the

North. Southern novelists had long written northern women as publicly minded, sometimes protofeminist characters and southern women as family oriented or even subservient.[22] Democrats had used such tropes against Republicans in 1856; southern Democrats had used them against northerners in 1860. Now southerners used them to build a sense of nationhood. One secessionist complained of northern women, "The Yankee ladies are good enough in a utilitarian sense, but how can you expect delicacy or refinement from young women who are taught from childhood to fight the world with its own weapons?" He went on to insult them as "self-reliant, shrewd, and energetic." Benjamin Dill, the secessionist editor of the *Memphis Daily Appeal*, similarly criticized northern and western women — this time, the ones who attended an early reception at the Lincoln White House. "Some of the strong[-]minded women from the West insisted on dancing the rail splitter's dance," Dill scoffed. "It certainly was the most undignified and childish performance ever seen in the White [H]ouse."[23] Alongside the characters in popular domestic novels, years of Democratic campaign rhetoric denigrating the "strong-minded women" of the North had finally made their mark on southern Democrats, who now used them to split the nation in two.

By contrast, southern Democrats constructed an image of southern women as pure, moral, and submissive. In early January, South Carolina lawyer and Democrat John Smythe Richardson received a letter from a contact who was working to raise a regiment of troops who could fight if war arrived. After praising the men for volunteering, the writer praised southern women for giving their brothers, husbands, and sons so willingly to the fight. "Our women are worthy of the best days of Rome or Sparta," he declared. "They give their best and dearest treasures ungrudgingly to the state." This letter built a kind of circular logic for southern nationalism. On the one hand, the new southern nation demanded that women give up their sons and husbands. On the other, by giving up their sons and husbands, southern women brought to life all that was good, pure, and worth defending in the South.[24] While northern society produced viragos who demanded women's rights, southern society produced moral, self-sacrificing women. To southern Democrats, the difference between northern and southern women spoke to the difference between northern and southern society.

In reality, southern women were often just as invested in politics as their northern counterparts, especially in the fall and winter following the election of 1860.[25] As South Carolinian Ada Bacot wrote in her diary, "I wonder some times if people think it is strange that I should be so warm a secessionist. But why should they, has not every woman a right to express opinions on some subjects, in private if not in public[?]" But even if offered in public, secessionist southern Democrats welcomed women's support as proof of the righteousness of their movement. In February, when Louisianan Judah P. Benjamin gave his final speech in the Senate before leaving to support the South, a paper described how in the gallery, "the ladies stood upon the seats, and, waving their hankerchiefs [sic], shouted as loud as the men." When the people of New Orleans lit up their city with candles, bonfires, and torches to celebrate Louisiana's secession, the local paper boasted that "thousands of people, half of them ladies, assembled from all quarters of the city to see the display." And while Georgia's secession convention was debating over whether to leave the union, a group of teachers and their students showed their support for secession by weaving their own cloth to avoid purchasing northern goods. A reporter noted with pride that "at a recent State Fair, not the least attractive feature was the appearance on the grounds of a party of thirty-seven ladies . . . attired in a substantial check homespun dress." By spinning their own fabric, the women took concrete action to support southern independence. They also provided a powerful visual—of "thirty-seven blooming, bright-eyed southern lasses, in clothing of southern manufacture"—for secessionists to deploy in their efforts to consolidate support for leaving the Union.[26]

The proceedings of a secessionist meeting in Concord, North Carolina, reveal how southern Democrats justified southern women's politicking— which they rejected among northern women—as falling within women's sphere. The women of Cabarrus County had organized the gathering at a local hotel and invited North Carolina House of Commons member William S. Harris and North Carolina state senator Victor Clay Barringer to attend as the guests of honor. Barringer remarked "that he was proud to see that the ladies of old Cabarrus awakened on the subject of their rights, (not *woman's rights*, for that is a *plant* that is indigenous to abolition *soil*, and cultivated in the general crop of rank fanaticism and infidelity)" but rather "of Southern rights." Barringer believed it augured "well for the country when the voice of women was heard, not attempting to guide the 'Ship of State' . . . but commingling together for its peace and safety in the domestic circle."[27]

In just one speech, Barringer twice denigrated northern women as power hungry and twice praised southern women as domestic. By hosting a pro-secession meeting, these women had participated in partisan politics. But the women's blessing affirmed the morality of secession, and Barringer would be a fool to reject their support. So Barringer claimed that the women supported secession only because they wanted to protect southern homes — not because they wanted to steer the ship of state. It is not difficult to see through Barringer's self-deception: he accepted women's activism, but only when the women were on his side. That tortured logic speaks to the significant malleability in what Americans meant by womanhood in the mid-nineteenth century. White southern women were no less political than northern women. But their political style — which mostly forwent public speaking or calls for suffrage — distinguished them from northern women. This allowed southern men to deny that white southern women were political at all, and therefore fit within their definition of womanhood.

Secessionists believed that slavery allowed white women to live as God intended: in the home as daughters, wives, and mothers, protected from the hurly-burly of the modern economy. On March 4, North Carolina's *Newbern Daily Progress* reported with dismay on the classified ads posted in a New York newspaper. According to the *Progress*, the ads "show[ed] how much valuable talent in the professional and domestic arts i[s] 'wasting its sweetness' in vain quest of some occupation sufficient to keep soul and body together." That is: the free economy in New York forced too many women to work outside the home to feed their families. The *Progress* cited examples of "a Lady of education and refinement, twenty-four years of age," "a 'Young American' widow," "a respectable married woman," and more, all of whom sought paying work. These classifieds represented "a fearful testimony to the widespread distress and suffering from want of employment which pervades Northern Society." "Happily for us," the southern paper continued, "these specimens are rare in our latitude. . . . We have within us all the elements of increasing prosperity, and we have peace and harmony among ourselves."[28]

This image of southern slavery and white southern womanhood was fictional. As Jeanne Boydston has shown, women's unpaid domestic labor drove American economic growth. This held true up and down the southern social ladder. The wives of small freeholders worked on family farms, doing essential tasks ranging from cooking to working in the fields. As the wives of plantation owners and as slave owners themselves, wealthy white women managed and often brutalized enslaved workers. And of course, editors at papers like the *Newburn Daily Progress* were not considering enslaved and free Black women, whom whites expected would work on farms and in factories. Southern women thus contributed immensely to the region's economy. If elite white southern women were able to stay home, it was only because their homes were places of work.[29] Erasing southern women's economic contributions and slavery's brutality allowed men to idealize white southern womanhood as unique and worthy of protection.

"Firesides" in the Winter:
The Deep South Pushes for Secession

Events on the ground made it clear that many in the Border South rejected the secessionists' case for ripping the nation apart. Texas had seceded on February 1, capping a six-week period in which seven Deep South states left the Union. But for the next two and a half months, not a single additional state seceded. Historians have explained the Upper South's hesitation in a few ways. William Link argues that in Virginia, slaveholders had adapted slavery to a more industrial economy, strengthening their desire to remain attached to the Union. William Freehling, meanwhile, has pointed to the rising price of slaves in the 1850s, which he contends drove down rates of slave ownership and therefore support for a new slaveholders' republic.[30] Whatever the cause, many southerners living in border states, including many Democrats, acknowledged that Lincoln had been elected according to the Constitution and resolved to wait and see whether the Lincoln administration would commit an "overt act" against slavery. As one Virginia planter wrote in his diary, "As we had gone into the election with the B[lack] Republican party it was but fair that we should submit being vanquished until some act was committed against our institutions." Democratic newspapers in Virginia also championed a wait-and-see attitude throughout November and December of 1860.[31]

Convincing the Border and Upper South to leave the Union was going to require a bit of work, especially as politicians in those states debated over whether and when to assemble secession conventions. In February, secessionists in Tennessee's state government—led by Democrat Isham Harris—sought voter approval for such a convention, but Tennesseans rejected the measure 54 to 46 percent. Virginia's secession convention met for the first time on February 13 and ground on for months after. Arkansas's convention met for the first time on March 4, the day of Lincoln's inauguration. Secessionists had already constructed a national identity that idealized white southern womanhood. Now they promised fence-sitters in the Border and Upper South that real southern women—their wives and daughters—would be safer in the Confederacy than in the Union.

In January 1861, John Tyler Jr., the son of the former president, drafted a pro-secession speech that warned of the devastation that would befall white Virginian women if Republicans abolished slavery. "Our present Patriarchal system of slave labor [will be] broken up, and our present race of planters [will be] destroyed, and their children beggared," he wrote. By seceding, men in the Deep South had protected themselves and their families from this fate. "The early secession of the Planting States will have saved their Patriarchal Institutions, their Family altars, their home life," Tyler declared. Now was the time for Upper South states like his native Virginia to act. Given the "differences and distinctions, moral, social, and political, existing between the non-slaveholding and slaveholding states," Tyler argued, "the Border States must either accept emancipation and join the North, or maintain the patriarchal institution of negro slavery and join the South."[32] In this passage, Tyler appealed directly to Virginia's slaveholders who still cleaved to the Union. Those men were willing to wait and see if Lincoln would move to abolish slavery, but Tyler sensed the chance to secede had finally arrived. So he reminded them of the system that slavery undergirded—a system that installed them as patriarchs, provided for their families, and protected their wives and children from abolition and insurrection. Of course, Republicans committed not to interfere with slavery where it already existed. But were Virginia's slaveholders willing to gamble their families' safety on northern politicians' promises?

In a December letter to Kentucky governor Beriah Magoffin, Alabama secession commissioner Stephen F. Hale conjured the same fabricated threat to white women that secessionists had used in the wake of John Brown's raid. According to Hale, Republican rule would "[inaugurate] all the horrors of a San Domingo servile insurrection, consigning her citizens to assassinations, and her wives and daughters to pollution and violation, to gratify the lust of half-civilized Africans." Hale warned that this would inevitably lead to race mixing: "In the South, where in many places the African race largely predominates, and, as a consequence, the two races would be continually pressing together, amalgamation, or the extermination of the one or the other, would be inevitable. Can Southern men submit to such degradation and ruin?" he asked. "God forbid that they should."[33] Hale's letter is appallingly racist. Yet its shamelessness reveals the core secessionist argument: Republican rule would lead to slave insurrection; slave insurrection would lead to the rape of white women; the rape of white women would result in race mixing; and race mixing would diminish white's absolute control over southern society. Hale was counting on the fact that Magoffin would find this vision of violence and racial equality as horrifying as he did.

Even within families, men divided between Lower and Border South, between secession and union. In these cases, secessionists' appeal to protect southern families took on a deeper meaning. Mississippian Robert

Holt was an early supporter of secession. His brother Joseph had moved to Kentucky about twenty years earlier and by 1860 was serving as post-master general for the Buchanan administration. Joseph did not believe Lincoln's election alone justified disunion.

In a November 9 letter, Robert tried to change his brother's mind. "[Lincoln's] election is a declaration by northern people . . . of a purpose to emancipate the slaves of the South, and to involve southern states in all the horror which that event would plainly entail," he warned. "I know your heart is altogether southern," he assured Joseph. "You cannot but abhor the fanatics and assassins by whom our rights and firesides are invaded." Anticipating that Joseph, like many Kentuckians, might hope to remain neutral in the coming conflict, Robert finished by pleading with Joseph to side with the South to protect his brother's family. "The issue involves . . . the safety of my roof from the fire brand, and of my wife and children from the poison and dagger, and I would like to hear from you the assurance that you are with us and that you demand no Moloch-like sacrifice upon the altar of the Union," Robert wrote.[34]

Robert Holt supported secession to preserve slavery and protect his wife and children from insurrection. Joseph did not—perhaps because he did not believe Republicans would abolish slavery, perhaps because of his staunch Unionism, or likely because both. So Robert combined his political appeal for secession with a personal appeal to protect his family. Southerners believed that abolitionist agitation gave enslaved workers the hope and information they needed to rise up against their enslavers. As David Potter has argued, southerners like Holt feared not so much what Lincoln might do as what his election might encourage their enslaved workers to do. They feared that, as Potter puts it, "the election to the presidency of a man who stated flatly that slavery was morally wrong might have a more inciting effect upon the slaves than denunciatory rhetoric from the editor of an abolitionist weekly in Boston."[35] For Robert Holt, then, there could be no delay: the South must secede before Lincoln took office or else face the threat of slave insurrection. He implored his brother to think of the issue as a choice not between Union and secession but between slave insurrection—with its threat to the lives of his wife and children—and safety.

On other occasions, secessionists pleaded their case by conjuring the image of bloodthirsty northern soldiers raping and murdering white southern women. On December 26, Raleigh's secessionist *Spirit of the Age* beseeched readers to support secession so they could prepare themselves to protect their families against a northern invasion. "Do we not all love our homes, our hearths, and our blessed father-land[?]" the paper asked. "Supposed the startling news was received that the black republican hordes of the abolition North, were on their way, in hostile array, to steal our slaves, burn our towns, desolate our fields, and slaughter our wives and children! How soon would every man rally to a common standard of resistance."[36] According to the paper, abolitionists would stop at nothing in their quest to impose their social order on the South—even if it meant marching into the South and doing it themselves. The threat was utterly absurd, not least because one cannot imagine the balding, humorless, fifty-five-year-old abolitionist William Lloyd Garrison leading the charge on horseback. Yet it forced readers to consider whose side they would be on if the North invaded. Would they allow the Lincoln administration to trample South Carolina's right to secede? And would they be ready to protect their wives and families from harm?

Most often, the cries about protecting southern families drew on no specific threat at all, instead simply evoking a vague fear of violence and rape. A patriotic ballad circling in the South in the month after the election called on men to save their wives and children from ruin: "Ye sons of the South, awake to glory! . . . Prevent their tears and save their cries!" Another one exhorted men to honor "the noble mothers, at whose fond breast ye hung" and the "wives and daughters, and by the ills they dread" by "driv[ing] deep that good secession steel right through the monster's head." Secessionists warned darkly that they needed to protect their families, without explaining exactly from whom or what their families required protection. On January 8, Louisiana senator Judah P. Benjamin wrote to Samuel Barlow, a New York lawyer and financial backer for Democratic candidates, that "one million of men" in the South would rise up to "[defend] themselves at home against invasion." Two days later, a South Carolinian wrote that "the community believe that their personal safety, and the security of their families, are seriously threatened." Even northern Democrats recognized the growing power of this rhetoric in the South: James Buchanan fretted to Pennsylvania district attorney George Wharton that "the people of the South are daily more and more confirmed in the opinion that the security of the domestic fireside requires a separation from the Northern States."[37] Whether summoning southerners' old fear of slave insurrection, calling to life a new fear of abolitionist invasion, or invoking a vague fear of rape, all of these secessionists accomplished the same objective: they created a false choice between secession, on the one hand, and the rape and murder of southern women, on the other.

Upper South unionists agreed that southern women required their protection. But through the winter and spring of 1861, they continued to believe that secession posed a greater threat to their wives and daughters than remaining in the Union did. Raleigh's *Semi-weekly Standard* had railed against John Brown in 1859 and supported Breckinridge in 1860. Yet even as tensions were rising in Charleston harbor, the paper refused to condone secession. On April 10, the *Standard* printed a poem that warned readers of the fate that would befall southern wives and children if the state seceded and war arrived at their doorstep. In the poem, four characters—Discord, Famine, Slaughter, and the Devil—describe with glee the apocalyptic scene that secession has wrought. Slaughter says, "The mother gave her babe one parting glance / The soldier spitted both upon his lance." Famine adds, "Beside [the farmers] sat their wives, whose starving babes / Like withered lilies lay upon their laps / Seeking the breasts that gave no nourishment."[38] The editors of the *Standard* agreed with secessionists that southern women needed their protection. They simply concluded that the best way to protect them was to stay in the Union.

Beyond appealing to fellow southerners to protect their wives and daughters, secessionists also declared that a man's bravery could be measured in terms of his willingness to fight for the South. On December 26, Marylander Jefferson Martenet wrote to his mother from San Francisco, promising that, if war arrived, he would fight to defend southerners' right to own property in slaves. "If our Country is invaded we fight . . . there could be no patriotism, nothing to strive for if we know we had no security in possession, the South is right and I would not consider a southerner a man who would not fight for her rights," he wrote. Martenet presented a stark choice: be a man and fight for the South, or refuse to fight and be called a coward. Southern men pushed each other to support secession and join the army, but they also felt pressure from southern women. Writing to the editor of Jackson's *Weekly Mississippian*, one woman "challenge[d] to chivalric and generous emulation the true knights of Mississippi," promising that "to him that plants his standard in the thickest of the fight be the award of valor." And one secessionist in North Carolina warned his brother at West Point that a pretty girlfriend back home "says if this state would go out of [of the Union] she intends to marry a secessionist," even if he were "as poor and ugly as a Black snake."[39]

Finally, secessionists trotted out the same tactic they had used to force a split in the party in 1860: declaring that compromise was equivalent to submissiveness. During the nominating conventions of 1860, southern Democrats discouraged delegates from compromising with northerners by characterizing intransigence as masculine and compromise as feminine. Now, even as northern Democrats proclaimed that compromise was manly, secessionists contended it was weak and feminine. Secessionists repeatedly used this language to explain their position and to cajole others to support the Confederacy. On November 10, one South Carolinian reported that there was not a "southerner who does not prefer disunion, before submission to the incoming administration." He exaggerated—there were plenty—but the way he framed a political decision as a question of masculine honor hinted at things to come. Secessionists continued to use this language throughout the winter. Democratic newspaperman William Montague Brown had immigrated to the United States from Ireland. After moving to Washington, D.C., to write for the proadministration *Constitution*, he became a strong partisan of the South. On November 22 and again on December 10, Brown fumed to New Yorker Samuel Barlow that he would not submit to northern rule. "I am a citizen of a southern state," he wrote. "I should suffer anything rather than submit to Lincoln's election." The second letter read, "Ought you [give] them . . . the left cheek, because you have endeavored in vain to prevent their being smitten on the right cheek?" Clearly not, according to Brown. "The South will never bend the knee again and beg for her rights." On December 2, as South Carolina began to assemble a secession convention, a Democrat from Virginia's Tidewater wrote to a friend in South Carolina, praising South Carolina for putting Virginians in a position where they would have to stand like men. "If left to herself [Virginia] would do nothing but 'pass resolutions' and let all her courage rage out through them . . . but thanks to South Carolina (God bless her) she (Virginia) will not be permitted to 'brag and back out.'" But the writer worried that "the state is full of submissionists," who might delay Virginia's secession. The fire-eater Edmund Ruffin shared the same concern in a letter to his friend John Perkins, decrying Virginia's secession convention as a "Submission Convention" that is "regarded with scorn and contempt by every man true to the South."[40]

As winter wore into spring, the submissionist rhetoric put the heat on unionist southern Democrats. They were frustrated that their lifelong commitment to the Union should suddenly be cause for censure by their fellow southerners. On April 10, Raleigh's Democratic *Semi-weekly Standard* quoted a threat against Union men run by the secessionist *Richmond Examiner*. The *Standard* cried, "Union men . . . you are abused and branded as submissionists to unjust power, simply because you are true to the Constitution and obedient to its laws! Such is the mad spirit of disunion."[41] The *Standard* saw secessionists' gendered insults for what they were: attempts to manipulate men's pride and pressure the Upper South into seceding from the Union.

On and on secessionists railed against the so-called submissionists.[42] The rhetorical device accomplished two things. First, it feminized those who wanted to give the Lincoln administration an opportunity to govern before quitting the Union. These men were conditional unionists: they supported the Union as long as the Union supported slavery. They were not convinced that the Republican government represented an existential threat to slavery or to slave society. By calling these men submissionists, secessionists made their position seem cowardly rather than reasonable. Second, the secessionists justified their own position. For many years, Americans across the political spectrum had dismissed calls for disunion as radical—even treasonous. Among contemporaries, the mere word "disunion" conjured up images of chaos, death, anarchy, and war.[43] And now, the secessionists wanted to make disunion a reality by seceding from the Union. They needed a way to sell this program. Reframing themselves as courageous—rather than treasonous—and those who wished to stay in the Union as submissive—rather than loyal—helped them do just that. They convinced sufficient numbers of men in the Lower South states to secede, and they primed the pump for secession in the Upper South, too.

"Firesides" in the Spring:
The Upper South Joins the Confederacy

After Lincoln's election, as states seceded and Congress argued over how to save the Union, trouble had begun to brew in Charleston's harbor. After South Carolina left the Union in December, its government demanded that the U.S. Army abandon its facilities on the islands in the harbor— facilities that South Carolina now claimed as its own. The federal government refused. Supplies on Fort Sumter dwindled. On April 4, a month after taking office, Lincoln ordered a relief expedition sent to Sumter. The Confederate government responded by demanding the federal troops evacuate Fort Sumter, U.S. Major Robert Anderson refused, and on April 12, Confederate troops opened fire on the fort. Anderson surrendered thirty-four hours later. On April 15, Lincoln issued a call for 75,000 volunteers to defend Washington, D.C., and suppress the rebellion. Though Confederate troops had fired the first shots, southerners perceived Lincoln's call for troops as an act of aggression. Virginia voted to secede on April 17, Arkansas on May 6, North Carolina on May 20, and Tennessee on June 8. The gender tactics deployed over the previous five years, and especially over the previous five months, primed Upper South Democrats to see secession and war as the only way to defend southern women and homes from an invading northern menace.[44]

Four days after Lincoln's call for troops, the secessionist editor J. O. Griffith urged readers of his *Nashville Union and American* to consider their families' safety in the war that was sure to come. Griffith could not believe that "some half dozen or so of old grannies, hold the opinion that in the present conflict . . . the true policy of Tennessee is to take no part in the fight." But having spent much of the winter working himself into a lather over the supposed preponderance of free love and abolitionism in the North, Griffith believed that Lincoln had called for troops to impose that radical social order on the South. "Black Republicanism," he warned readers, represented "a crime against the peace and safety, not only of the State, but of the domestic circle." On the same page, a separate article commented on the special legislative session called in response to the raising of Union troops. "It behooves Tennessee to place herself on a footing of defense, and to make herself ready to protect her hearthstones and her homes against the invader," it declared.[45] Griffith had long supported secession. But Lincoln's call for troops made it easier for him to claim that the North would impose by force its radical social program on "the domestic circle"—eliminating the system of slavery and patriarchy that sustained southern homes. To protect their homes, Tennesseans must support secession and prepare for war. If they did not, they were nothing but "old grannies" who lacked the strength, courage, and virility to protect southern homes from invading northerners.[46]

An article in Raleigh's *Semi-weekly Standard* demonstrates the versatility of calls to protect southern women. Whereas Griffith had long supported secession, *Standard* editor William W. Holden had opposed it. Indeed, just days before Fort Sumter, Holden published a poem painting a picture of the hunger, death, and destruction that secession would wreck on North Carolina's women and children. But in the wake of Lincoln's call for troops, Holden reluctantly came out in favor of leaving the Union. At a public meeting in Lumberton, North Carolina, on April 20, a man gave a speech declaring that men should be "willing to die . . . for the honor and safety of the State," and that "the State ought to throb as it were with on[e] heart, and that heart should be for the safety of their firesides." In reprinting the speech, the *Standard* praised it as "very able and patriotic."[47] In a matter of weeks, Holden had moved from opposing secession because it would devastate North Carolina's women to supporting secession because it would protect them. Historians recognize that Lincoln's call for troops effected a sea change in southern public opinion. This example from the *Standard* elucidates how gendered language facilitated that change by encouraging men to see Lincoln's call for troops as a threat to their families—a perception that persisted throughout the war.[48]

Not content to serve as mere symbols of the new Confederacy, white southern women proclaimed their wholehearted support for secession and war. Twenty-two-year-old Amanda Virginia Edmonds of Fauquier County in northern Virginia praised her state's vote to secede from the Union. "Virginia today is numbered with her Southern Sister states, and a revolution the intelligence brings in political affairs," she wrote in her diary. Ten days later in South Carolina, Mary Boykin Chesnut, the wife of former South Carolina senator James Chesnut Jr., expressed irritation that her husband's contacts were not more excited by the success of the secession movement and the prospect of a coming war. "Fears for the future and not exultation at our successes pervade [Alexander Stephens's] discourse," she complained to her diary. Later that same day, she snapped, "It is very tiresome to have these people always harping on this: 'The enemy's troops are the finest body of men we ever saw.' 'Why did you not make friends of them,' I feel disposed to say. We would have war, and now we seem to be letting our golden opportunity pass."[49]

Even though law barred them from voting and custom prevented them from speaking in public, southern women organized to support preparations for the war effort. In South Carolina, women attended military drills, sewed uniforms, and fashioned patriotic cockades. One group of women sewed a Palmetto flag for the cadets at the Anderson Military Academy. Careful not to defy contemporary mores by speaking in public, the women asked the cadets' leader to present the flag for them. The leader held forth on "the emotions of pleasure and gratification, which spring from the depths of our hearts for this beautiful embodiment of the approbation of the fair ladies." One of the cadets at the gathering also thanked the women—but then moved quickly to remind them of their appropriate place in southern society. "While history records many illustrious examples of woman's capacity to guide and control the destinies of nations . . . the appropriate sphere of woman will be found in the exercise of those gentle and benign affections peculiar to her sex, which constitutes the charm and solace of domestic life."[50] In the South, women could care about politics, but only if they supported the Confederacy. Women could even participate in politics—but only in silence, and only if they did so knowing their participation constituted an anomalous foray outside of their proper sphere.

Southern volunteers appreciated women's enthusiasm. In June, a group of Confederate volunteers camped at Manassas Junction wrote to the women members of Richmond churches who had sewn uniforms for the company. The volunteers thanked the women for their support, "evinced not only in their smiles and promised prayers, but in acts of substantial kindness." But as they went off to war, southern men wanted more: they wanted women to become flesh-and-blood representatives of the southern womanhood the men idealized and idolized. So if sexual purity differentiated idealized southern womanhood from northern womanhood, then southern women must abstain from extramarital sex while their husbands fought on their behalf. The company of soldiers wrote to the Richmond women, "There is nothing truer than that women are the tutors and guardians of our Race"—that is, of white southerners. "So absorbing is her influence upon Youth that patriotic intelligent woman has never been known as the mother of a bastard boy." In case that did not make the imperative to abstain clear, the men went on, "As [woman] has been elevated or depraved—licentious or pure, so has risen or fallen the morals, the manners, and the character of a people."[51]

The letter served a few purposes. The first was undisguised sexual control. As men left their homes, they wanted to make sure women did not find company elsewhere. To accomplish this, men tied sexual loyalty to husbands to political loyalty to the Confederacy: women could demonstrate the latter by performing the former. Second, the men needed women to act as the men had imagined them: as pure, almost untouchable goddesses who could bear witness to men's greatness in war.[52] The women's witness gave the men's efforts deeper meaning. And finally, the letter defined women's roles in the new nation. In the North, women projected their virtuous nature into the public sphere by supporting reform programs such as women's rights and abolition. According to southerners, this had created a disordered and chaotic society. So, in the South, women would demonstrate their virtue in the domestic sphere, by raising virtuous children and refraining from extramarital affairs. This marked a return to the early republican vision of patriotic womanhood.[53] Southern Democratic women, and now most southern women, had proven themselves willing supporters of secession. Now secession demanded just as much from them.

Conclusion

By June 8, 1861, eleven slaveholding states had seceded from the Union—
and the Lincoln administration worried that Maryland, Kentucky, and
Missouri would follow. But even as Americans prepared for war, they could
not escape the politics of the recent past. The gender tactics of the preceding five years guided northern and southern Democrats' perception of
their enemy and their prosecution of the war.

Northern and southern Democrats shared a vision of white manhood
based on their status as autonomous household heads, their ability to
provide for their families, and the maintenance of their political freedom.
Slavery had rendered the lived experience of these prerogatives mutually incompatible. But northern Democrats still respected southerners
as equals in the national family. A June 1861 letter from a New England
woman to Kentucky Democrat Joseph Holt represents this sense of equality. She thanked Holt for cleaving to the Union. "I must return you my
thanks for the noble stand you have taken for our country," she wrote. And
after blaming the southern aristocracy for secession, she wished "that our
southern brethren could read our hearts, and hear the prayers that are
offered in their behalf! . . . I love them as fellow countrymen and many of
them as brethren in Christ."[1]

This continued respect for their estranged southern counterparts led
northern Democrats to articulate a unique vision of the Union War. As
Jack Furniss has demonstrated, northern Democrats continued to push
for compromise as an honorable war aim—an effort that was distinctly
gendered, and which echoed the procompromise rhetoric of the secession
winter. In 1861, the New York Democratic State Committee adopted a
platform entreating the Lincoln administration to remember that "our
political system was founded in compromise, and it can never be dishon-
orable in any Administration to seek to restore it by the same means." If
administration men reached a compromise with the South, they would
be no more dishonored than the Founders themselves. In 1863, New York
governor Horatio Seymour echoed this language in his inaugural address,
claiming that the advance of the armies "must be accompanied by a firm
and conciliatory policy" to bring the South back into the Union.[2] Though

war had arrived, northern Democrats still believed compromise could save the Union, so they reassured northern politicians that doing so would constitute a "firm" and honorable course of action.

In addition to supporting compromise, northern Democrats pushed for a restrained war that would spare white men and their families the heaviest burdens of the conflict. This attitude was based in part on the assumption that, in Mark Grimsley's words, "most white Southerners were lukewarm about secession, and if handled with forbearance, would withdraw their allegiance from the Confederacy." But it also stemmed from northern Democrats' respect for white southern men as brothers in the American family and fellow patriarchs. On April 22, the *Brooklyn Daily Eagle* described the war fever in New York following Lincoln's call for troops. "Brooklyn is one scene of commotion," the paper reported. But as the soldiers marched off to war, the *Eagle* hoped that men on both sides would "restrain all barbarities, and keep the contest within the rules of manly and honorable warfare." This attitude persisted into the fall, when Horatio Seymour wrote of the need to protect the "freedom of conscience, the protection of our persons, the sacredness of our homes, the trial by jury, [and] the freedom from arbitrary arrests."[3] To modern readers, it is strange to see the "sacredness of homes" mentioned in the same breath as trial by jury. But to Seymour, both of these were key components of white manhood. Seymour and his fellow northern Democrats would fight to bring southern men back into the Union, but they would not bring them to their knees.

Finally, a sense of shared white manhood led northern Democrats to oppose immediate emancipation, even as a war measure. Many northern Democrats believed in the superiority of the free labor system. But they feared emancipation because they believed it would lead to servile insurrection and race war. This was a terrifying prospect in and of itself. It also threatened white southern men's status as heads of households and protectors of southern women. Before Abraham Lincoln issued the Emancipation Proclamation, Seymour referred to immediate emancipation and the arming of slaves as a "proposal for the butchery of women and children, for scenes of lust and rapine, and of arson and murder." And after the proclamation had been issued, Seymour claimed it had only served to "humiliate and mortify the loyal men of the South"; a more conservative war policy would "kindle anew the fires of patriotism" among the "many thousand loyal men" in the Confederacy.[4] Seymour vastly overestimated Unionist sentiment in the Confederacy. But he correctly surmised the effect of emancipation on white southern men's psyches. By denying them the right to enslave and by exposing their wives to the specter of rape, emancipation struck at the very heart of white southern manhood.

The party's gender tactics predisposed northern Democrats to support compromise and a restrained war effort and oppose emancipation. For southerners, however, the party's gender tactics had the opposite effect. Southern Democrats extended their election-year critique of a fanatical northern society into the war years. Southerners' accusations against northern society were multifarious and often contradictory, ranging from Puritanism to infidelity, socialism to tyranny, abolitionism to free love.[5]

An engraving by the Confederate-sympathizing Marylander Aldabert Volck illustrates southerners' kitchen-sink critique of northern fanaticism. An offensively ape-like Black man sits atop a throne with the words "Chicago Platform." In front of him, a white man lies bleeding to death on an altar made of stones etched with "negro worship," "spirit rapping," "free love," "witch burning," "atheism," "rationalism," and "Puritanism." Around the altar, a cast of characters—including Horace Greeley, Harriet Beecher Stowe, Abraham Lincoln, John Frémont, Benjamin Butler, and Charles Sumner—looks on, and an idol statue of John Brown with a pike stands in the background. Taken together, the set of tropes is strikingly similar to those northern Democrats published in their anti-Republican cartoons in the past two elections. As for Lincoln, southerners described him at turns as a "Baboon Despot," an "unprincipled tyrant," or as Satan carrying off the white Goddess of Liberty. Born of the Democrats' 1856 and 1860 campaigns, these racialized and gendered critiques of northern fanatics and of Lincoln as their leader "laid the groundwork," in George Rable's words, "for a war carried on at ever-mounting cost and with ever greater cruelty."[6]

During the war years, southerners also continued to appeal to protect white southern women. For decades, southern men had exalted white women as the sacred vessels of their civilization's best instincts. After Lincoln's election, secessionists had pleaded with southerners to leave the Union to protect their wives and daughters from women's rights, free love, and abolition. Confederates adopted and adapted this view during the war, conceptualizing military service as a way to literally protect white southern women from the advancing Union army. White southerners like twenty-year-old Sarah Morgan agonized over the ransacking of their family homes. After Union troops searched their home in Baton Rouge, Morgan was mortified to think of "the Yankee stamp of dirty fingers" on her sister's correspondence and the women's clothes "used for the vilest purposes, and spread in every corner" of the house.[7] Ironically, the war the South

"Worship of the North," 1861. Library Company of Philadelphia.

started wrought exactly what southern men had feared: a desecration of their firesides and a loss of control over their homes.

Fear of assault, rape, and murder loomed even larger in the southern imagination, fueled by dark rumors and breathless newspaper reports. Some of this propaganda played on the fear of the rape of white women by enslaved men. Reports in Mississippi and Tennessee told of enslaved men raping white women while Union soldiers either did nothing to stop them or looked on approvingly. And a correspondent for a Mobile newspaper asked southern men to "think of a negro, your slave, gratifying his hellish lust upon one of your countrywomen! Think of her future degradation through life; fancy her cry for rescue [from] his fiendish embrace." The correspondent denied that he had invented the story as propaganda for the southern cause. But generals and politicians realized that the ability to protect—and control—women was central to Confederates' identity as free men, and they frequently conjured images of rape when recruiting and addressing troops. Incensed by General Benjamin Butler's infamous woman order in New Orleans, General P. G. T. Beauregard asked his men, "Shall our mothers, our wives, our daughters, and our sisters be thus outraged by the ruffianly soldiers of the North, to whom is given the right to treat at their pleasure the ladies of the south as common harlots?"[8] The answer, of course, was no.

Other propaganda capitalized on the fear of Union troops, describing bestial northern soldiers raping beautiful, helpless white women. In August 1861, one Richmond paper reported, "We have heard of an outrage perpetrated upon one of the most respectable married ladies of Fairfax, in the presence of her children, which has no parallel except among the atrocities of the Sepoys and Druses."[9] Longer accounts described five soldiers gang-raping a Tennessee woman, holding pistols to women's heads while assaulting them, or attacking women with their children present. The fearmongering obscured the truth: during the Civil War, as before, Black women, not white women, were most vulnerable to attacks by white men. As Thavolia Glymph has explained, white men's ideas about Black women's sexuality normalized sexual assaults on Black women by Union and Confederate soldiers. Esther Hawks, a northern woman working with the National Freedman's Relief Association in South Carolina, observed that "no colored woman or girl was safe from the brutal lusts of the soldiers — and by soldiers I mean both officers and men." Union soldiers assaulted so many women that in 1863 President Lincoln signed the Lieber Code, prohibiting the rape of women. Following the code's issuance, hundreds of Black women sought legal protections against rape.[10] Despite this serious threat to Black women, southern newspaper editors played up the much less serious threat to white women. In so doing, they urged fellow Confederates to fight to the death to protect white southern womanhood — and to save themselves from the emasculation of seeing southern women dishonored.

The Union split in two. Northern Democrats urged compromise and opposed emancipation. Confederates insisted on an all-out fight to defend the South from northern fanaticism and northern soldiers. The Democratic Party bore special responsibility for this shambolic state of affairs. Since the Lecompton crisis, southern Democrats had demanded increasingly vigorous protections for slavery — from a guarantee that slavery could extend to the territories, to a stronger fugitive slave law, to a southern nominee for president. In so doing, they put northern Democrats in an impossible position: support southern demands and lose their seats or deny southern demands and alienate one-half of their party — and one section of the country. And when southern Democrats led the charge toward secession and then attacked a federal fort, they both caused and started the Civil War.

But northern Democrats played a critical role in this chain of events. They collaborated with southern Democrats to bring forth a powerful gendered language that southerners then used to express and intensify their alienation within and ultimately from the Democratic Party and the Union. In 1856, northern Democrats differentiated themselves from their new Republican competitors by condemning the Republicans as radicals on gender and slavery alike, claiming that Republican rule would result in an upside-down world in which Black men were equal to white men and wives were equal to their husbands. Southern Democrats did the same, and together, northern and southern Democrats elected James Buchanan president and affirmed popular sovereignty as the law of the land. But then came the perceived betrayal of Lecompton and the shock of John Brown's raid. After both events, southern Democrats co-opted the gendered language from the previous presidential election to question northern Democrats' loyalty. Southern Democrats wondered whether their northern counterparts truly cared about protecting southern slavery, southern patriarchy, and southern women from the onslaught of Republican radicalism; they even worried that northern Democrats themselves subscribed to radical beliefs. Southern Democrats continued to use that language against Republicans and northern Democrats throughout the election of 1860. And finally, southern Democrats combined a gendered explanation with a political one to justify their support for secession, push wavering southern moderates toward war, and inflame the passions of Confederate soldiers against northern fanatics and Yankee soldiers. Against that emotional and political juggernaut, northern Democrats' belated motions toward compromise rang hollow.

The fracturing and collapse of the Democratic Party offers a sober warning to modern politicians: the political rhetoric they use and the concessions they make can lead to disaster for party and country. Animated by personal ambition, an obsession with winning the next election, and the desire to secure key legislative victories, Democrats described Republicans as dangerous extremists whose ascendancy would bring the country to ruin. The cynical tactic ultimately did the party far greater harm than good, as northern Democrats found themselves accused of the same radical misreading of the North in 1860 that they had advocated in 1856. To be clear, it was southerners who drove a wedge in the Democratic Party with their manifold demands to protect and extend slavery. But northern Democrats' appeasement emboldened southerners. They made endless concessions to the radical elements in their party. They used racist and sexist language and tropes to gin up support. And they insisted on trying to find a middle ground on issues where, increasingly, there was none. By prioritizing their political survival over the preservation of the Union, northern Democrats enabled an extremist movement that rejected core American principles to metastasize into a serious threat to the republic. By the time they finally condemned the antidemocratic elements in their party, it was too late: their party and their country had split in two.

Notes

Introduction

1. Maurer, "The Great Republican Reform Party."
2. Maurer, "The Republican Party Going to the Right House."
3. "Northern Slavery," *Daily Delta* (New Orleans), April 18, 1860, 4; John Tyler Jr., "The Secession of the South," *DeBow's Review*, April 1860, 390, Virginia Historical Society.
4. Cott, *The Bonds of Womanhood*; Douglas, *The Feminization of American Culture*; DuBois, *Feminism and Suffrage*; Varon, *We Mean to Be Counted*; Edwards, *Angels in the Machinery*.
5. Whites, *The Civil War as a Crisis in Gender*; McCurry, *Masters of Small Worlds*; Greenberg, *Manifest Manhood and the Antebellum American Empire*; Pierson, *Free Hearts and Free Homes*, 3. See also Gail Bederman's work on turn-of-the-century America, which argues that America's imperial conquest pushed white, middle-class Americans to redefine masculinity in terms of racial dominance and "civilization." Those ideas about white masculinity and femininity, in turn, contributed to America's nationalist and imperialist crusade: Gail Bederman, *Manliness and Civilization*.
6. For a review of works by Whites and McCurry, including a critique of the way they at times suppress nonwhite perspectives, see Edwards, "Review: You Can't Go Home Again," 570–76.
7. Scott, *Gender and the Politics of History*, 31; Butler, *Gender Trouble*, x; Connell, *Masculinities*.
8. Beard and Beard, *The Rise of American Civilization*; for the most influential examples of the argument that the Civil War was needless and avoidable, see Craven, *The Repressible Conflict*; and Randall, "The Blundering Generation." See also Du Bois, *Black Reconstruction*; McPherson, *Battle Cry of Freedom*; and Foner, *Free Soil, Free Labor, Free Men*.
9. Potter, *The Impending Crisis*; Holt, *The Political Crisis of the 1850s*; Freehling, *Road to Disunion*.
10. Edward Ayers calls on historians to focus "on the connection between structure and event, on the relationships between the long-existing problem of slavery and the immediate world of politics" in the two or three decades before 1861. See Ayers, *What Caused the Civil War?*, 138; and Varon, *Disunion!*
11. For studies on Republicans, see Foner, *Free Soil, Free Labor, Free Men*; and Pierson, *Free Hearts and Free Homes*. On southern Democrats, see, for instance, Walther, *The Fire-Eaters*. There are also a few cultural and political biographies of influential southern Democrats. See Faust, *James Henry Hammond and the Old South*; and Walther, *William Lowndes Yancey and the Coming of the Civil War*.

12. On northern Democrats, see Baker, *Affairs of Party*; Eyal, *The Young America Movement*; Smith, *The Stormy Present*; Peck, *Making an Antislavery Nation*; and Neely, *Lincoln and the Democrats*. Joshua A. Lynn's dissertation examines the whole party and pays attention to how a commitment to patriarchy helped shape Democrats' political identity, but Lynn emphasizes the party's unity, leaving the party's 1860 schism unexplained. See Lynn, "Preserving the White Man's Republic." For the only book-length study of the national party, see Woods, *Arguing until Doomsday*.

13. Circulation numbers from American Antiquarian Society, "The Early Nineteenth-Century Newspaper Boom"; Daniel Walker Howe has argued that these revolutions in transportation and communication both bound Americans together and—by nationalizing politics and boosting the reform impulse—encouraged controversy and contest. See Howe, *What Hath God Wrought?*. "Literally drenched in politics" quote in Gienapp, "'Politics Seem to Enter into Everything,'" 41. Literacy numbers cited in Graff, *The Legacies of Literacy*, 344.

14. Robertson, *The Language of Democracy*, 11; Rachel Shelden, quoted in Maizlish, *A Strife of Tongues*, 3. Maizlish argues that discourse revealed the values of speakers as well as of their constituents—and I agree. For a full expression of this methodological argument, see Maizlish, 2–5.

15. Quoted in McClintock, *Lincoln and the Decision for War*, 268–69.

Chapter 1

1. Politicians from states all along the Mississippi Valley had spent the previous decade jockeying to have the railroad line begin in their cities, hoping to advance their own political prospects and share in the inevitable profits. Douglas pushed for the railroad to begin in Chicago, where he owned significant land and property; Louisiana's Judah P. Benjamin was deeply involved in the Tehuantepec Railroad Company; and Missouri's Thomas Hart Benton advocated for St. Louis. See Potter, *The Impending Crisis*, 148–49. In 1849, Douglas said that the Missouri Compromise was "canonized in the hearts of the American people as a sacred thing which no ruthless hand would ever be reckless enough to disturb." Quoted in Potter, 156n23.

2. Recently, historians have debated why Douglas and the northern Democrats battled so tenaciously to support popular sovereignty. Adam I. P. Smith argues that northern Democrats believed that popular sovereignty would result in the restriction of slavery from the territories where it was formerly prohibited by the Missouri Compromise. "The challenge of the Democratic Party after 1854," Smith writes, "was to exploit the underlying acceptance of the principle of popular sovereignty and to try to argue that in practice it worked, both in the sense of giving settlers real power, and also—as a presumed consequence—by prohibiting the expansion of slavery." On the other side of the debate, Graham Peck asserts that Douglas's personal toleration of slavery "emboldened him to risk the possibility of slavery's expansion." Peck supports this claim by pointing to Douglas's admission that some slaveholders had already established themselves in Kansas and Nebraska; Peck also notes that northern free-soil opposition to the Kansas-Nebraska bill actually deepened Douglas's resolve to get it passed. I believe that timing is critical in resolving this debate. Between 1854 and 1857, Douglas had no way of knowing for sure whether Nebraska would end up a free or slave territory—and his

rhetoric indicates that he did not care much about the morality or the expansion of slavery either way, as long as it did not interfere with national expansion and the endurance of the Union. Moreover, it seems illogical that free soilers would have so passionately opposed the Kansas-Nebraska Act if people believed that popular sovereignty guaranteed a free-soil outcome. Only in 1858—when Kansans roundly rejected the proslavery Lecompton Constitution—did it become clear that popular sovereignty would lead to more free territory. See Smith, *The Stormy Present*, 104; and Peck, *Making an Antislavery Nation*, 117.

3. "Republican Party Platform of 1856."

4. "From Philadelphia," *New York Tribune*, June 21, 1856, 5; "Rallying Song," *New York Herald*, June 26, 1856, 1; "Give 'Em Jessie," *Burlington (Vt.) Free Press*, July 14, 1856, 2; "Fremont at Cincinnati," *Hartford Courant*, July 4, 1856, 2.

5. "What Abolition Has Effected," *Richmond Enquirer*, October 24, 1856, 1.

6. "Visit to Col. Fremont," *Hartford Courant*, August 20, 1856, 2. "Col. Fremont," *Wisconsin State Journal* (Madison), June 10, 1856, 2; "Gen. Scott, Col. Fremont and His Wife," *True American* (Steubenville, Ohio), August 6, 1856, 2; "What Sort of a Man Is Col. Fremont," *True American*, August 6, 1856, 2.

7. William Bradford Reed, "The Appeal to Pennsylvania. A Speech by William B. Reed. Delivered at a Meeting of the Friends of Buchanan and Breckenridge, at Somerset, Pa., September 25, 1856," 1856, 27, Massachusetts Historical Society. "Fremont's Religion—Two Fremonts in the Field," *Brooklyn Daily Eagle*, October 11, 1856, 2. An article in the *Cincinnati Daily Enquirer* implied that Democratic hero Andrew Jackson would never have bothered to part his hair down the middle. See "Fremont," *Cincinnati Daily Enquirer*, October 9, 1856. "Prospects in New York," *Cincinnati Daily Enquirer*, August 20, 1856, 4. Friend and Glover, *Southern Manhood*, xiii.

8. Quote on Jessie's charm from Pierson, *Free Hearts and Free Homes*, 126. Republican newspaper article is "We Own Up—He Will Do It," *St. Albans (Vt.) Weekly Messenger*, September 4, 1856, 2.

9. *O, Jessie Is a Sweet, Bright Lady*; "Gen. Scott, Col. Fremont and His Wife," *True American*, August 6, 1856, 2. "Jessie Fremont," in Drew, *The Campaign of 1856*. "Give 'Em Jessie," *Burlington Free Press*, July 14, 1856, 2. Information on "Jessie Circles" from Pierson, *Free Hearts and Free Homes*, 109. Quote on composition of the ticket is of Allan Nevis, quoted in Pierson, 129.

10. For examples of Democratic women's partisanship during the Second Party System, see "Where Is the Democrat That Would Not Be Proud of Such a Wife?," *United States Magazine and Democratic Review*, September 1841, 350; "Democratic Meeting at Daviston, Talbot County," *Federal Union* (Milledgeville, Ga.), September 24, 1844, 3; "Houston Barbecue," *Georgia Telegraph* (Macon), September 24, 1844, 2; and "The Illumination," *Federal Union*, November 19, 1844, 3.

11. "New Election 'Wrinkle'—'Our Jessie,'" *Cincinnati Daily Enquirer*, July 9, 1856, 2. A similar article questions why Jessie appeared at a campaign rally on her own, as a stand-in for John, after John was forced to cancel. See "New Mode of Electioneering for the Presidency," *Cincinnati Daily Enquirer*, July 13, 1856, 2.

12. Rynders quoted in "The Fourteenth Ward Democracy in a Glow of Enthusiasm," *Brooklyn Daily Eagle*, August 15, 1856, 2. Song from "Saline Lake," *Boston*

Post, October 30, 1856, 4. The following articles referred to Jessie's power over John, John's foppishness or emasculation, or both: "New Election 'Wrinkle'—'Our Jessie,'" *Cincinnati Daily Enquirer*, July 9, 1856, 2; "New Mode of Electioneering for the Presidency," *Cincinnati Daily Enquirer*, July 13, 1856, 2; "The Closing Scenes of the Monster Democratic Meeting at Indianapolis," *Cincinnati Daily Enquirer*, July 19, 1856, 4; "Prospects in New York," 4; "A Chance for the Police," *Cincinnati Daily Enquirer*, August 23, 1856, 2; "What a Pretty Man!," *Cincinnati Daily Enquirer*, August 28, 1856, 2; and "Extraordinary Freak of Nature," *Cincinnati Daily Enquirer*, September 2, 1856, 3.

13. See "The Closing Scenes of the Monster Democratic Meeting at Indianapolis," *Cincinnati Daily Enquirer*, July 19, 1856, 4; and "Inasmuch as the Black Republicans," *Cincinnati Daily Enquirer*, July 4, 1856, 2.

14. "Grand Rally in the Fifth Ward," *Brooklyn Daily Eagle*, September 19, 1856, 2.

15. "John C. Fremont's Mother," *Richmond Enquirer*, October 24, 1856, 4. "Grand Rally in the Fifth Ward," *Brooklyn Daily Eagle*, September 19, 1856, 2.

16. Lovejoy, *The True Democracy*, 1. On the Frémonts' elopement, see Pierson, *Free Hearts and Free Homes*, 124–26.

17. As retold in Pierson, *Free Hearts and Free Homes*, 106.

18. "The Family," *Richmond Enquirer*, July 1, 1856, 1.

19. Pierson, *Free Hearts and Free Homes*, 107–8.

20. On Buchanan as a compromise candidate, see Smith, *The Stormy Present*, 90. Anti-Buchanan language from "Give 'Em Jessie," *Rutland (Vt.) Weekly Herald*, July 4, 1856, 2; "A Shot at the Nominee," *Pomeroy (Ohio) Weekly Telegraph*, July 8, 1856, 1; "Mittened," *Enterprise and Vermonter* (Vergennes), August 15, 1856, 2; "It Is Proposed," *St. Albans (Vt.) Weekly Messenger*, June 26, 1856, 2; "A Shot at the Nominee," 1.

21. Denby quoted in "Fun among the Democracy," *Evansville (Ind.) Daily Journal*, November 5, 1856, 3. Lynn, "A Manly Doughface."

22. "Why Buchanan Is a Bachelor," *Ottawa (Ill.) Free Trader*, August 9, 1856, 1. "Personal and Political Abuse," *Brooklyn Daily Eagle*, August 7, 1856, 2.

23. "Mr. Buchanan's Charities," *Richmond Enquirer*, September 26, 1856, 2. A similar article published in the same paper one month later praised Buchanan's charitable activities. See "Buchanan at Home," *Richmond Enquirer*, October 24, 1856, 1. Capen, *Plain Facts and Considerations*, 6; James Buchanan, quoted in Capen, 6.

24. "Declaration of Sentiments." Lisa Tetrault shows how Elizabeth Cady Stanton, Susan B. Anthony, and Lucretia Mott popularized the myth that Seneca Falls marked the beginning of the women's suffrage movement in response to post–Civil War racial politics and dynamics in the women's rights movement. See Tetrault, *The Myth of Seneca Falls*.

25. Isenberg, *Sex and Citizenship in Antebellum America*, 20, 189.

26. "No. 2: Will the Union Be Preserved? If Dissolved Can the South Maintain Herself?," *Richmond Enquirer*, September 9, 1856, 2. "Woman's Rights," *Richmond Enquirer*, April 15, 1856, 2.

27. "Women's Rights and Married Men's Notions," *Belvidere (Ill.) Standard*, April 1, 1856, 4.

28. "Woman's Rights, or, the History of a Visit to Utopia," *Carlisle (Penn.) Weekly Herald*, June 25, 1856, 2. "Anti-'Woman's Rights' Lecture," *Belvidere Standard*, April 1, 1856, 2.

29. Benevolent sexism characterizes women as sensitive, affectionate individuals who need to be protected and cared for. Although benevolently sexist beliefs can sometimes encompass traits that seem to favor women, benevolent sexism is just as oppressive as hostile sexism. See Glicke and Fiske, "The Ambivalent Sexism Inventory."

30. "The Masculine and Feminine Mind," *Carroll Free Press* (Carrollton, Ohio), January 3, 1856, 1.

31. "Woman's Rights Convention," *New York Tribune*, November 26, 1856, 5. "Legislative Doings—Rush for Land," *New York Tribune*, February 18, 1856, 6. Pierson, *Free Hearts and Free Homes*, 116.

32. My analysis here is based on Cott, *Public Vows*, 63–68.

33. "The Rights of Women," *North Star* (Rochester, N.Y.), July 28, 1848. "Marriage Gaolers," *National Era* (Washington, D.C.), September 11, 1856, 1. Robinson editorial is "A Word for Men's Rights," *Anti-slavery Bugle* (New Lisbon, Ohio), February 9, 1856, 4.

34. "The Black-Republican Party and the Strong-Minded Woman," *Cincinnati Daily Enquirer*, November 29, 1856, 4.

35. "Women's Rights," *Brooklyn Daily Eagle*, August 2, 1856, 2. Another *Brooklyn Daily Eagle* article punned that a women's rights convention had been called off after the women had become "palpabl[y] split" over Frémont's center part, condemning the women as silly and Frémont as feminine in one turn of phrase. See "'Take Your Time, Miss Lucy,'" *Brooklyn Daily Eagle*, October 14, 1856, 1. "Free Love and Fremont," *Richmond Enquirer*, September 16, 1856, 1. "No. 2: Will the Union Be Preserved? If Dissolved Can the South Maintain Herself?," *Richmond Enquirer*, September 9, 1856, 2. As Steven Hahn has written, "In the patriarchal household economy, relations of legal and customary dependency, not equality, linked all to the male head." Democrats would have considered women's rights activists' calls for equality subversive because women and children were supposed to depend on men, not relate to them as equals. Hahn, *The Roots of Southern Populism*, 31. Rebecca Edwards's study of gender in post–Civil War partisanship affirms that Democrats believed Republicans would undermine men's control over their wives. She writes, "The logical end of Republicanism, its opponents warned, was that husbands would lose authority over wives. If any man needed further proof, he could look to the northern legislatures that were meddling with their marriage laws." See Edwards, *Angels in the Machinery*, 20.

36. "Lady's Logic, or Miss Murray on Liberty," *Richmond Enquirer*, July 4, 1856, 1. "A Home Picture," *Brooklyn Daily Eagle*, September 2, 1856, 1.

37. "Obituary," *Richmond Enquirer*, October 3, 1856, 2. "Lady's Logic, or Miss Murray on Liberty," *Richmond Enquirer*, July 4, 1856, 1.

38. "The Mass Meeting of the Democracy in Providence," *Boston Post*, September 6, 1856, 2, Boston Athenaeum—Vershbow Special Collections. For similar articles, in which Democratic newspapers praised women for appearing at campaign rallies bearing signs that read "White Husbands or None," see "The Democracy of Preble

County," *Boston Post*, September 11, 1856, 2, Boston Athenaeum—Vershbow Special Collections; and "The Right Way to Talk," *Richmond Enquirer*, September 30, 1856, 1.

39. On the free love movement's development and relationship to other reform movements, see Spurlock, "The Free Love Network in America."

40. Indeed, Michael Pierson believes that the free love movement, not women's rights activists, represented "the era's most explicit threat to marriage as an institution." It was thus easy to unite around marriage as the "only bastion of legitimate sexual activity." See Pierson, *Free Hearts and Free Homes*, 105. As Rebecca Edwards puts it, in midcentury politics, "good government depended on proper household order; tyranny or anarchy, as threats to the republic, appeared in the guise of sexual sin." See Edwards, *Angels in the Machinery*, 17.

41. "A Chance for the Police," *Cincinnati Daily Enquirer*, August 23, 1856, 2.

42. "The Black Republicans on Polygamy," *Richmond Enquirer*, June 27, 1856, 2.

43. "Out for Fremont," *Brooklyn Daily Eagle*, September 23, 1856, 3. "To the Editor of the Eagle," *Brooklyn Daily Eagle*, September 9, 1856, 2.

44. Maurer, "The Great Republican Reform Party." The cartoon made a sufficient splash that two newspapers described it in depth to their readers. See "A Capital Political Caricature," *Wilmington (N.C.) Daily Herald*, August 18, 1856, 2; and "The Great Republican Reform Party Calling on Their Candidate," *Daily American Organ* (Washington, D.C.), August 19, 1856, 1.

45. "James Buchanan: The North, the South, and the Union," *Richmond Enquirer*, October 10, 1856, 2. "The Effects of Disunion on the South," *Richmond Enquirer*, August 29, 1856, 2. "The Evils and Dangers of the Times," *Richmond Enquirer*, August 26, 1856, 2.

46. "To Annie B*******, of Charleston, S.C.," *Richmond Enquirer*, September 9, 1856, 4. "The Lily of Heaven," *Richmond Enquirer*, September 30, 1856, 4. This intense veneration of women also appears in Southern men's diaries, with men sometimes allowing women's faith to become their own. Stephen Berry writes that men's "love of woman . . . did not replace organized religion but bled into it until the two were indistinguishable. Their wives became their conduits to God, and that was often as close to Him as they really wanted to be." See Berry, *All That Makes a Man*, 92.

47. "President Pierce," *Brooklyn Daily Eagle*, October 14, 1856, 2.

48. Summary of women's antislavery activism and its backlash from Varon, *Disunion!*, 131–35, 144–45, 245–46; on women's support for the Republican Party, see Pierson, *Free Hearts and Free Homes*, 139–63.

49. As Elizabeth Varon shows, William Lloyd Garrison himself was "profoundly ambivalent about the [Republican] party." Garrison believed no moral Union could coexist with slaveholders; Republicans believed in the perpetuity of the Union. But Garrison appreciated the rise of an antislavery political party, seeing it as an outgrowth of immediatist abolition and therefore as a step toward his desired end of either abolition or disunion. See Varon, *Disunion!*, 277. Democrats were not the only ones to link slavery, abolition, and gender issues. Kristin Hoganson argued that Garrisonian abolitionists needed to prove their political legitimacy over objections that supporting women's rights made them womanish radicals. To do this, Hoganson writes that Garrisonians "drew on conventional middle-class gender

beliefs to combat their own marginality as desexed freaks; prove black people's full humanity; and make their religious, economic, social, and moral arguments more compelling." By arguing that slavery desexed both slaves and owners, Garrisonians "shifted the tables so that the slave-holding South became the seat of gender radicalism." Hoganson, "Garrisonian Abolitionists," 559–60.

50. "Nigger Worship and Nigger Worshippers," *Brooklyn Daily Eagle*, September 9, 1856, 2. "Our New York Correspondence," *Washington Union*, December 4, 1856, 3. "Almagamation Meeting on Sunday," *Southern Banner* (Athens, Ga.), December 25, 1856, 2.

51. "The Right Way to Talk," *Richmond Enquirer*, September 30, 1856, 1. A story published in the *Cincinnati Daily Enquirer* played on Democrats' horror of both racial amalgamation and Republicanism. Allegedly, an innkeeper did not believe a Black man when he called at the inn, claiming that a white female lodger was his wife. The woman assured the innkeeper that the man was her husband, and the innkeeper was incredulous. But the tension is diffused when the woman said that marrying a Black man was far better than marrying a Republican—something she and the innkeeper could agree on. "Truly a Hard Case," *Cincinnati Daily Enquirer*, September 5, 1856, 3. "The Right Way to Talk," *Star of the North* (Bloomsburg, Penn.). September 3, 1856, 2; "The Right Way to Talk," *Wilmington (N.C.) Journal*, October 3, 1856, 2; "Political Items," *Evening Star* (Washington, D.C.), September 17, 1856, 2; "The Democracy of Preble County," 2.

52. "The True State of the Case," *Richmond Enquirer*, September 23, 1856, 2. "The Electoral Question," *Charleston (S.C.) Mercury*, May 29, 1856.

53. "An Undivided and Conservative South," *Richmond Enquirer*, June 24, 1856, 1. In her study of gender in politics in the postwar years, Rebecca Edwards argues that the Civil War only intensified Democrats' belief that federal power too frequently intruded on private life and men's control. Abolitionism offended these Democrats because, whether from the North or South, they "defined slavery as a household or family institution, [and] they viewed Emancipation and black male suffrage as threats to patriarchal as well as racial order." Edwards, *Angels in the Machinery*, 6.

54. "The Tribune and Its Political Blunders," *New York Herald*, December 2, 1856. "Our New York Correspondence," 3.

55. "Letter to Charles James Faulkner," September 29, 1856, Virginia Historical Society. "1852 Democratic Party Platform."

56. "The Strangest Thing in the World," *Richmond Enquirer*, September 19, 1856, 2. "An Undivided and Conservative South," *Richmond Enquirer*, June 24, 1856, 1.

57. "The Man of Toil," *Belvidere (Ill.) Standard*, June 10, 1856, 1.

58. "The Contrast," *Indiana Herald* (Indianapolis), October 22, 1856, 2. For a variation on this argument, which portrays southern slaveholders as domineering and southern yeomen as submissive, see "Changing Front," *Kansas Herald of Freedom* (Lawrence), November 22, 1856, 4.

59. "The Hon. Bayard Clarke on the Presidency," *New York Tribune*, September 15, 1856, 5.

60. "Honest Laborers, Look at This," *Alton (Ill.) Weekly Telegraph*, September 25, 1856, 1. "The Buchanan Democracy Hate Freedom," *Holmes County Republican* (Millersburg, Ohio), September 25, 1856, 1.

61. "Jersey and Calhoun," *Alton Weekly Telegraph*, October 30, 1856, 2.

62. "The Buchanan Democracy Hate Freedom," *Holmes County Republican*, September 25, 1856, 1. The *Republican* seems to have misconstrued or even misquoted Butler's words from a speech he gave in July. Butler had argued that South Carolina's constitution was very democratic—allowing all white men to vote and only imposing minimal property requirements on office-holding. For Butler's speech, see "Copious Extracts from the Speech of Hon. A. P. Butler, of South Carolina," *Edgefield (S.C.) Advertiser*, July 2, 1856, 1.

63. "Is This Democracy?," *Buffalo Daily Republic*, September 25, 1856, 2.

64. "A Thought for the Reflecting," *Aurora of the Valley* (Newbury, Vt.), September 27, 1856, 1.

65. *Democratic Review*, quoted in Varon, *Disunion!*, 287. Luby, *Welcome Buchanan!*

Chapter 2

1. "Michigan for Buchanan!," *McArthur Democrat* (Logan, Ohio), May 29, 1856, 3. "The Young Men," *Buffalo Morning Express*, July 2, 1856, 2. "For President," *South-Western* (Shreveport, La.), June 18, 1856, 2. "Additional California News," *Baltimore Sun*, December 30, 1856, 1.

2. "Among the Late Arrivals," *McArthur Democrat*, May 29, 1856, 3. "Excitement at Beaver Islands, and Arrest of the Mormons by the Sheriff of Mackinaw," *Buffalo Morning Express*, July 2, 1856, 2. "General Intelligence," *South-Western*, June 18, 1856, 2. "Judge Drummond and the Mormons," *Baltimore Sun*, December 30, 1856, 2.

3. Pierson argues, and I agree, that gender served as an easy yet important marker of party identity. For Republicans, this meant identifying men as "the champions of female morality, male restraint, and sentimental marriage while stating [their] opposition to tyrannical marriages in the North and patriarchal abuses in the South"; Pierson, *Free Hearts and Free Homes*, 116. I would add that it also meant opposing polygamous marriages in the West. See Foner, *Free Soil, Free Labor, Free Men*. Of Leonard Arrington's two works on Mormon history, *Brigham Young: American Moses* comes closest to dealing with Mormonism and federal politics in the 1850s with its narrative of the Utah War, plus one paragraph each on the Republican and Democratic positions on popular sovereignty and polygamy. But Arrington argues that Democrats "became just as outspoken in denouncing Mormon marriage practices" (251). I would amend that statement to argue that Democrats did not like polygamy, but they did not want to be seen as interfering to stop it. J. Spencer Fluhman offers one of the few book-length treatments of anti-Mormonism, yet he moves through the antebellum years quickly and offers only two paragraphs on popular sovereignty and the state. David T. Smith and Kathleen Flake likewise focus on the post-1879 era. See Fluhman, *"A Peculiar People,"* 107–8; Smith, *Religious Persecution and Political Order in the United States*; and Flake, *The Politics of American Religious Identity*. One chapter of Sarah Barringer Gordon's *The Mormon Question* does deal with the relationship between the "domestic institutions" of polygamy and slavery. But my work differs in focus and therefore in findings. Gordon is most interested in polygamy as a moral and legal issue. As a result, she attends

only briefly to southern resistance to antipolygamy action and does not consider the northern Democratic response. Additionally, though Gordon writes briefly on how southerners believed intervention in polygamy could justify intervention in slavery, she does not explain why northern Democrats resisted antipolygamy laws. Yet if we put Republicans' focus on polygamy into its political context—a presidential campaign focused on Kansas and popular sovereignty—understanding the northern Democrats' reaction is crucial to our understanding of that election as a whole. See Gordon, "The Twin Relic of Barbarism."

4. "Republican Party Platform of 1856."

5. "An Act to Organize the Territories of Nebraska and Kansas," 283.

6. My analysis here is based on Wardle, "From Slavery to Same-Sex Marriage." On the power of the states to regulate domestic institutions, see Wardle, 1881. For two examples of *domestic relations* being used to describe family relations, see "Mr. Gaston's Speech," *Carolina Federal Republican* (New Bern, N.C.), April 9, 1814, 1; "Obituary," *North-Carolina Star* (Raleigh), November 11, 1814, 3. For two instances where *domestic relations* describes the relationship among the states, see "Report of the Committee of Senate. Appointed to Inquire into the Extent and Causes of the Present General Distress," *Wyoming Herald* (Wilkes-Barre, Penn.), March 10, 1820, 3; and "The New Year," *Democrat* (Huntsville, Ala.), January 6, 1824, 2.

7. For instances in which Americans used *domestic relations* to talk about slavery, see "The Legislature of South Carolina," *Pittsburgh Weekly Gazette*, January 7, 1825; for instances of Americans using *domestic institutions* to describe slavery in this period, see "Colonization Society," *Pensacola (Fla.) Gazette*, May 15, 1830, 2; "An Incendiary Article," *Liberator*, September 21, 1833, 3. For an example of *domestic relations* being used to talk about a man's family life, see "Proceedings in Relation to the Editor of the Telegraph," *Adams (Penn.) Sentinel*, January 26, 1835, 3. "Abolition in All Its Branches," *Long-Island Star*, September 11, 1835, 2. Another article on a court case dealing with whether a master had the right to beat his enslaved workers acknowledged that lawyers had argued in favor of that right on the grounds that slavery was a domestic relation. "This has indeed been assimilated at the bar to the other domestic relations; and arguments drawn from the well-established principles which confer and restrain the authority of the parent over the child, the tutor over the pupil, the master over the apprentice," the article reported. See "At the Late Session of the Supreme Court of This State," *National Gazette* (Philadelphia), June 30, 1830, 1.

8. "An Act to Organize the Territories of Nebraska and Kansas," 283.

9. Kirtland population figures from "Kirtland, Ohio," in *Encyclopedia of Mormonism*, 795. "Quasi-genocidal" quote in Smith, *Religious Persecution and Political Order in the United States*, 44. Executive Order 44, quoted in Smith, 44.

10. In the early colonial era, Native Americans occasionally took European settlers captive; some those who escaped wrote captivity narratives about their experiences. In the nineteenth century, American Protestants adapted this form to describe— and hyperbolize—the threat Catholicism posed to the American Republic. Writers described in lurid detail the supposed sexual exploitation of Protestant women held captive in Catholic convents, producing literature that was at once a warning about the Catholic faith and a form of popular pornography. For more on this

genre, see Appleby, Chang, and Goodwin, "Captivity Narratives"; Regan, "Runaway Nuns, Runaway Bestsellers"; and Dorsey, *Reforming Men and Women*, 239. *Nauvoo Expositor*, quoted in Smith, *Religious Persecution and Political Order in the United States*, 60.

11. For a survey of the history of the Latter-Day Saints between 1830 and 1848, see Smith, *Religious Persecution and Political Order in the United States*, 44–63. Brigham Young, quoted in PBS, "Utah."

12. "The Mormons in Utah," *New York Times*, June 30, 1854, 2.

13. *Yankee Notions* circulation from Caron, *Mark Twain, Unsanctified Newspaper Reporter*, 175; *Harper's* and *Leslie's* circulation numbers from Bunker and Bitton, "Illustrated Periodical Images of Mormons," 83–84; "Mormon Breastworks and U.S. Troops," 1852, priAPC 0099, American Political Cartoons, Huntington Library, San Marino, California.

14. Bell, *Boadicea*; Belisle, *The Prophets*; Victor, *Mormon Wives*. Circulation information from Ulrich, *A House Full of Females*, 337. Burgett, "On the Mormon Question," 87.

15. "Republican Party Platform of 1856."

16. Quoted in "Interesting from Washington. The Immediate Admission of Kansas into the Union. Speech of Hon. William H. Seward," *New York Times*, April 10, 1856, 2. "An Act to Organize the Territories of Nebraska and Kansas," 283.

17. "Utah Forming a State Constitution," *Buffalo Daily Republic*, March 20, 1856, 2.

18. Lieber quote and analysis of xenophobia in anti-Mormonism from Ulrich, *A House Full of Females*, 336–37; Megan Sanborn Jones argues that popular culture Orientalized Mormons in order to create a visual distinction between Mormon and gentile Americans. "Assigning Mormons a Turkish identity," she writes, "associated Mormons with a group already viewed with extreme prejudice" and "tainted [Mormonism] by the Orientalist assumption of gross treachery, carnality, and indolence already associated with Turks." See Jones, *Performing American Identity in Anti-Mormon Melodrama*, 123. "Philadelphia National Convention," *National Era* (Washington, D.C.), April 24, 1856, 4.

19. "A Trap to Catch Gudgeons," *Anti-slavery Bugle* (New Lisbon, Ohio), February 2, 1856, 1. "Utah and Popular Sovereignty," *National Era*, April 30, 1857, 2.

20. Ward, *Female Life among the Mormons*, 105, 289. For a useful summary of another popular anti-Mormon novel, Metta Victor's 1856 *Mormon Wives*, see Burgett, "On the Mormon Question," 87–89.

21. For more on contemporary anti-Shaker, anti-Catholic, and anti-Oneida literature, see Kern, *An Ordered Love*, 52–65. Kennedy, "The Nun, the Priest, and the Pornographer," 4. For more information on how contemporary authors wrote and thought about rape, see Sielke, *Reading Rape*.

22. Arrington and Haupt, "Intolerable Zion," 245–48.

23. Quoted in Ward, *Female Life among the Mormons*, 102. William Lysander Adams's 1852 satire *Treason, Stratagems, and Spoils* expressed similar concerns about Mormons' loyalty to the Union. See Jones, *Performing American Identity in Anti-Mormon Melodrama*, 95.

24. Childs, "The Cincinnati Platform." John Childs was an artist and lithographer who worked in New York, Boston, and Philadelphia. He published lithographic

cartoons, like this one, as well as genre scenes and social satires. Most of his cartoons are moderately favorable toward the Republican Party. See "Childs, John,"
in *Philadelphia on Stone.*

25. Magee, "Liberty, the Fair Maid of Kansas." John Magee was a prolific engraver
and lithographer who worked in New York and Philadelphia in the mid-nineteenth
century. His cartoons frequently, though not always, demonstrated support for
the Republican Party. See "Magee, John L.," in *Philadelphia on Stone.* For further
analysis of these cartoons, as well as of reports on sexual aggression in Kansas
more generally, see Arnold, "'To Inflame the Mind of the North,'" 30–33. A thorough search of contemporary newspapers did not turn up any discussion, let alone
reprints, of either "Liberty, the Fair Maid of Kansas" or "The Cincinnati Platform."
But this makes sense: a study of lithography in antebellum America has shown that
shops began selling separately issued lithographs in the 1830s, some for as little
as twenty-five cents (about eight dollars in 2022 money). Thousands of copies of a
cartoon could be printed and sold in a short period. Though this information does
not answer exactly how many people saw the cartoons discussed above, it does
show that political lithographs often reached a wide audience, particularly during
elections or times of political scandal. See Piola, "The Rise of Early American
Lithography," 129–30.

26. "1856 Democratic Party Platform."

27. Pierce, "Third Annual Message."

28. "Offensive Language and Personal Responsibility," *Brooklyn Daily Eagle*, June
12, 1856, 2. "Congressional," *Washington Union*, December 18, 1856, 1.

29. William MacKinnon argues that "the social conduct of the U.S. Army's Steptoe Expedition of 1854–1855 created a civil affairs atmosphere so poisonous that
it aggravated deteriorating Mormon-federal relations while stiffening Brigham
Young's resolve to bar the U.S. Army from Utah." See MacKinnon, "Sex, Subalterns,
and Steptoe," 228. I have drawn this summary of events from Smith, *Religious
Persecution and Political Order in the United States*, 65–66.

30. Douglas, *Remarks of the Hon. Stephen A. Douglas*, 12–13.

31. "Great Debate in the U.S. Senate," *Mississippi Free Trader* (Natchez), April
25, 1859, 1.

32. Smith, *Religious Persecution and Political Order in the United States*, 65–66.
For an example of protagonists supporting the federal government in anti-Mormon
literature, see Ward, *Female Life among the Mormons*, 102. "Utah Forming a State
Constitution," *Buffalo Daily Republic*, March 20, 1856, 2. Here I am disagreeing with
Sarah Barringer Gordon's analysis that "Democrats began to feel that by quelling
insubordination in Utah, they could distance themselves from the more unsettling
aspects of the notion that 'domestic' government should be left to local majorities.
Polygamy, at least, would no longer be paired with slavery in Republican rhetoric."
As I have shown, Democrats did not want to interfere with local majorities' control over domestic institutions—which is precisely why Stephen Douglas justified
intervention on other grounds. See Gordon, "The Twin Relic of Barbarism," 60.

33. Kimball Young, quoted in Smith, *Religious Persecution and Political Order
in the United States*, 68. Kenneth Stampp concludes, "Public sentiment favoring
both a firm assertion of federal authority in Utah and the curbing of Brigham

Young's political power had made some kind of response on [Buchanan's] part almost mandatory." See Stampp, *America in 1857*, 200. Laurel Thatcher Ulrich writes, "President James Buchanan had decided to tackle the one issue on which everyone seemed to agree—something had to be done about the Mormons." See Ulrich, *A House Full of Females*, 338. Nancy Cott offers a more nuanced analysis of the decision to intervene in Mormon polygamy—though she focuses on the anti-polygamy Morrill bill, which was introduced in Congress in 1860. Cott notes that opposing polygamy was a winning issue but that many southern Democrats made sure to distinguish between polygamy and slavery when offering their support for the bill to ensure that they were not setting a precedent for intervening in southern slavery. See Cott, *Public Vows*, 74–75.

34. I have based my analysis here on Cott, *Public Vows*, 61–63.

35. "Correspondence of the Sun," *Baltimore Sun*, November 25, 1856, 4. "Affairs in Utah. Interesting from Salt Lake City," *New Orleans Times-Picayune*, August 17, 1858, 2. Carl Osthaus explains that during the crisis of 1850, "the *Picayune* adopted a middle course, seeking to encourage Northern and Southern moderates and isolate and defeat extremists in both sections." Osthaus writes that "the only topic that provoked the *Picayune* to characteristically Southern tirades was abolitionism." For more on the *Picayune* and its editors in the 1850s, see Osthaus, *Partisans of the Southern Press*, 66–68.

36. "The Mormons," *Washington Union*, June 10, 1857, 2. "Does the Authority of the Federal Government Extend Over the Mormons?," *Weekly Mississippian* (Jackson), July 14, 1858, 3. *Mercury* quoted in "The Mormons," 2.

37. Cott, *Public Vows*, 28. John Taylor, quoted in Ulrich, *A House Full of Females*, 353.

38. Quoted at length in "Polygamy and Slavery," *National Era* (Washington, D.C.), December 24, 1857, 2.

39. "A New Question," *Nashville Union and American*, January 31, 1858, 2. Poindexter was ultimately murdered by a rival editor after accusing the man of being an abolitionist—the ultimate insult. For a contemporary report on the event, see "The Affray in Nashville," *New York Times*, November 23, 1859, 2.

40. As with the Republicans and their position on popular sovereignty and polygamy, the standard texts on antebellum Democrats contain almost no information on the Democrats' response to Utah or their belief in the application of popular sovereignty to both the Utah and the Kansas territories. Even David Potter's encyclopedic work on antebellum politics does not mention the connection. See, for instance, Baker, *Affairs of Party*; Eyal, *The Young America Movement*; and Potter, *The Impending Crisis*.

41. Etcheson, *Bleeding Kansas*, 141–42, 145; Potter, *The Impending Crisis*, 300, 314.

42. On southern threats, see Etcheson, *Bleeding Kansas*, 158. Buchanan, "First Annual Message."

43. Stephen Douglas, quoted in Etcheson, *Bleeding Kansas*, 160. Etcheson argues that the debates over and in Kansas were not about slavery and antislavery as much as they were about rights. For southerners, this meant the right to bring their property in slaves to Kansas. For northerners, this meant the right to vote freely and allow

for the freedom of speech. See Etcheson, *Bleeding Kansas*. The results of the 1858 midterms and the 1860 presidential election demonstrate the clear anti-Lecompton mood among northern Democrats. In the 1858 midterms, Republicans hammered Democrats, largely due to the Democratic split over Lecompton; in twenty-two seats, anti-Lecompton Democrats ran against pro-Lecompton Democrats, and in eight cases, they won. Taken together, the Republicans and the anti-Lecompton Democrats reduced the number of pro-Lecompton Democratic congressmen from fifty-three to twenty-six. By the election of 1860, Breckinridge (whom Buchanan supported) received only 8.1 percent of the vote in the North, compared to Douglas's 24.7 percent. Over half of Breckinridge's support came from Pennsylvania, where Pennsylvanian Buchanan had managed to retain some control over the state party. See Holt, *The Election of 1860*, 16, 194.

44. Douglas, *Remarks the Hon. Stephen A. Douglas*, 4.

45. Douglas, *Speech of Hon. S. A. Douglas*, 1; for similar language, see 8, 16.

46. "The Deficiency Bill," *Daily Delta* (New Orleans), March 27, 1858, 1.

47. Buchanan, "First Annual Message."

48. "Speech of Senator Douglas—Defence of Popular Sovereignty and the Will of the Majority," *Press* (Philadelphia), December 12, 1857, 1.

49. "Thirty-Fifth Congress, First Session," *Press*, January 29, 1858, 2.

50. "The Voice of an Original Buchanan Man," *Press*, December 31, 1857, 2.

51. "Speech of Senator Douglas—Defence of Popular Sovereignty and the Will of the Majority," *Press*, December 12, 1857, 1.

52. According to the *Daily Delta* (New Orleans). See "The Deficiency Bill," *Daily Delta*, March 27, 1858, 1.

53. "The Voice of the People," *Press*, December 12, 1857, 2.

54. On southern Democrats' belief Kansas would be admitted as a free state, see Potter, *Impending Crisis*, 302. On October 8, Kansans had elected an antislavery legislature. On December 21, an election called by the Lecompton convention took place. Because the election allowed no real choice, free-staters abstained; official returns showed 6,226 votes for the constitution with slavery and 569 for it without slavery. On January 4, 1858, there was more voting, this time called by the now-antislavery legislature. Proslavery voters abstained; returns showed 10,226 votes against Lecompton, 138 for it with slavery, and 24 for it without slavery. See Potter, 318.

55. "Letter from Postmaster General Brown," *Washington Union*, December 31, 1857, 2. "Speech of Henry S. Fitch, Esq.," *Charleston (S.C.) Mercury*, July 31, 1858, 2.

56. "Judge Douglas and the President's Message," *Washington Union*, December 16, 1857, 3. One source from a radical southern newspaper disagreed with Buchanan. "No tyro in politics, no one the least familiar with the political technology of the country and the times, can be ignorant that the terms quoted have been in common use for years to distinguish State from Federal institutions in general, and home from foreign matters in general." But the paper argued that the Kansas-Nebraska Act had not given the people the right to vote directly on any of their domestic institutions, anyway. See "The President and the Douglas-Walker Movement," *Daily Delta*, December 18, 1857, 2.

57. "An Act to Organize the Territories of Nebraska and Kansas," 283; "Thirty-Fifth Congress, First Session," *Press* (Philadelphia), December 17, 1857, 2.

58. "Debate in the Senate: Speech of Hon. G. N. Fitch, of Indiana, Delivered in the Senate Tuesday, Dec 22, 1857," *Washington Union*, December 30, 1857, 2. "The Kansas Question: Speech of Hon. James Hughes, of Indiana, at a Democratic Meeting in Mozart Hall, New York, March 2, 1858," *Washington Union*, March 6, 1858, 3.

Chapter 3

1. "Slave Insurrection at Harper's Ferry," *Baltimore Sun*, October 18, 1859, 1.

2. For a fuller description of Brown's raid, as well as a brief summary of historians' changing evaluations of Brown and his militant abolitionism, see Varon, *Disunion!*, 326–30.

3. Lincoln quoted in Paul Finkelman, "Manufacturing Martyrdom," 41; "Where the Responsibility Belongs," *Chicago Press and Tribune*, October 20, 1859, https://scholarexchange.furman.edu/secession-editorials/all/editorials/32/; David Davis, quoted in Finkelman, "Manufacturing Martyrdom," 41; "John Brown's Insanity," *New York Tribune*, November 25, 1859; Benjamin Wade Senate speech on December 14, 1859, in Rives, *The Congressional Globe*, 142.

4. "'The Cloud in the Distance No Bigger then [*sic*] a Man's Hand': The First Battle of the 'Irrepressible Conflict,'" *Cincinnati Enquirer*, October 19, 1859, https://scholarexchange.furman.edu/secession-editorials/all/editorials/177/. In 1860, the campaign biography of northern Democratic candidate Stephen A. Douglas asked readers to recall the raid, and then told them that such violence was the natural outgrowth of Republican ideology. See Sheahan, *The Life of Stephen A. Douglas*, 507.

5. "The Harper's Ferry Conspiracy," *Portsmouth (Ohio) Daily Times*, October 22, 1859, 2. "Writhing of the Serpent," *Illinois State Register* (Springfield), October 27, 1859, https://scholarexchange.furman.edu/secession-editorials/all/editorials/40/.

6. "The Cowardly Desertion of Capt. Brown by His Former Patrons," *Brooklyn Daily Eagle*, October 27, 1859, 2; "John Brown Was Sentenced," *Brooklyn Daily Eagle*, November 3, 1859, 2. Interestingly, neither northern nor southern Democrats castigated Brown in this way. While most Republican papers rushed to call Brown insane, Democratic papers offered him a grudging respect: at least he was willing to die for his beliefs. For instance, the same *Eagle* article that called Douglass cowardly described Brown as "a man of iron nerve and Roman firmness."

7. "John Brown Suffered the Extreme Penalty," *Brooklyn Daily Eagle*, December 3, 1859, 2; "Folly—Insanity—Blasphemy," *Daily Empire* (Dayton, Ohio), January 16, 1860, 2.

8. "Slave-hating northeast" quote in Greenberg, "Charles Ingersoll," 192. Charles Jared Ingersoll's son, Charles Ingersoll, became a prominent Copperhead Democrat during the Civil War. "From Hon. Charles Jared Ingersoll," *New York Times*, January 10, 1860, 5.

9. Focusing on the Shenandoah Valley, Edward Ayers argues that only the firing on Fort Sumter and Lincoln's call for troops moved Pennsylvanians and Virginians to commit themselves to the Union and the Confederacy, respectively. Christopher Phillips, meanwhile, contends that border slave and free states were more similar than different until emancipation. And William Freehling argues that white men in the Upper South were in most ways more like their counterparts in the North than those in the Deep South. See Ayers, *In the Presence of Mine Enemies*; Phillips,

The River Ran Backward; and Freehling, *The South versus the South*. Stanley Harrold argues that the border free states, including New Jersey, Pennsylvania, Ohio, Indiana, Illinois, and the border slave states, including Delaware, Maryland, Virginia, Kentucky, and Missouri, fought about slavery for decades before the Civil War. Interested more in cross-border conflict over slavery than in a state's loyalty to the Union, he does not include Upper South states such as North Carolina and Tennessee in his analysis. See Harrold, *Border War*. Robinson, *A Union Indivisible*. For an examination of how infrapolitics could push a border state to side with the Confederacy, see Link, *Roots of Secession*.

10. Woods, *Emotional and Sectional Conflict*. "Mr. Lovejoy's Address," *Lancaster (Penn.) Intelligencer*, December 13, 1859, 1. "Speech of James S. Thayer," *New York Daily Herald*, December 20, 1859, 4. "Immense Union Demonstration," *Gettysburg (Penn.) Compiler*, December 12, 1859, 2. W. R. Stark to Thomas L. Clayton, November 29, 1859, Clayton Family Papers, Southern Historical Collection at the University of North Carolina at Chapel Hill.

11. "Senators Bigler and Iverson," *Rock Island (Ill.) Argus*, December 23, 1859, 2.

12. "The Conservative Movement—The Great Union Demonstration at Boston," *Baltimore Sun*, December 10, 1859, 1; see also "Union Demonstration at Boston," *Richmond Dispatch*, December 13, 1859. For more on Cushing's Faneuil Hall speech, see Belohlavek, *Broken Glass*, 300–302. As the election of 1860 neared, a Democratic paper in Pennsylvania tried a similar approach, publishing a drawing of a large dagger it claimed was the size of the one carried by Brown at Harpers Ferry. See "Black Republican Argument," *Pennsylvania Statesman* (Philadelphia), October 20, 1860, http://elections.harpweek.com/1860/cartoon-1860-large.asp?UniqueID =14&Year=1860.

13. "The Insurrection at Harper's Ferry," *Public Ledger* (Philadelphia), October 19, 1859, 2.

14. "The Insurrection at Harper's Ferry." The *Ledger* would go on to oppose the Civil War and support a negotiated peace with the Confederate States.

15. I am disagreeing here with historian Michael Todd Landis, who argues that northern Democrats smeared Republicans to draw themselves closer to southern Democrats—rather than, as I argue, to win elections in the North. I believe northern Democrats did not yet fully understand the extent of southern Democrats' sense of alienation from the national party and the Union. See Landis, *Northern Men with Southern Loyalties*, 216–17.

16. Harrold, *Border War*, 15. "Conspicuous anomaly" quote in Fields, *Slavery and Freedom on the Middle Ground*, xi.

17. Jefferson Martenet to Catherine M. Richardson, December 14, 1859, Jefferson Martenet Correspondence, Huntington Library, San Marino, California. "The John Brown Party," *Nashville Union and American*, September 8, 1860, 2. Torbett became editor of the paper after its previous editor, George Poindexter, was murdered by a rival paper's editor.

18. *Governor's Biennial Messages to the General Assembly of the State of Virginia, December 5, 1859* (Richmond: James E. Goode, 1859), 5, 75520, Huntington Library, San Marino, California. For a fuller explanation of Wise's politics in the winter following John Brown's raid, see Link, *Roots of Secession*, 195–200.

19. "Soul of border state moderation" quote in Knupfer, "A Crisis in Conservatism," 123. "Is John Brown a Representative Man?," *Baltimore Sun*, November 28, 1859, 2. Tell-all account is *Startling Incidents and Developments of Osowotomy Brown's Insurrectory and Treasonable Movements at Harper's Ferry, Virginia, October 17, 1859, with a True and Accurate Account of the Whole Transaction by a Citizen of Harper's Ferry* (Baltimore: John W. Woods, 1859), Huntington Library, San Marino, California.

20. P. C. Massie to William Massie, December 2, 1859, William Massie Papers, 1747–1919, Dolph Briscoe Center for American History, University of Texas at Austin. Fettman, "Harper's Weekly," 931. Quote in "John Brown's Insanity," *New York Tribune*, November 25, 1859. For similar, see "The Harper's Ferry Affair," *Daily Evening Transcript* (Boston), October 24, 1859, in which the reporter claims to have uncovered a long history of mental illness in Brown's family. Lincoln disavowed Brown in his now-famous speech at Cooper Union in New York City on February 27, 1860. For more on the Republican Party's response to Brown's raid, see Varon, *Disunion!*, 332–35.

21. Hentz, *The Planter's Northern Bride*. Catherine M. Richardson to Jefferson Martenet, November 17, 1859, Jefferson Martenet Correspondence, Huntington Library, San Marino, California.

22. Portia L. Baldwin, "Portia L. Baldwin to Henry A. Wise," December 17, 1859, Mss1W7547bFA2, Virginia Historical Society. Elizabeth Varon points out that Virginians had been making this argument since the 1830s. At that juncture, southerners had not yet solidified behind the positive good argument for slavery; many Virginians, for instance, hoped they could diversify their state's economy to create an all-white Virginia, free of both slaves and free Blacks. Yet in 1831, they blamed "abolitionist agitation" for Nat Turner's rebellion—showing the beginning of the transition to the positive good argument. See Varon, *Disunion!*, 78–85.

23. "Action Wanted, and Not Sympathy," *Charlotte Evening Bulletin*, December 15, 1859, 2.

24. "The Harper's Ferry Affair," *New Orleans Times-Picayune*, October 25, 1859. (In 1859, George Wilkins Kendall and Francis Asbury Lumsden edited the *Picayune*.) "Where Is the Responsibility?," *New Orleans Times-Picayune*, October 25, 1859. For similar, see "The True Lesson," *New Orleans Times-Picayune*, October 30, 1859.

25. "The Tragedy at Harper's Ferry," *Liberator*, October 28, 1859, http://fair-use.org/the-liberator/1859/10/28/the-tragedy-at-harpers-ferry. Emerson quoted in Cooke, *Ralph Waldo Emerson*, 140. "The Execution of Brown—The Hostile Camps," *Semi-weekly Mississippian* (Jackson), December 2, 1859, 2.

26. The American Anti-slavery Society eventually published this correspondence, from which I quote here. See *Correspondence between Lydia Maria Child and Gov. Wise and Mrs. Mason, of Virginia* (Boston: American Anti-slavery Society, 1860), box 1860, Massachusetts Historical Society, 4, 5. The pamphlet ultimately sold 300,000 copies—see Venet, "'Cry Aloud and Spare Not,'" 109. Republican papers reprinted the correspondence, apparently believing that Child's sense of moral obligation bolstered the justice of their cause. See "Gov. Wise Catches a Tartar," *Janesville (Wisc.) Daily Gazette*, November 24, 1859; and "Lydia Maria Child's Reply to Gov. Wise," *Fremont (Ohio) Weekly Journal*, November 25, 1859.

27. On the publication of the letters, see Venet, "Cry Aloud and Spare Not," 108. Eliza Margaretta Chew Mason, in *Correspondence between Lydia Maria Child and Gov. Wise and Mrs. Mason, of Virginia*, box 1860, Massachusetts Historical Society, 16.

28. *Correspondence between Lydia Maria Child and Gov. Wise and Mrs. Mason, of Virginia*, box 1860, Massachusetts Historical Society, 16, 17.

29. Venet, "Cry Aloud and Spare Not," 108. Glymph states simply, "White women wielded the power of slave ownership." Obviously, this violence also flagrantly contradicted the notion that that white women were pious and gentle. See Glymph, *Out of the House of Bondage*, 4. And as Stephanie Jones-Rogers writes, "Slave-owning women not only witnessed the most brutal features of slavery, they took part in them, profited from them, and defended them." Jones-Rogers, *They Were Her Property*, ix.

30. "We Have Seldom Seen," *Alexandria (Va.) Gazette*, November 16, 1859, 2. "A Woman's View of a Woman's Duty, in Connection with the John Brown Crime, &c., &c.," *Newbern (N.C.) Daily Progress*, December 6, 1859, 2. "Mrs. Child and the Insurgent Brown," *Richmond Enquirer*, November 8, 1859, 1.

31. "Modern Philanthropy Illustrated," *Macon (Ga.) Daily Telegraph*, April 28, 1860, 2. Joseph Clisby, who purchased the newspaper in 1855, believed that newspapers should communicate news rather than shape public opinion. See "Clisby, Joseph," in *Georgia Info*. The modern iteration of the *Telegraph* reports that the paper's editor, Philemore Tracy, wrote upon leaving for the Civil War that "I shall cherish with satisfaction . . . that I have never been found occupying the extreme Southern ground." See Grisamore, "85 Things You May Have Not Known about the *Telegraph* and Macon."

32. "Where Is Mrs. Child?," *Richmond Dispatch*, January 20, 1860, 1. The *Dispatch* had been a Whig paper until that party crumbled earlier in the decade. This article reveals why: southern Whigs could not abide their northern counterparts' growing support for antislavery ideology. In 1859, the *Dispatch* was a proslavery opposition paper; by 1860, it endorsed John Breckinridge.

33. *Picayune* quoted in Venet, "Cry Aloud and Spare Not," 110. It was not uncommon for people to use animalization as a way to unsex opponents: Evan Kutzler has shown that reducing Civil War prisoners of war to animals—even figuratively—unmanned them. See Kutzler, *Living by Inches*. In 1977, Barbara Welter identified what she called the "cult of true womanhood." The attributes of true womanhood, by which a woman judged herself and was judged by others, included four virtues: piety, purity, submissiveness, and domesticity. See Welter, "The Cult of True Womanhood"; and Cott, *The Bonds of Womanhood*.

34. Lacy K. Ford argues that this tendency to see forcibly enslaved people as members of an extended family developed in the years following the War of 1812, and especially during the Missouri debates of 1820 and 1821. During those debates, southern slaveholders used the language of paternalism to characterize the master-slave relationship. They insisted, as Ford puts it, "that when governed by paternalism, slavery became a domestic institution that recognized the humanity of slaves and treated them accordingly"; Ford, *Deliver Us from Evil*, 203.

35. A Virginia woman, identified in an Ohio Republican newspaper as Mrs. Marm, wrote to Child to say that no southern lady should read any of Child's works after

she demonstrated sympathy for John Brown. See "Mrs. Marm," *Ashtabula (Ohio) Weekly Telegraph*, December 31, 1859, 2. American Anti-slavery Society publication numbers from Venet, "Cry Aloud and Spare Not," 109. Republican papers reprinted the correspondence, apparently believing that Child's sense of moral obligation bolstered the justice of their cause. See "Gov. Wise Catches a Tartar," *Janesville (Wisc.) Daily Gazette*, November 24, 1859; and "Lydia Maria Child's Reply to Gov. Wise," *Fremont (Ohio) Weekly Journal*, November 25, 1859.

36. History of abolitionist women's support for Brown as well as newspaper quote from Venet, "Cry Aloud and Spare Not," 100–104.

37. "Correspondence of the Daily Progress," *Newbern (N.C.) Daily Progress*, February 1, 1860, 2.

38. Portia L. Baldwin, "Portia L. Baldwin to Henry A. Wise," December 17, 1859, Mss1W7547bFA2, Virginia Historical Society. Again, southerners believed Child represented a broader problem with northern women. One man wrote to his mother reasoning that an acquaintance in South Carolina was not making friends easily because his mother was a "strong-minded" Yankee woman. See Jefferson Martenet to Catherine M. Richardson, January 3, 1860, Jefferson Martenet Correspondence, Huntington Library, San Marino, California.

39. Moss, *Domestic Novelists in the Old South*, 60.

40. Stephen Berry argues that southern men elevated women as near-deities to whom they could offer up their efforts. "Men believed that women were supposed to bear witness to male becoming, to cheer men to greatness"; Berry, *All That Makes a Man*, 85. Berry argues that this forced women into subservient roles that made their worlds smaller and less significant. In terms of the personal relationships between southern men and women, I do not disagree with Berry. But in terms of the politics, the above research shows that women were sometimes complicit in this quest for southern male greatness, themselves providing men with an image of southern womanhood that was worth fighting for.

41. For reporting on the trial, including language imagining the rape of white women, see "Trial of John Brown," *Richmond Dispatch*, November 2, 1859, 1; and "Trial of the Harper's Ferry Insurgents," *Baltimore Sun*, November 1, 1859, 1. Andrew Hunter and Charles B. Harding prosecuted Brown's case. For slaveholders' anxieties, see Link, *Roots of Secession*, 9. Henry Wise, quoted in "Message of the Governor of Virginia," *Richmond Dispatch*, December 5, 1859, 1. Conspiracy theories abounded in the weeks and months following Brown's raid. Paranoid southerners also worried about a rumored attempt by abolitionists to free Brown from prison. On November 22, less than two weeks before Brown's scheduled execution, sixteen-year-old Hope Massie wrote to his father, Piedmont planter William Massie that "there is a great excitement over here about the abolitionists trying to rescue Brown." Of course, they did not, nor was any such plan afoot. See Hope Massie to William Massie, November 22, 1859, William Massie Papers, box 2E492, Dolph Briscoe Center for American History, University of Texas at Austin. "The Outbreak at Harpers Ferry," *Wilmington (N.C.) Journal*, October 21, 1859, 2. Sensationalist account is *Startling Incidents and Developments of Osowotomy Brown's Insurrectory and Treasonable Movements at Harper's Ferry, Virginia, October 17, 1859, with a True and Accurate*

Account of the Whole Transaction by a Citizen of Harper's Ferry (Baltimore: John W. Woods, 1859), Huntington Library, San Marino, California, 1, 39.

42. John Tyler Jr., "The Secession of the South," *DeBow's Review*, April 1860, 390, Virginia Historical Society, 380. "Pardon for John Brown," *New Orleans Times-Picayune*, November 16, 1859. "Letter from New York," *New Orleans Times-Picayune*, December 1, 1859, 6.

43. "The Abolition Insurrection at Harper's Ferry—The Irrepressible Conflict Begun," *Federal Union*, November 1, 1859. "The Federal Union (Milledgeville, Ga.) 1830–1861," *Georgia Historic Newspapers*, https://gahistoricnewspapers.galileo.usg .edu/lccn/sn86053071/.

44. For more on interracial relationships both before and after the Civil War, see Hodes, *White Women, Black Men*.

45. Amanda Virginia Edmonds Chappelear, "Amanda Virginia Edmonds Chappelear Diary," Mss1C3684a2, Virginia Historical Society. Ed Gallaher to Andrew Hunter, Esq., November 26, 1859, John Brown Collection, Massachusetts Historical Society.

46. Fox-Genovese, *Within the Plantation Household*, 291. Kathleen Brown has traced the beginnings of white society's hypersexualization of Black men to the late seventeenth century, when Virginia's lawmakers and courts began to regulate female sexuality. In 1662, Virginia's colonial assembly doubled the fines for interracial fornication; in 1691, it outlawed interracial marriage. Together, these secured the sexual rights of white men to white women, while Black men could be executed, or worse, for rape. This, in turn, created a sense of Black men as rapists. See Brown, *Good Wives, Nasty Wenches and Anxious Patriarchs*, 196. Eugene D. Genovese points out that the idea of Black male hypersexuality only fully formed after emancipation. See Genovese, *Roll, Jordan, Roll*, 422, 461–62.

47. The *Cincinnati Daily Press* reported that "the ladies of Richmond, Va., [were] about to form a Southern Rights Association." See "Pen and Scissors," *Cincinnati Daily Press*, December 3, 1859, 1. As Elizabeth Varon has explained, the raid "accelerated an ongoing process of political reorientation, in which women cast off old political allegiances and came to embrace the cause of southern nationalism." See Varon, *We Mean to Be Counted*, 139.

48. *Governor's Biennial Messages to the General Assembly of the State of Virginia, December 5, 1859*, 75520, Huntington Library, San Marino, California, 17–18, 23. Here, because it suited his purposes, Wise cried for federal intervention in a state's domestic affairs. Southerners also called for federal intervention in the Lecompton affair, even if they refused to call it that. Yet southerners decried other moves by the federal government to intervene in slavery, which they claimed fell under the purview of the states. Similarly, abolitionists believed the federal government should abolish slavery yet cried state's rights when northern states passed personal liberty laws protecting residents from having to cooperate in the return of fugitive slaves to their southern owners. In short, both sides called on federal power when they stood to benefit from it and decried federal intervention when they did not.

49. "P. C. Massie to William Massie," December 2, 1859. Analysis of political divisions in Virginia from Link, *Roots of Secession*, 191–94.

50. As Eric Walther writes, "By the time the first state seceded in 1860 many south-erners"—that is, the fire-eaters—"had spent over thirty years preparing their people to deal with the sectional crisis and lead them out of the Union. They indoctrinated the people with arguments for state sovereignty, issued warnings about hostile sectional majorities, and argued for the necessity of perpetuating and protecting slavery." The only way to do this, they believed, was by seceding from the Union. See Walther, *The Fire-Eaters*, 8.

51. "Virginia," *Charleston (S.C.) Mercury*, November 28, 1859, https://scholarexchange.furman.edu/secession-editorials/all/editorials/239/. For simi-lar, see "The Plan of Insurrection," *Charleston Mercury*, November 1, 1859, https://scholarexchange.furman.edu/secession-editorials/all/editorials/233/.

52. "The Harper's Ferry Insurrection," *Charleston Mercury*, October 19, 1859. "The Plan of Insurrection," *Charleston Mercury*, November 1, 1859. The *Mercury* reprinted the article from the Richmond *Whig* in its own article, "The Blind Receive Their Sight," *Charleston Mercury*, December 6, 1859, 1.

53. Tyler, "The Secession of the South," 380, 367, 368.

54. Wagner's resolution quoted in "Evening Session," *Charleston Mercury*, Decem-ber 20, 1859, 3. Mississippi resolutions in "Resolutions Reported from the Joint Committee on State and Federal Relations," *Semi-weekly Mississippian* (Jackson), December 5, 1859, 2.

55. Richard Thompson Archer to the Editors of the *Sun*, December 8, 1859, Rich-ard Thompson Archer Family Papers, box 2E647, folder 5, Dolph Briscoe Center for American History, University of Texas at Austin. For "patriarchal tenure" as reported by a Republican paper, see "The Patriarchal Tenure," *Chicago Press and Tribune*, October 26, 1859.

Chapter 4

1. "More Trouble," *Independent* (Montgomery), January 7, 1860, 1.

2. James W. Singleton to Stephen Douglas, February 20, 1859, Stephen A. Doug-las Papers, Special Collections Research Center, University of Chicago.

3. For specifics on the content of the platforms and the political maneuverings in committee, see Holt, *The Election of 1860*, 56–59. Women laying flowers from Egerton, *Year of Meteors*, 77.

4. "The Meeting To-night," *Daily Delta* (New Orleans), May 12, 1860, 4; "Senator Toombs' Position," *Macon (Ga.) Daily Telegraph*, May 10, 1860, 2.

5. "Senator Toombs' Position," *Macon Daily Telegraph*, May 10, 1860, 2. John Townsend, "The South Alone, Should Govern the South: And African Slavery Should Be Controlled by Those Only, Who Are Friendly to It" (Charleston, S.C.: Steam-Power Presses of Evans and Cogswell, 1860), box 1860, Massachusetts His-torical Society, 6, 9.

6. *Mobile Register*, quoted in "[Illegible]," *Daily Confederation* (Montgomery), May 30, 1860, 2. Forsyth went on to support Stephen Douglas in the election. For more on Forsyth and his career, see Burnett, *The Pen Makes a Good Sword*.

7. "Our Oregon Correspondence," *New York Herald*, April 6, 1860, 2.

8. "Political," *Wisconsin Patriot* (Madison), May 17, 1860, 7. After northern Dem-ocrats nominated Douglas, the same paper extolled Douglas's "bravery, an energy,

and an unflinching back-bone, an unyielding firmness . . . to his friends, to his principles, and to his country"—more gendered language implying that Douglas's unwillingness to compromise made him a real man. See "Judge Douglas' Last Speech," *Wisconsin Patriot*, June 16, 1860, 5.

9. For more on the ins and outs of the Baltimore convention, see Holt, *The Election of 1860*, 115–28. Davis, *Breckinridge*, 224–26. Another Breckinridge biographer believes that Breckinridge "thought of his acceptance as a necessary preliminary to the withdrawal of his candidacy, as well as Bell's and Douglas's, in order to concentrate the opposition to Lincoln on a single candidate" to be determined at a later date. See Heck, *Proud Kentuckian*, 85. Either interpretation shows that Breckinridge accepted the nomination with the hope of uniting the Democratic Party—whether under himself or someone else—rather than simply running to lose.

10. Had Frémont also won Pennsylvania and either Illinois or Indiana, he would have won the election.

11. "Republican Party Platform of 1860," May 17, 1860, https://www.presidency .ucsb.edu/node/273296. James Oakes describes the Republican constellation of beliefs—including no constitutional right to property in man, due process for fugitive slaves, citizenship for free Blacks, and freedom in the territories—as antislavery constitutionalism. See Oakes, *The Crooked Path to Abolition*, 98. Clay quoted in Pierson, *Free Hearts and Free Homes*, 170. "The Last Rail Split by 'Honest Old Abe,'" *Wide-Awake Pictorial*, November 1, 1860, 6, https://elections.harpweek.com /1860/cartoon-1860-medium.asp?UniqueID=19&Year=1860. For more on the single-issue periodical that published the cartoon, see West, "Wide-Awake Pictorial." For a similar depiction of Lincoln as a rail-splitting backwoodsman, see "Abraham Lincoln as 'Railsplitter': Cartoon Image from the Masthead of the Railsplitter, 1860," House Divided: The Civil War Research Engine at Dickinson College, n.d., http://hd.housedivided.dickinson.edu/node/34101.

12. Fessenden quoted in "Invasion of States," *Rock Island (Ill.) Argus*, February 6, 1860, 2. Evarts reprinted in "Speech of Wm M. Evarts, Esq., at Auburn," *New York Times*, October 19, 1960, 1. "Labor—Degrading!," *Racine (Wisc.) Advocate*, July 4, 1860, 1.

13. Hammond, "The 'Mudsill' Theory." "New Jersey for Old Abe," *Chicago Tribune*, June 11, 1860, 2.

14. "Brief Reminiscences of the Congo-Democracy," *Gazette and Democrat* (Lancaster, Ohio), September 27, 1860, 1.

15. "Progress," *Pomeroy (Ohio) Weekly Telegraph*, September 14, 1860, 2. "Northern Slaves," *Cedar Falls (Iowa) Gazette*, November 2, 1860, 2. A paper in Vermont similarly denigrated northern Democrats as "servile tools" of the South. See "Virginia Again," *Green-Mountain Freeman* (Montpelier, Vt.), January 12, 1860, 6. A paper in New York described northern Democrats as "servile tools of power in a corrupt administration." See "Rally for Action!," *Poughkeepsie (N.Y.) Journal*, November 3, 1860, 2.

16. Quotes found in Pierson, *Free Hearts and Free Homes*, 168–69.

17. Currier and Ives sold prints for prices ranging from five cents to three dollars (between about $1.52 and $91.14 in 2018 money). The prints were available retail

as well as wholesale at outlets throughout the country and in London. See "Currier and Ives," in *Encyclopaedia Britannica*.

18. "The Famous Gurney Letter," *New York Herald*, August 13, 1860, 2; "Lincoln's Radicalism Proved," *New York Herald*, September 6, 1860, 6. For similar, see "The Presidential Contest," *New York Herald*, May 21, 1860, 4, which claims that Republicans would turn "government into a great promoter of religious and moral reform, of woman's rights . . . and the displacement of the family by social phalanxes."

19. Wisconsin correspondent: "Chicago Convention," *Wisconsin Daily Patriot* (Madison), May 24, 1860, 2. "Free love manifesto" is "The Famous Gurney Letter," *New York Herald*, August 13, 1860, 2. "Ulcerous abomination" quote in "Free Love," *New York Times*, September 21, 1860, 5. The *Chicago Tribune* reprinted the article: "Expose of the Affairs of the Late 'Unitary Household,'" *Chicago Tribune*, September 26, 1860, 3. An earlier *Times* article detailed a murder-suicide committed by a jilted husband whose wife had allegedly adopted free love principles. See "News of the Day," *New York Times*, March 9, 1860, 4.

20. Seward, "William Henry Seward's Higher Law Speech."

21. "Amalgamation in Lake County," *Daily Ohio Statesman* (Columbus), May 29, 1860, 2. For a similar story, see also "Another Judson Affair," *Wisconsin Daily Patriot*, April 30, 1860, 1. For a reported case involving a Black woman and a white man, see "One of the Cases of Amalgamation in Oberlin," *Daily Ohio Statesman*, November 10, 1860, 2. Other articles simply claimed that the Republican Party supported amalgamation. See "Union Now and Forever! Tremendous Uprising of the People," *New York Herald*, October 24, 1860, 3.

22. Sheahan, *The Life of Stephen A. Douglas*, 438.

23. Benjamin Wade, quoted in Quitt, *Stephen A. Douglas and Antebellum Democracy*, 189. Douglas's speech is Douglas, "Execution of United States Laws," 330. Sheahan, *The Life of Stephen A. Douglas*, 437.

24. Daniel Walker Howe argues that the Whigs had a coherent political culture that focused simultaneously on innovation and social control and self-control. He argues that Republicans reflected this Whiggish impulse for social reform. See Howe, *The Political Culture of the American Whigs*. I have based this paragraph's analysis of manhood on Amy Greenberg's typology of "restrained manhood." Restrained men, she writes, "could be found in all political parties, but the reform aspects of the Whig, Know-Nothing, and Republican parties held a special appeal." See Greenberg, *Manifest Manhood and the Antebellum American Empire*, 11–12.

25. Howe writes that Whigs "synthesized innovation with the maintenance of control. . . . It was precisely this emphasis on controlling others that the Jacksonians objected to in Whig reforms." Democrats opposed these moves. See Howe, *The Political Culture of the American Whigs*, 300.

26. "The Douglas Barbecue. Twenty to Thirty Thousand People in Jones' Wood," *New York Herald*, September 13, 1860, 3. "Cheer Up, My Lively Lads" and "The Douglas Campaign Rolling," in *The Democratic Campaign Songster*.

27. "Constitutional Union Party Platform of 1860." "Intentional brevity" quote in Holt, *The Election of 1860*, 80.

28. "Granny-dears" quote in Holt, *The Election of 1860*, 84. For "fogies" and "old fossils," see, for instance, "Houston on Bell and Everett," *Nashville Union and*

American, July 22, 1860, 2; and "The Great Union Rally," *Louisville Daily Courier*, July 4, 1860, 1. Constitutional Union papers tried to combat these insults by adopting them as a badge of pride. See "It Is Obvious," *Alexandria Gazette*, June 5, 1860, 2. For more on the language of age and the generational politics of the Constitutional Union Party, see Knupfer, "Aging Statesmen."

29. Quote from Constitutional Union organ the *Rome (Ga.) Courier* in "The Fusion in Georgia," *Nashville Union and American*, July 29, 1860, 2. Republican quoted in "Fusion in Pennsylvania," *Pomeroy (Ohio) Weekly Telegraph*, August 21, 1860, 2. Stephen Douglas, quoted in Egerton, *Year of Meteors*, 192. For a description of the various fusion attempts and why they failed, see Egerton, 188–92.

30. Conlin, "The Dangerous Isms and the Fanatical Ists."

31. Davis and Mason quoted in Walther, *The Shattering of the Union*, 140.

32. "Letter from New York," *Weekly Houston Telegraph*, May 29, 1860, 1.

33. "Letter from New York," *Weekly Houston Telegraph*, May 29, 1860, 1. One historian has written that "no man on the Gulf Coast was a more energetic advocate for the institution of slavery, the reopening of the African slave trade, and eventually for secession, than was editor Cushing." See Fornell, *The Galveston Era*, 152–53. For anti-women's rights articles in Breckinridge papers, see "Woman's Rights Conventions," *San Joaquin (Calif.) Republican*, June 23, 1860, 2, which reported the following on the convention at the Cooper Institute: "Among the resolutions adopted by these strong minded women and weak minded men who associate with them . . . was a series repudiating the present obligations of the marriage contract and denouncing our divorce laws as unjust to women. . . . When our laws are altered in accordance with the wishes of these fanatics, Free Love will indeed prevail without any restraint, and it will indeed not only be a wise child that will know its own father, but a wise man who will know his children." The *Daily Delta*, an extreme southern organ, claimed that in the North, any man who "will not submit to be led by demagogues and masculine women" is expelled from his community—implying broad support for women's rights. "Northern Slavery," *Daily Delta* (New Orleans), April 18, 1860, 4.

34. Norton, "The Evolution of White Women's Experience in Early America," 613.

35. Allgor, *Parlor Politics*. Unknown to Wife, May 18, 1860, William Chestnut Manning Family Papers, South Caroliniana Library. Unknown to Wife, May 29, 1860, William Chestnut Manning Family Papers, South Caroliniana Library.

36. "Black-Republican (Negro) Equality," *Constitution* (Washington, D.C.), June 30, 1860, 2.

37. Article reprinted in "Texas Items," *Weekly Telegraph* (Houston), May 29, 1860, 1. Gage, "The Texas Road to Secession and War," 198.

38. Stephen Douglas, as reprinted in "Second Debate: Freeport, Illinois."

39. "Speech of Hon. Thomas L. Clingman of North Carolina," *Weekly Standard* (Raleigh), May 23, 1860, 4.

40. James Williams, "Letters on Slavery from the Old World. Written during the Canvass for the Presidency of the United States in 1860" (Nashville: Southern Methodist Pub. House, 1861), 120–21, Massachusetts Historical Society. Though I disagree with Michael Conlin's broader thesis—that social conservatism held the Democratic Party and the United States together—he offers extensive evidence

demonstrating that southern men believed "the essential conservatism of slavery protected the South—and thus at least half of the United States—from these dangerous isms." See Conlin, "The Dangerous Isms and the Fanatical Ists," 218–19.

41. For a description of Douglas's Norfolk speech and a summary of southern responses to the "Norfolk Doctrine," see Johannsen, *Stephen A. Douglas*, 788–89. The *Baltimore Sun* reported that Wise's speech lasted for four hours and was witnessed by 3,000 people; the *Semi-weekly Standard* (Raleigh) reported it lasted for three and a half hours. See "Governor Wise," *Semi-weekly Standard*, October 31, 1860, 3; and "First Campaign Speech of Governor Wise, of Virginia," *Baltimore Sun*, September 29, 1860, 1. For text of the speech, see "Gov. Wise's Speech at Norfolk," *Richmond Enquirer*, October 12, 1860, 3, Robert Mercer Taliaferro Hunter Papers, Virginia Historical Society.

42. For more on these novels, see Moss, *Domestic Novelists in the Old South*.

43. Quoted in Moss, *Domestic Novelists in the Old South*, 148.

44. In 1860, for instance, abolitionist Lydia Maria Child wrote a pamphlet for the American Anti-slavery Society that included dozens of ads for runaway slaves who were thought to have left to find their spouse, who had been sold away, as well as stories of light-skinned slaves thought to be the children of notable politicians and landowners. See Child, "The Patriarchal Institution."

45. Caleb Cushing, "Speech of Hon. Caleb Cushing, in Norombega Hall, Bangor, October 2, 1860, before the Democracy of Maine" (s.n., 1860), 12, Massachusetts Historical Society. "Mr. Breckinridge's Letter of Acceptance," *Constitution* (Washington, D.C.) July 12, 1860, 2. Cushing, "Speech of Hon. Caleb Cushing," 12, Massachusetts Historical Society. Robert McClane, quoted in "Letter from Minister McLane," *Constitution*, October 18, 1860, 2. James Henry Hammond to Milledge Luke Bonham, October 3, 1860, Milledge Luke Bonham Papers, South Caroliniana Library.

46. "The Part Which Mr. Douglas Will 'Do All in His Power to Aid,'" *Constitution*, September 1, 1860, 2. "The South to Be Subjugated—Douglasism and Abolitionism on the Same Track," *Constitution*, October 24, 1860, 2.

47. "Congressional Speech of Hon. Jefferson Davis, of Mississippi," *Constitution*, May 9, 1860, 2. "The Canvass of 1860," *Constitution*, November 6, 1860, 2.

48. Olsen, *Political Culture and Secession in Mississippi*, 12.

49. "Madison's Views on Slavery," *Tri-weekly Telegraph* (Houston), October 27, 1860, 3. "What Shall the South Do If Lincoln Be Elected?," *Tri-weekly Telegraph*, November 8, 1860, 3. For more on Cushing, including his work to publicize an alleged plot between abolitionists and enslaved people to overthrow slavery in Texas, see Reynolds, "Cushing, Edward Hopkins." McCurry argues that yeomen "found common cause with planters in maintaining and policing the class, gender, and racial boundaries of citizenship in the slave republic. In the end, their commitment to the slave regime owed as much to its legitimation of dependence and inequality in the private sphere as to the much-lauded vitality of male independence and formal 'democracy' in the public sphere." See McCurry, *Masters of Small Worlds*, 228.

50. John Townsend to Milledge Luke Bonham, October 10, 1860, Milledge Luke Bonham Papers, South Caroliniana Library.

51. Edward Rugemer has argued that the "boundaries of the United States were permeable," allowing news of other slave rebellions to reach southern slaveholders. The more slaveholders learned about other rebellions, the more they came to believe that abolitionist agitation (not the daily atrocities of slavery) caused slaves to rebel. This made them retrench against abolition. See Rugemer, *The Problem of Emancipation*, 7. John Tyler Jr., "The Secession of the South," *DeBow's Review*, April 1860, 390, Virginia Historical Society, 381. "Speech of Hon. Wm. L. Yancey," *Constitution* (Washington, D.C.), September 22, 1860, 6. "Mr. Editor," *Semi-weekly Standard* (Raleigh), November 3, 1860, 2.

52. "Letter from Gov. Wise," *Macon (Ga.) Daily Telegraph*, September 3, 1860, 1. "Presentation," *Daily Confederation* (Montgomery), April 1, 1860, 2.

53. A. G. Baskin to John Lawrence Manning, October 27, 1860, Chestnut-Miller-Manning Papers, South Carolina Historical Society; for more on this exchange, see Bowman, *At the Precipice*, 64–65.

54. William Tennent Jr. to Milledge Luke Bonham, October 10, 1860, Milledge Luke Bonham Papers, South Caroliniana Library. For more on the 1860 Association and its influence, see Cauthen, *South Carolina Goes to War*, 35. Townsend, *The South Alone*, 8, 9.

Chapter 5

1. "Let the People Rejoice: Lincoln Elected," *Freeport (Ill.) Wide Awake*, November 17, 1860, 3.

2. "Is the Democratic Party Defunct?," *Brooklyn Daily Eagle*, November 10, 1860, 2.

3. Holmes, *The Diary of Miss Emma Holmes*, 1.

4. Democrat at Albany convention quoted in *Proceedings of the Democratic State Convention, Held in Albany*, 13, Albert and Shirley Small Special Collections Library, University of Virginia. "Help for the South!," *Sun* (New York City), January 9, 1861, 2. For further articles blaming fire-eaters for Lincoln's victory or for the secession frenzy, see "The Union," *Democrat and Sentinel* (Ebensburg, Penn.), November 14, 1860, 2; and "Threatened Reign of Terror," *Brooklyn Daily Eagle*, December 20, 1860, 2.

5. "The Meeting of Congress," *Brooklyn Daily Eagle*, December 3, 1860, 2. "Masterly Inactivity," *Brooklyn Daily Eagle*, September 5, 1860, 2.

6. "The Remedy," *Democrat and Sentinel* (Ebensburg, Penn.), December 26, 1860, 2.

7. "Reactionary Symptoms at the North," *New York Daily Herald*, December 29, 1860, 6.

8. As Russell McClintock writes, through January and February, "under the growing pressure for compromise, most Republicans clung to their party's core doctrines all the more tightly. This was a testament to their devotion to those principles and the party that represented them, and also to their deep-seated distrust of their opponents' motives." See McClintock, *Lincoln and the Decision for War*, 151. "Hon. S. A. Douglas, of Illinois, on the State of the Union, Delivered in the Senate, January 3, 1861," 1861, 17, Stephen A. Douglas Papers, University of Chicago

Library, Special Collections Research Center. For the text of the proposed bill, see "S.R. 52: Joint Resolution Proposing Certain Amendments to the Constitution of the United States," December 24, 1860, Stephen A. Douglas Papers, University of Chicago Library, Special Collections Research Center.

9. Buchanan, "Fourth Annual Message." Buchanan repeated the sentiment a month later as he explained why he refused to resupply the forts in Charleston's harbor. See Buchanan, "Message on Threats to the Peace and Existence of the Union." Van Anden quoted in "A Military Despotism," *Brooklyn Daily Eagle*, January 11, 1861, 2.

10. Howe, "The Evangelical Movement and Political Culture in the North," 1228. On southern men opposing intervention in their private affairs, Stephanie McCurry has written, "Within the boundaries of the household . . . in daily governance of wives, children, and in some cases, slaves, yeomen both produced the material basis of independence and practiced its considerable prerogatives." McCurry, *Masters of Small Worlds*, 61.

11. "The Present Juncture of Our Political Affairs," *Brooklyn Daily Eagle*, January 18, 1861, 2. Lynn Hunt has argued that something similar happened in the years before, during, and following the French Revolution. According to Hunt, changing understandings of the proper roles of family members consciously and subconsciously affected the way the French understood the course of their Revolution. "Authority in the state was explicitly modeled on authority in the family," she argues. Once the king had been deemed a "bad father," revolutionaries had to draw governing authority from a different family model. They found it in brotherhood, but brotherhood was a necessarily less stable, less hierarchal model than fatherhood. See Hunt, *The Family Romance of the French Revolution*, 3.

12. For a full explanation of the affective theory of Union, see the prologue of Woods, *Emotional and Sectional Conflict*. Rogan Kersh also briefly touches on this idea. He describes how the affective theory of union—or "voluntary national solidarity," as he calls it—provided a basis for nationalism beyond ancestry or ethnicity in the early days of the Republic and throughout the antebellum era. See Kersh, *Dreams of a More Perfect Union*, 292. Dowdell, Douglas, Buchanan, and Lincoln quoted in Woods, *Emotional and Sectional Conflict*, 22–23.

13. Adams quoted in Woods, *Emotional and Sectional Conflict*, 24. As Phillip Paludan has argued, northerners worried that secession would produce "disorder, anxiety, and a general disrespect for democratic government." If the North accepted the principle that states could quit the Union, then there would be nothing to enforce law and order in the future. See Paludan, "The American Civil War Considered as a Crisis in Law and Order,"1017.

14. "Notes of the Rebellion," *New York Times*, December 18, 1861, 3. "Special Correspondence of the Union and American," *Nashville Union and American*, December 2, 1860, 2. "Interesting Correspondence," *Nashville Union and American*, January 4, 1861, 2. In an 1862 letter to Andrew Johnson, then the governor of Tennessee, Adrian V. S. Lindsley reported that southern Methodists and their publishing houses continued to foment disloyalty among Tennesseans. "The Reverent dignitaries who presided over it & controlled all its movements were the most noisy secessionists & the most active, inveterate & working rebels that we had in our midst." Lindsley

singled out McFerrin as a particularly strong secessionist, describing him as "head devil & the master spirit of all the wicked," whose work at the Methodist Publishing House "scattered the seeds of rebellion far & wide over this once happy land." See letter from Adrian V. S. Lindsley to Andrew Johnson in Graf, Haskins, and Clark, *The Papers of Andrew Johnson*, 319–20.

15. Richard Thompson Archer, "Editors of the Mississippian," Richard Thompson Archer Family Papers, Dolph Briscoe Center for American History, University of Texas at Austin. Jefferson Martenet to Catherine M. Richardson, January 14, 1861, Jefferson Martenet Correspondence, Huntington Library, San Marino, California. Theophilus Nash to Margaret Stanly Beckwith, March 2, 1861, Margaret Stanly Beckwith Papers, Virginia Historical Society.

16. Seward, "On the Irrepressible Conflict."

17. "Address of the Executive Committee of the Southern Rights Association, Parish of Jefferson," *Daily Delta* (New Orleans), December 7, 1860, 1. For similar commentary on the election, see "The 'Union Meeting' at Vicksburg," *Daily Mississippian* (Jackson), December 12, 1860, 1. Speech in North Carolina reprinted in "Remarks of Mr. Slade, of Rockingham," *Semi-weekly Standard* (Raleigh), January 26, 1861, 3.

18. For an overview of this scholarship, see Sinha, "Gender and Nation," 229–39. David Potter pushes historians to pay attention to the importance of shared interests—especially shared economic interests—in creating a national identity. For the South, that shared economic interest was, of course, slavery. See Potter, "The Historian's Use of Nationalism and Vice Versa," 933–35. The development of southern nationalism through a sense of shared culture and interests aligns with Benedict Anderson's definition of the nation as an "imagined political community." See Anderson, *Imagined Communities*, 6–7. "Attachments to modern gender . . ." in Sinha, "Gender and Nation," 231.

19. This overall thesis owes much to the work of Paul Quigley, who argues that "white southerners increasingly defined their national identity in gendered terms"; Quigley, *Shifting Grounds*, 10. This, combined with his insight that southerners defined their nationalism in opposition to northerners, helped me connect the denigration of northern women to the praise of southern women and to the growth of southern nationalism.

20. Jefferson Martenet to Catherine M. Richardson, December 26, 1860, Jefferson Martenet Correspondence, Huntington Library, San Marino, California. Francis Pickens to Jefferson Davis, January 23, 1861, Francis Pickens Papers, South Caroliniana Library.

21. Potter, *The Impending Crisis*, 456.

22. For a thorough summary and analysis of many of these works, see Moss, *Domestic Novelists in the Old South*.

23. Jefferson Martenet to Catherine M. Richardson, January 20, 1861, Jefferson Martenet Correspondence, Huntington Library, San Marino, California. Indeed, Martenet said as much when enumerating to his mother his requirements in his search for a wife a few years earlier. See Jefferson Martenet to Catherine Richardson, January 31, 1855, Jefferson Martenet Correspondence, Huntington Library, San Marino, California. "High Life in Washington," *Memphis Daily Appeal*, April 19, 1861, 2.

24. John W. Ervin to John Smythe Richardson, January 3, 1861, John Smythe Richardson Papers, South Caroliniana Library. In this paragraph, I am building on Stephen Berry's argument. Berry contends that southern men conflated women and eminence; I argue that they also fused women and the South. See Berry, *All That Makes a Man*, 171–72.

25. Melissa DeVelvis argues that in 1860, elite South Carolinian women harnessed familial and religious language to express their political consciousness without transgressing their gender roles. See DeVelvis, "'May the Lord Shield and Protect Us from the Terrible Storm Ahead of Us.'"

26. Ada Bacot, quoted in DeVelvis, 993. For report on Benjamin's speech, see "From Washington," *Charlotte Evening Bulletin*, January 3, 1861, 3. New Orleans coverage from "The Illumination Last Night," *New Orleans Crescent*, February 7, 1861, 1. "The Georgia Girls," *Vicksburg (Miss.) Whig*, December 15, 1860, 2. For another example of a publication approving of southern women who supported secession, see "South Carolina Convention," *Vicksburg Whig*, December 26, 1860, 2. It reported, "The galleries of the hall of the House of Representatives were densely crowded, many ladies being present. Gov. Pickens read his inaugural, the sentiments of which were decidedly firm for secession. The address was warmly applauded." Southern women who supported remaining in the Union also participated in out-of-doors politics. See, for example, this story of Tennessee women presenting a national flag, and then removing and burning a Palmetto one: "A Palmetto Flag Burned," *Tennessean* (Nashville), February 1, 1861, 2. Women also attended pro-Union meetings in the South. See "Another Great Union Meeting," *Weekly Raleigh Register*, December 5, 1860, 3.

27. "Complimentary Party," *Charlotte Evening Bulletin*, March 13, 1861, 2.

28. "Life in New York," *Newbern (N.C.) Daily Progress*, March 4, 1861, 2.

29. Boydston, *Home and Work*. Thavolia Glymph argues that even historians have been tripped up by the idealization of the southern home as separate from the public sphere of work, assuming because southerners said so that work took place in the fields, not in the home. Glymph proves that this is not the case: southern homes were places of work and, therefore, of brutality against enslaved workers. See Glymph, *Out of the House of Bondage*.

30. Link, *Roots of Secession*. See especially the second chapter of Freehling, *Road to Disunion*.

31. "Diary of Richard Eppes," 1862, 1859, Virginia Historical Society. For more on Eppes's political views at this juncture, see Bowman, "Conditional Unionism and Slavery in Virginia," 34–39. Virginia Democratic senator Robert M. T. Hunter also spent the winter rejecting calls for immediate secession. On December 9, one of Hunter's friends needled him on the point. "I do not agree with you on one thing—that the election of Lincoln is not sufficient cause for disruption. I think that election with its surroundings is enough[,] more than enough," his friend wrote. See "George Booker to R. M. T. Hunter," December 9, 1860, Virginia Historical Society. For instances of Democratic papers in Virginia expressing a wait-and-see attitude, see "The Meeting To-Morrow," *Staunton Vindicator*, November 16, 1860; and "Disunion from a Love of Disunion—Disunion by Reason of a Failure to Correct the Breaches of the Constitution," *Staunton Vindicator*, December 21, 1860.

32. John Tyler Jr., "Virginia and Her Responsibilities!," January 1861, Virginia Historical Society.

33. Stephen F. Hale to Beriah Magoffin, December 27, 1860, reproduced in full in Charles B. Dew, *Apostles of Disunion*, 91–103.

34. R. S. Holt to Joseph Holt, November 9, 1860, Milledge Luke Bonham Papers, South Caroliniana Library.

35. Potter, *The Impending Crisis*, 454–55.

36. "Temperance and the Times," *Spirit of the Age* (Raleigh), December 26, 1860, 2.

37. "Words of a Patriotic Song," *New York Herald*, November 29, 1860, Henry Campbell Davis Scrapbook, 1850–1865, South Caroliniana Library. "A Secession Ballad," *New York Herald*, November 29, 1860, Henry Campbell Davis Scrapbook, 1850–1865, South Caroliniana Library. Judah P. Benjamin to Samuel Barlow, January 8, 1861, Samuel Barlow Collection, Huntington Library. J. W. Claxton to Mr. Jones, November 10, 1860, Milledge Luke Bonham Papers, South Caroliniana Library. James Buchanan to George M. Wharton, December 16, 1860, James Buchanan Papers, Historical Society of Pennsylvania.

38. "The Disunion Banner—A One-Act Drama," *Semi-weekly Standard* (Raleigh), April 10, 1861, 2.

39. Jefferson Martenet to Catherine M. Richardson, December 26, 1860, Jefferson Martenet Correspondence, Huntington Library, San Marino, California. "A Cheering Voice from Texas," *Weekly Mississippian* (Jackson), January 16, 1861, 2. Secessionist in North Carolina is Edwin M. Clayton to Brother, March 9, 1861, Clayton Family Papers, Southern Historical Collection at the University of North Carolina at Chapel Hill.

40. South Carolinian is J. M. Claxton to Mr. Jones. William Montague Brown to Samuel Barlow, November 22, 1860, and December 10, 1860, Samuel Barlow Collection, Huntington Library. Unknown to Unknown, December 2, 1860, John L. Manning Papers, South Carolina Historical Society. Locations identified by dateline and by presence in John L. Manning Papers. Edmund Ruffin to John J. Perkins, March 2, 1861, John Perkins Papers, Southern Historical Collection at the University of North Carolina at Chapel Hill.

41. "The Reign of Terror," *Semi-weekly Standard*, April 10, 1861, 3.

42. See also Richard Thompson Archer, "The Friends of Southern Rights," n.d., Richard Thompson Archer Family Papers, box 2E647, folder 5, Dolph Briscoe Center for American History, University of Texas at Austin; Richard Thompson Archer, n.d., Richard Thompson Archer Family Papers, box 2E647, folder 5, Dolph Briscoe Center for American History, University of Texas at Austin.

43. For more on the uses of the word "disunion," see Varon, *Disunion!*

44. By so arguing, I am building on William Link's thesis: that men enlisted because of cultural and social concerns that went beyond political and ideological debates. See Link, *Roots of Secession*.

45. "Discretion, the Better Part of Valor," *Nashville Union and American*, April 19, 1861, 2. "Extra Session of the Legislature," *Nashville Union and American*, April 19, 1861, 2.

46. The word "granny" denoted age, and, indeed, young southerners were impatient with their parents' and grandparents' "old fogey" leadership, which they

believed had cost the South some of its power and standing within the Union. Peter Carmichael traces the influence of this generation of young Virginians in Carmichael, *The Last Generation.*

47. Poem is "The Disunion Banner—A One-Act Drama," 2. Praise for speech in "Public Meeting in Robeson," *Semi-weekly Standard*, May 1, 1861, 2.

48. Aaron Sheehan-Dean's work on Virginia men during the Civil War supports this notion. He writes, "Virginians' tenacity on the battlefield belies the simplistic notion that they fought solely for the defense of a loving family. Their antebellum families were organized within a slave society and the two were inseparable, as Virginians recognized. The interdependence of Virginians' intimate households and the slave society that sustained them compelled Virginians to reject return to the Union. Appreciating this reality helps explain why Confederates fought for their independence with such determination." See Sheehan-Dean, *Why Confederates Fought*, 194.

49. Amanda Virginia Edmonds Chappelear, "Amanda Virginia Edmonds Chappelear Diary," Virginia Historical Society. Chesnut had spoken with Stephens at a reception in the spring of 1861. See Chesnut, *A Diary from Dixie*, 49–50. For another example of support for the war, see Unknown to Margaret Stanly Beckwith, n.d., Margaret Stanly Beckwith Papers, Virginia Historical Society.

50. "Presentation of a Flag to the Cadets of Anderson Military Academy—Interesting Speeches on the Occasion, &c., &c," *Intelligencer* (Anderson, S.C.), April 11, 1861, 2. For more examples of women in South Carolina supporting the Confederacy, see DeVelvis, "'May the Lord Shield and Protect Us from the Terrible Storm Ahead of Us,'" 998.

51. Sumter Volunteers of SoCa. to the Ladies of the First and Second Baptist Churches and the Four Methodist Churches of Richmond, Va., June 9, 1861, John Smythe Richardson Papers, South Caroliniana Library.

52. Stephen Berry argues that having a woman's undying support allowed southern men to conceptualize their sufferings in pursuit of éclat as sacrifices on the altar of love. Women, in turn, were expected to be mere witnesses to male becoming: essential, but sidelined. But as Berry argues, and as this passage affirms, this idealized vision of southern womanhood put pressure on flesh-and-blood southern women to behave in certain ways. See Berry, *All That Makes a Man.*

53. Linda Kerber and Mary Beth Norton have described this as "Republican Motherhood." See Kerber, *Women of the Republic*; and Norton, *Liberty's Daughters.*

Conclusion

1. Anonymous to Joseph Holt, June 15, 1861, Joseph Holt Papers, Huntington Library, San Marino, California. Two months earlier, John Porter Brown, the nephew of a U.S. diplomat in Turkey, also wrote Holt (though he from Constantinople) to thank Holt for his tireless Unionism. See John Porter Brown to Joseph Holt, March 28, 1861, Joseph Holt Papers, Huntington Library, San Marino, California.

2. Quoted in Furniss, "To Save the Union 'in Behalf of Conservative Men,'" 170.

3. Grimsley, *The Hard Hand of War*, 3. Grimsley argues that this conciliatory phase of the Union war effort ran through the middle of 1862, when it was overtaken by a pragmatic phase and finally, in 1864, by a hard war policy. Even during the hard

war, however, the idea was never to attack civilians. And indeed, in almost no cases did Union soldiers kills southern civilians without provocation. "The Impending Conflict," *Brooklyn Daily Eagle*, April 22, 1861, 2. Seymour quoted in Furniss, "To Save the Union 'in Behalf of Conservative Men,'" 173.

4. Seymour quoted in Furniss, "To Save the Union 'in Behalf of Conservative Men,'" 176, 179.

5. On the southern critique of "Yankees," see Rable, *Damn Yankees!*, 8–30.

6. Volck, "Worship of the North." Southern descriptions of Lincoln from Rable, *Damn Yankees!*, 24–25. Rable quoted in *Damn Yankees!*, 8.

7. On white southerners' exaltation of white women, see Berry, *All That Makes a Man*, 112–13. Morgan quoted in Rable, *Damn Yankees!*, 69.

8. Examples and Beauregard quote drawn from Rable, *Damn Yankees!*, 72–73. Known officially as General Order No. 28, the Woman's Order stated that any woman insulting or showing contempt for Union troops should be treated as "a woman of the town plying her avocation"—that is, as soliciting prostitution.

9. *Richmond Daily Dispatch*, quoted in Rable, 72.

10. Esther Hawks, quoted in Glymph, *The Women's Fight*, 109. On the Lieber Code, see Crystal N. Feimster, "Rape and Justice in the Civil War," *New York Times*, April 25, 2013, https://opinionator.blogs.nytimes.com/2013/04/25/rape-and-justice-in -the-civil-war/. On the surge in Black women seeking legal protection from rape following the passage of the Lieber Code, as well as the vulnerability of Black women in refugee camps, see Taylor, *Embattled Freedom*, 85–86.

Bibliography

PRIMARY SOURCES

Manuscript and Archival Sources

California

  Huntington Library, San Marino

    American Political Cartoons Collection

    Jefferson Martenet Correspondence

    Joseph Holt Papers

    Samuel Barlow Collection

    *Governor's Biennial Messages to the General Assembly of the State of
      Virginia, December 5, 1859.* Richmond: James E. Goode, 1859.

    *Startling Incidents and Developments of Osowotomy Brown's Insurrectory
      and Treasonable Movements at Harper's Ferry, Virginia, October 17,
      1859, with a True and Accurate Account of the Whole Transaction by a
      Citizen of Harper's Ferry.* Baltimore: John W. Woods, 1859.

Illinois

  University of Chicago Library, Special Collections Research Center

    Stephen A. Douglas Papers

Massachusetts

  Massachusetts Historical Society, Boston

    Box 1856

    Box 1860

    Box 1861

    Caleb Cushing. "Speech of Hon. Caleb Cushing, in Norombega Hall,
      Bangor, October 2, 1860, before the Democracy of Maine." n.p., 1860.

    James Williams. "Letters on Slavery from the Old World. Written during
      the Canvass for the Presidency of the United States in 1860." Nashville:
      Southern Methodist Pub. House, 1861.

    John Brown Collection

North Carolina

  Southern Historical Collection, University of North Carolina, Chapel Hill

    Clayton Family Papers

    John Perkins Papers

Pennsylvania

  Historical Society of Pennsylvania, Philadelphia

    James Buchanan Papers

South Carolina

  South Caroliniana Library, Columbia

Henry Campbell Davis Scrapbook, 1850–1865
Francis Pickens Papers
Milledge Luke Bonham Papers
John Smythe Richardson Papers
William Chestnut Manning Family Papers
South Carolina Historical Society, Charleston
Chestnut-Miller-Manning Papers
John L. Manning Papers
Texas
Dolph Briscoe Center for American History, University of Texas at Austin
Hugo, Victor. "Victor Hugo's Letter on John Brown, with Mrs. Ann S.
Stephens' Reply." New York: Irwin P. Beadle, 1860.
Richard Thompson Archer Family Papers
William Massie Papers
Virginia
Virginia Historical Society, Richmond
Amanda Virginia Edmonds Chappelear Diary
Faulkner Family Papers
John Tyler Papers
Margaret Stanly Beckwith Papers
Richard Eppes Diary
Robert Mercer Taliaferro Hunter Papers
Wise Family Papers
Albert and Shirley Small Special Collections Library, University of Virginia,
Charlottesville
*Proceedings of the Democratic State Convention, Held in Albany, January
21, and February 1, 1861.* Albany, N.Y.: Comstock & Cassidy, 1861.

Newspapers and Periodicals

Alabama
  Daily Confederation (Montgomery)
  Democrat (Huntsville)
  Independent (Gainesville)
California
  San Joaquin Republican
Connecticut
  Hartford Courant
Florida
  Pensacola Gazette
Georgia
  Federal Union (Milledgeville)
  Georgia Telegraph (Macon)
  Macon Daily Telegraph
  Southern Banner (Athens)
Illinois
  Alton Weekly Telegraph

  Belvidere Standard
  Chicago Press and Tribune
  Chicago Tribune
  Freeport Wide Awake
  Illinois State Register (Springfield)
  Ottawa Free Trader
  Rock Island Argus
Indiana
  Evansville Daily Journal
  Indiana Herald (Indianapolis)
Iowa
  Cedar Falls Gazette
Kansas
  Kansas Herald of Freedom
    (Lawrence)
Kentucky
  Louisville Daily Courier

Louisiana
  Daily Delta (New Orleans)
  New Orleans Crescent
  New Orleans Times-Picayune
  South-Western (Shreveport)
Maryland
  Baltimore Sun
Massachusetts
  Boston Post
  Daily Evening Transcript (Boston)
  Liberator (Boston)
Mississippi
  Daily Mississippian (Jackson)
  Mississippi Free Trader (Natchez)
  Semi-weekly Mississippian
    (Jackson)
  Vicksburg Whig
  Weekly Mississippian (Jackson)
New York
  Brooklyn Daily Eagle
  Buffalo Daily Republic
  Buffalo Morning Express
  Long-Island Star
  New York Herald
  New York Times
  New York Tribune
  North Star (Rochester)
  Poughkeepsie Journal
  Sun (New York City)
  Wide-Awake Pictorial (New York
    City)
North Carolina
  Carolina Federal Republican (New
    Bern)
  Charlotte Evening Bulletin
  Newbern Daily Progress
  North-Carolina Star (Raleigh)
  Semi-weekly Standard (Raleigh)
  Spirit of the Age (Raleigh)
  Weekly Raleigh Register
  Weekly Standard (Raleigh)
  Wilmington Daily Herald
  Wilmington Journal
Ohio
  Anti-slavery Bugle (New Lisbon)
  Ashtabula Weekly Telegraph

Carroll Free Press
Cincinnati Daily Enquirer
Cincinnati Daily Press
Cincinnati Enquirer
Daily Empire (Dayton)
Daily Ohio Statesman (Columbus)
Fremont Weekly Journal
Gazette and Democrat (Lancaster)
Holmes County Republican
  (Millersburg)
McArthur Democrat (Logan)
Pomeroy Weekly Telegraph
Portsmouth Daily Times
True American (Steubenville)
Pennsylvania
  Adams Sentinel (Gettysburg)
  Carlisle Weekly Herald
  Democrat and Sentinel (Ebensburg)
  Gettysburg Compiler
  Lancaster Intelligencer
  National Gazette (Philadelphia)
  Pennsylvania Statesman
    (Philadelphia)
  Pittsburgh Weekly Gazette
  Press (Philadelphia)
  Public Ledger (Philadelphia)
  Star of the North (Bloomsburg)
  Wyoming Herald (Wilkes-Barre)
South Carolina
  Charleston Mercury
  Edgefield Advertiser
  Intelligencer (Anderson)
Tennessee
  Memphis Daily Appeal
  Nashville Union and American
  Tennessean (Nashville)
Texas
  Tri-weekly Telegraph (Houston)
  Weekly Telegraph (Houston)
Vermont
  Aurora of the Valley (Newbury)
  Burlington Free Press
  Enterprise and Vermonter
    (Vergennes)
  Green-Mountain Freeman
    (Montpelier)

Rutland Weekly Herald
St. Albans Weekly Messenger
Virginia
 Alexandria Gazette
 Richmond Dispatch
 Richmond Enquirer
 Staunton Vindicator
Washington, D.C.
 Constitution
 Daily American Organ
 Evening Star

National Era
United States Magazine and
 Democratic Review
Washington Union
Wisconsin
 Janesville Daily Gazette
 Racine Advocate
 Wisconsin Daily Patriot (Madison)
 Wisconsin Patriot (Madison)
 Wisconsin State Journal (Madison)

Other Published Primary Sources

"1852 Democratic Party Platform." June 1, 1852. http://www.presidency.ucsb.edu
 /ws/index.php?pid=29575.
"1856 Democratic Party Platform." June 2, 1856. http://www.presidency.ucsb.edu
 /ws/index.php?pid=29576.
"An Act to Organize the Territories of Nebraska and Kansas." In *Public Acts of
 the Thirty-Third Congress of the United States*, 277–90. Boston: Little, Brown,
 n.d, https://memory.loc.gov/ll/llsl/010/0300/03050283.tif.
Belisle, Orvilla S. *The Prophets; or, Mormonism Unveiled*. Philadelphia:
 Wm. White Smith, 1855. https://ia600303.us.archive.org/20/items
 /prophetsormormoooobeligoog/prophetsormormoooobeligoog.pdf.
Bell, Alfred Eva. *Boadicea the Mormon Wife: Life-Scenes in Utah*. Baltimore:
 Arthur R. Orton, 1855. https://ia800504.us.archive.org/0/items
 /boadiceamormonwioobell/boadiceamormonwioobell.pdf.
Buchanan, James. "First Annual Message to Congress on the State of the Union."
 December 8, 1857. http://www.presidency.ucsb.edu/ws/index.php?pid=29498.
———. "Fourth Annual Message." December 3, 1860. Miller Center: Presidential
 Speeches. https://millercenter.org/the-presidency/presidential-speeches
 /december-3-1860-fourth-annual-message.
———. "Message on Threats to the Peace and Existence of the Union." January
 8, 1861. https://millercenter.org/the-presidency/presidential-speeches
 /january-8-1861-message-threats-peace-and-existence-union.
Caen, Nahum. *Plain Facts and Considerations: Addressed to the People of the
 United States, without Distinction of Party, in Favor of James Buchanan, of
 Pennsylvania, for President and John C. Breckinridge, of Kentucky, for Vice
 President. By an American Citizen*. Boston: Brown, Bazán, 1856. Box 1856,
 Massachusetts Historical Society.
Chesnut, Mary Boykin. *A Diary from Dixie, as Written by Mary Boykin Chesnut,
 Wife of James Chesnut, Jr., United States Senator from South Carolina, 1859–
 1861, and Afterward an Aide to Jefferson Davis and a Brigadier-General in the
 Confederate Army*. Edited by Isabella D. Martin and Myrta Lockett Aviary.
 New York: D. Appleton, 1905. http://docsouth.unc.edu/southlit/chesnut
 /maryches.html#mches42.

Child, Lydia Maria Francis. "The Patriarchal Institution, as Described by Member of Its Own Family." American Anti-slavery Society, 1860. http://lincoln.lib.niu.edu/object/niu-lincoln:35182.

Childs, John. "The Cincinnati Platform, or the Way to Make a New State in 1856." Library Company of Philadelphia, 1856. https://digital.librarycompany.org/islandora/object/Islandora%3A65073.

"Constitutional Union Party Platform of 1860." May 9, 1860. https://www.presidency.ucsb.edu/documents/constitutional-union-party-platform-1860.

Cooke, George Willis. *Ralph Waldo Emerson: His Life, Writings, and Philosophy.* 2nd ed. Honolulu: University Press of the Pacific, 2003.

"Declaration of Sentiments." July 19, 1848. http://ecssba.rutgers.edu/docs/seneca.html.

The Democratic Campaign Songster: Douglas and Johnson Melodies. New York: P. J. Cozzens, 1860. http://lincoln.lib.niu.edu/islandora/object/niu-lincoln%3A36028.

Douglas, Stephen A. "Execution of United States Laws. Speech of Hon. S. A. Douglas, of Illinois, Friday, February 23, 1855." In *Appendix to the Congressional Globe for the Second Session, Thirty-Third Congress, Containing Speeches, Important State Papers, Laws, Etc.*, 31:330–31. Washington, D.C.: John C. Rives, 1855.

———. *Remarks of the Hon. Stephen A. Douglas, on Kansas, Utah, and the Dred Scott Decision, Delivered at Springfield, Illinois, June 12, 1857.* Chicago: Daily Times Book and Job Office, 1857.

———. *Speech of Hon. S. A. Douglas, of Illinois, against the Admission of Kansas under the Lecompton Constitution, Delivered in the Senate of the United States, March 22, 1858.* Washington, D.C.: n.p., 1858.

Drew, Thomas, ed. *The Campaign of 1856: Fremont Songs for the People.* Boston: John P. Jewett, 1856.

Graf, LeRoy P., Ralph W. Haskins, and Patricia P. Clark, eds. *The Papers of Andrew Johnson.* Vol. 5, *1861–1862.* Knoxville: University of Tennessee Press, 1979.

Hammond, James Henry. "The 'Mudsill' Theory." March 4, 1859. https://www.pbs.org/wgbh/aia/part4/4h3439t.html.

Hentz, Caroline Lee. *The Planter's Northern Bride.* Philadelphia: T. D. Peterson, 1854. http://utc.iath.virginia.edu/proslav/hentzhp.html.

Holmes, Emma. *The Diary of Miss Emma Holmes.* Edited by John F. Marszalek. Baton Rouge: Louisiana State University Press, 1979.

Lovejoy, Joseph C. *The True Democracy: A Speech Delivered at East Cambridge, Sept. 29, 1856.* Boston: n.p., 1856. Box 1856, Massachusetts Historical Society.

Luby, Katy. *Welcome Buchanan!* New York: Horace Waters, 1857. http://lcweb2.loc.gov/diglib/ihas/loc.music.sm1857.631020/default.html.

Maurer, Louis. "The Great Republican Reform Party, Calling on Their Candidate." 1856. https://www.loc.gov/item/2003656588/.

———. "The Republican Party Going to the Right House." 1860. https://www.loc.gov/pictures/item/2003674590/.

Magee, John L. "Liberty, the Fair Maid of Kansas, in the Hands of the 'Border Ruffians.'" 1856. https://digital.librarycompany.org/islandora/object/digitool %3A130222.

O, Jessie Is a Sweet, Bright Lady. Boston: John P. Jewett, 1856. http://lincoln.lib .niu.edu/Songs/jessieisasweetbrightlady.html.

Pierce, Franklin. "Third Annual Message." December 31, 1855. http://www .presidency.ucsb.edu/ws/index.php?pid=29496.

"Republican Party Platform of 1856." June 18, 1856. http://www.presidency.ucsb .edu/ws/?pid=29619.

"Republican Party Platform of 1860." May 17, 1860. https://www.presidency.ucsb .edu/node/273296.

Rives, John C., ed. *The Congressional Globe, Containing the Debates and Proceedings of the First Session of the Thirty-Sixth Congress: Also, of the Special Session of the Senate.* Washington, D.C.: John C. Rives, 1860.

"Second Debate: Freeport, Illinois." August 27, 1858. National Park Service, Lincoln Home National Historic Site. https://www.nps.gov/liho/learn /historyculture/debate2.htm.

Seward, William Henry. "William Henry Seward's Higher Law Speech." In *The Works of William H. Seward*, vol. 1, edited by George E. Baker, 70–93. New York: Redfield, 1853. http://history.furman.edu/~benson/docs/seward.htm.

———. "On the Irrepressible Conflict." October 25, 1858. http://www.nyhistory .com/central/conflict.htm.

Sheahan, James W. *The Life of Stephen A. Douglas.* New York: Harper and Brothers, 1860. Huntington Library, San Marino, Calif.

Townsend, John. *The South Alone, Should Govern the South. And African Slavery Should Be Controlled by Those Only, Who Are Friendly to It.* Charleston, S.C.: Steam-power presses of Evans & Cogswell, 1860. Box 1860, Massachusetts Historical Society. Victor, Metta Victoria Fuller. *Mormon Wives: A Narrative of Facts Stranger Than Fiction.* New York: Derby & Jackson, 1856.

Volck, Aldabert John. "Worship of the North." Library Company of Philadelphia, 1861. https://digital.librarycompany.org/islandora/object/Islandora%3A65185.

Ward, Maria. *Female Life among the Mormons: A Narrative of Many Years' Personal Experience, by the Wife of a Mormon Elder, Recently from Utah.* New York: J. C. Derby, 1855. https://catalog.hathitrust.org/Record/005777264.

SECONDARY SOURCES
Books, Book Chapters, and Articles

Allgor, Catherine. *Parlor Politics: In Which the Ladies of Washington Help Build a City and a Government.* Charlottesville: University Press of Virginia, 2000.

Anderson, Benedict. *Imagined Communities: Reflections on the Origin and Spread of Nationalism.* London: Verso, 1983.

Appleby, Joyce Oldham, Eileen K. Chang, and Joanne L. Goodwin, eds. "Captivity Narratives." In *Encyclopedia of Women in American History*, 59–60. New York: Routledge, 2015.

Arnold, Brie Swenson. "'To Inflame the Mind of the North': Slavery Politics and the Sexualized Violence of Bleeding Kansas." *Kansas History* 38, no. 1 (Spring 2015): 22–39.

Arrington, Leonard J. *Brigham Young: American Moses*. New York: Alfred A. Knopf, 1985.

Arrington, Leonard J., and Jon Haupt. "Intolerable Zion: The Image of Mormonism in Nineteenth Century American Literature." *Western Humanities Review* 22, no. 3 (Summer 1968): 243–60.

Ayers, Edward L. *In the Presence of Mine Enemies: War in the Heart of America, 1859–1863*. New York: W. W. Norton, 2003.

———. *What Caused the Civil War? Reflections on the South and Southern History*. New York: W. W. Norton, 2005.

Baker, Jean H. *Affairs of Party: The Political Culture of Northern Democrats in the Mid-Nineteenth Century*. New York: Fordham University Press, 1983.

Beard, Charles, and Mary Beard. *The Rise of American Civilization*. New York: Macmillan, 1927.

Bederman, Gail. *Manliness and Civilization: A Cultural History of Gender and Race in the United States, 1880–1917*. Chicago: University of Chicago Press, 1995.

Belohlavek, John M. *Broken Glass: Caleb Cushing and the Shattering of the Union*. Kent, Ohio: Kent State University Press, 2005.

Berry, Stephen W. *All That Makes a Man*. Oxford: Oxford University Press, 2002.

Bowman, Shearer Davis. "Conditional Unionism and Slavery in Virginia, 1860–1861: The Case of Dr. Richard Eppes." *Virginia Magazine of History and Biography* 96, no. 1 (January 1988): 31–54.

———. *At the Precipice: Americans North and South during the Secession Crisis*. Chapel Hill: University of North Carolina Press, 2010.

Boydston, Jeanne. *Home and Work: Housework, Wages, and the Ideology of Labor in the Early Republic*. New York: Oxford University Press, 1990.

Brown, Kathleen M. *Good Wives, Nasty Wenches and Anxious Patriarchs: Gender, Race and Power in Colonial Virginia*. Chapel Hill: University of North Carolina Press, 1996.

Bunker, Gary L., and Davis Bitton. "Illustrated Periodical Images of Mormons, 1850–1860." *Dialogue: A Journal of Mormon Thought* 10, no. 3 (Spring 1977): 82–94.

Burgett, Bruce. "On the Mormon Question: Race, Sex, and Polygamy in the 1850s and the 1990s." *American Quarterly* 57, no. 1 (March 2005): 75–102.

Burnett, Lonnie A. *The Pen Makes a Good Sword: John Forsyth of the Mobile Register*. Tuscaloosa: University of Alabama Press, 2006.

Butler, Judith. *Gender Trouble: Feminism and the Subversion of Identity*. New York: Routledge, 1990.

Carmichael, Peter S. *The Last Generation: Young Virginians in Peace, War, and Reunion*. Chapel Hill: University of North Carolina Press, 2005.

Caron, James E. *Mark Twain, Unsanctified Newspaper Reporter*. Columbia: University of Missouri Press, 2008.

Cauthen, Charles Edward. *South Carolina Goes to War, 1860–1865.* Columbia: University of South Carolina Press, 2005.

Conlin, Michael F. "The Dangerous Isms and the Fanatical Ists: Antebellum Conservatives in the South and the North Confront the Modernity Conspiracy." *Journal of the Civil War Era* 4, no. 2 (June 2014): 205–33.

Connell, R. W. *Masculinities.* Berkeley: University of California, 2005.

Cott, Nancy F. *The Bonds of Womanhood: "Woman's Sphere" in New England, 1780–1835.* New Haven, Conn.: Yale University Press, 1977.

———. *Public Vows: A History of Marriage and the Nation.* Cambridge, Mass.: Harvard University Press, 2000.

Craven, Avery O. *The Repressible Conflict.* Baton Rouge: Louisiana State University Press, 1939.

Davis, William C. *Breckinridge: Statesman, Soldier, Symbol.* Baton Rouge: Louisiana State University Press, 1974.

DeVelvis, Melissa. "'May the Lord Shield and Protect Us from the Terrible Storm ahead of Us': Elite South Carolina Women's Anticipation of Secession and War, 1860–1861." *Journal of American Studies* 54, no. 5 (2020): 981–1004.

Dew, Charles B. *Apostles of Disunion: Southern Secession Commissioners and the Causes of the Civil War.* Charlottesville: University Press of Virginia, 2001.

Dorsey, Bruce. *Reforming Men and Women: Gender in the Antebellum City.* Ithaca, N.Y.: Cornell University Press, 2002.

Douglas, Ann. *The Feminization of American Culture.* New York: Farrar, Straus and Giroux, 1977.

DuBois, Ellen Carol. *Feminism and Suffrage: The Emergence of an Independent Women's Movement in America, 1848–1869.* Ithaca, N.Y.: Cornell University Press, 1979.

Du Bois, W. E. B. *Black Reconstruction: An Essay toward a History of the Part Which Black Folk Played in the Attempt to Reconstruct Democracy in America, 1860–1880.* New York: Russell and Russell, 1935.

Edwards, Laura F. "Review: You Can't Go Home Again: Politics, War, and Domestic Life in the Nineteenth-Century South." *Reviews in American History* 25, no. 4 (December 1997): 570–76.

Edwards, Rebecca. *Angels in the Machinery: Gender in Party Politics from the Civil War to the Progressive Era.* New York: Oxford University Press, 1997.

Egerton, Douglas R. *Year of Meteors: Stephen Douglas, Abraham Lincoln, and the Election That Brought on the Civil War.* New York: Bloomsbury, 2010.

Etcheson, Nicole. *Bleeding Kansas: Contested Liberty in the Civil War Era.* Lawrence: University Press of Kansas, 2004.

Eyal, Yonatan. *The Young America Movement and the Transformation of the Democratic Party, 1828–1861.* Cambridge: Cambridge University Press, 2007.

Faust, Drew Gilpin. *James Henry Hammond and the Old South: A Design for Mastery.* Baton Rouge: Louisiana State University Press, 1982.

Fettman, Eric. "Harper's Weekly." In *Encyclopedia of the American Civil War: A Political, Social, and Military History*, edited by David S. Heidler and Jeanne T. Heidler, 931–32. New York: W. W. Norton, 2000.

Fields, Barbara Jeanne. *Slavery and Freedom on the Middle Ground: Maryland during the Nineteenth Century*. New Haven, Conn.: Yale University Press, 1985.

Finkelman, Paul. "Manufacturing Martyrdom: The Antislavery Response to John Brown's Raid." In *His Soul Goes Marching On: Responses to John Brown and the Harpers Ferry Raid*, edited by Paul Finkelman, 41–66. Charlottesville: University Press of Virginia, 1995.

Flake, Kathleen. *The Politics of American Religious Identity: The Seating of Senator Reed Smoot, Mormon Apostle*. Chapel Hill: University of North Carolina Press, 2004.

Fluhman, J. Spencer. *"A Peculiar People": Anti-Mormonism and the Making of Religion in Nineteenth-Century America*. Chapel Hill: University of North Carolina Press, 2012.

Foner, Eric. *Free Soil, Free Labor, Free Men: The Ideology of the Republican Party before the Civil War*. New York: Oxford University Press, 1970.

Ford, Lacy K. *Deliver Us from Evil: The Slavery Question in the Old South*. New York: Oxford University Press, 2009.

Fornell, Earl Wesley. *The Galveston Era: The Texas Crescent on the Eve of Secession*. Austin: University of Texas Press, 2011.

Fox-Genovese, Elizabeth. *Within the Plantation Household: Black and White Women of the Old South*. Chapel Hill: University of North Carolina Press, 1988.

Freeh ling, William W. *Road to Disunion: Secessionists Triumphant, 1854–1861*. New York: Oxford University Press, 1990.

———. *The South versus the South: How Anti-Confederate Southerners Shaped the Course of the Civil War*. New York: Oxford University Press, 2001.

Friend, Craig Thompson, and Lorri Glover, eds. *Southern Manhood: Perspectives on Masculinity in the Old South*. Athens: University of Georgia Press, 2004.

Furniss, Jack. "To Save the Union 'in Behalf of Conservative Men': Horatio Seymour and the Democratic Vision for War." In *New Perspectives on the Union War*, edited by Gary Gallagher and Elizabeth R. Varon, 63-90. New York: Fordham University Press, 2019.

Gage, Larry Jay. "The Texas Road to Secession and War: John Marshall and the Texas State Gazette." *Southwestern Historical Quarterly* 62, no. 2 (October 1958): 191–226.

Genovese, Eugene. *Roll, Jordan, Roll: The World the Slaves Made*. New York: Pantheon, 1974.

Gienapp, William E. "'Politics Seem to Enter into Everything': Political Culture in the North, 1840–1860." In *Essays on Antebellum Politics, 1840–1860*, edited by William E. Gienapp, Stephen E. Maizlish, and John J. Kushma, 14–69. College Station: Texas A&M University Press, 1982.

Glicke, Peter, and Susan T. Fiske. "The Ambivalent Sexism Inventory: Differentiating Hostile and Benevolent Sexism." *Journal of Personality and Social Psychology* 70, no. 3 (1996): 491–512.

Glymph, Thavolia. *Out of the House of Bondage: The Transformation of the Plantation Household*. New York: Cambridge University Press, 2008.

————. *The Women's Fight: The Civil War's Battles for Home, Freedom, and Nation*. Chapel Hill: University of North Carolina Press, 2020.

Gordon, Sarah Barringer. "The Twin Relic of Barbarism." In *The Mormon Question: Polygamy and Constitutional Conflict in Nineteenth Century America*, 55–83. Chapel Hill: University of North Carolina Press, 2002.

Graff, Harvey J. *The Legacies of Literacy: Continuities and Contradictions in Western Culture*. Bloomington: Indiana University Press, 1987.

Greenberg, Amy S. *Manifest Manhood and the Antebellum American Empire*. Cambridge: Cambridge University Press, 2005.

Greenberg, Irwin F. "Charles Ingersoll: The Aristocrat as Copperhead." *Pennsylvania Magazine of History and Biography* 93 (April 1969): 190–217.

Grimsley, Mark. *The Hard Hand of War: Union Military Policy toward Southern Civilians, 1861–1865*. New York: Cambridge University Press, 1995.

Hahn, Steven. *The Roots of Southern Populism: Yeoman Farmers and the Transformation of the Georgia Upcountry, 1850–1890*. New York: Oxford University Press, 1983.

Harrold, Stanley. *Border War: Fighting over Slavery before the Civil War*. Chapel Hill: University of North Carolina Press, 2010.

Heck, Frank H. *Proud Kentuckian: John C. Breckinridge, 1821–1875*. Lexington: University Press of Kentucky, 1976.

Hodes, Martha. *White Women, Black Men: Illicit Sex in the Nineteenth-Century South*. New Haven, Conn.: Yale University Press, 1997.

Hoganson, Kristin. "Garrisonian Abolitionists and the Rhetoric of Gender, 1850–1860." *American Quarterly* 45, no. 4 (1993): 558–95.

Holt, Michael F. *The Political Crisis of the 1850s*. New York: John Wiley and Sons, 1978.

————. *The Election of 1860: "A Campaign Fraught with Consequences."* Lawrence: University Press of Kansas, 2017.

Howe, Daniel Walker. *The Political Culture of the American Whigs*. Chicago: University of Chicago Press, 1979.

————. "The Evangelical Movement and Political Culture in the North during the Second Party System." *Journal of American History* 77, no. 4 (March 1991): 1216–39.

————. *What Hath God Wrought? The Transformation of America, 1815–1848*. New York: Oxford University Press, 2007.

Hunt, Lynn. *The Family Romance of the French Revolution*. Berkeley: University of California Press, 1992.

Isenberg, Nancy. *Sex and Citizenship in Antebellum America*. Chapel Hill: University of North Carolina Press, 1998.

Johannsen, Robert W. *Stephen A. Douglas*. New York: Oxford University Press, 1973.

Jones, Megan Sanborn. *Performing American Identity in Anti-Mormon Melodrama*. New York: Routledge, 2009.

Jones-Rogers, Stephanie E. *They Were Her Property: White Women as Slaveowners in the American South*. New Haven, Conn.: Yale University Press, 2019.

Kennedy, Kathleen. "The Nun, the Priest, and the Pornographer: Scripting Rape in Maria Monk's Awful Disclosures." *Genders*, May 2013. https://www.colorado.edu/gendersarchive1998-2013/2013/05/01/nun-priest-and-pornographer-scripting-rape-maria-monks-awful-disclosures.

Kerber, Linda. *Women of the Republic: Intellect and Ideology in Revolutionary America*. Chapel Hill: University of North Carolina Press, 1997.

Kern, Louis J. *An Ordered Love: Sex Roles and Sexuality in Victorian Utopias—The Shakers, the Mormons, and the Oneida Community*. Chapel Hill: University of North Carolina Press, 1981.

Kersh, Rogan. *Dreams of a More Perfect Union*. Ithaca, N.Y.: Cornell University Press, 2001.

Knupfer, Peter. "A Crisis in Conservatism: Northern Unionism and the Harpers Ferry Raid." In *His Soul Goes Marching On: Responses to John Brown and the Harpers Ferry Raid*, edited by Paul Finkelman, 119–48. Charlottesville: University Press of Virginia, 1995.

———. "Aging Statesmen and the Statesmanship of an Earlier Age: The Generational Roots of the Constitutional Union Party." In *Union and Emancipation: Essays on Politics and Race in the Civil War Era*, edited by David W. Blight and Brooks D. Simpson, 57–78. Kent, Ohio: Kent State University Press, 1997.

Kutzler, Evan A. *Living by Inches: The Smells, Sounds, Tastes, and Feeling of Captivity in Civil War Prisons*. Chapel Hill: University of North Carolina Press, 2019.

Landis, Michael Todd. *Northern Men with Southern Loyalties: The Democratic Party and the Sectional Crisis*. Ithaca, N.Y.: Cornell University Press, 2014.

Link, William A. *Roots of Secession: Slavery and Politics in Antebellum Virginia*. Chapel Hill: University of North Carolina Press, 2003.

Lynn, Joshua A. "A Manly Doughface: James Buchanan and the Sectional Politics of Gender." *Journal of the Civil War Era* 8, no. 4 (December 2018): 591–620.

MacKinnon, William P. "Sex, Subalterns, and Steptoe: Army Behavior, Mormon Rage, and Utah War Anxieties." *Utah Historical Quarterly* 76, no. 3 (Summer 2008): 227–46.

Maizlish, Stephen E. *A Strife of Tongues: The Compromise of 1850 and the Ideological Foundations of the American Civil War*. Charlottesville: University of Virginia Press, 2018.

McClintock, Russell. *Lincoln and the Decision for War: The Northern Response to Secession*. Chapel Hill: University of North Carolina Press, 2008.

McCurry, Stephanie. *Masters of Small Worlds: Yeoman Households, Gender Relations and the Political Culture of the Antebellum South Carolina Low Country*. New York: Oxford University Press, 1995.

McPherson, James M. *Battle Cry of Freedom: The Civil War Era*. New York: Oxford University Press, 1988.

Moss, Elizabeth. *Domestic Novelists in the Old South: Defenders of Southern Culture*. Baton Rouge: Louisiana State University Press, 1992.

Neely, Mark E., Jr. *Lincoln and the Democrats: The Politics of Opposition in the Civil War*. New York: Cambridge University Press, 2017.

Norton, Mary Beth. *Liberty's Daughters: The Revolutionary Experience of American Women, 1750–1800*. Boston: Little, Brown, 1980.

———. "The Evolution of White Women's Experience in Early America." *American Historical Review* 89, no. 3 (June 1984): 593–619.

Oakes, James. *The Crooked Path to Abolition: Abraham Lincoln and the Antislavery Constitution*. New York: W. W. Norton, 2021.

Olsen, Christopher J. *Political Culture and Secession in Mississippi: Masculinity, Honor, and the Antiparty Tradition, 1830–1860*. New York: Oxford University Press, 2000.

Osthaus, Carl R. *Partisans of the Southern Press: Editorial Spokesmen of the Nineteenth Century*. Lexington: University Press of Kentucky, 2015.

Paludan, Phillip S. "The American Civil War Considered as a Crisis in Law and Order." *American Historical Review* 77, no. 4 (October 1972): 1013–34.

Peck, Graham A. *Making an Antislavery Nation: Lincoln, Douglas, and the Battle over Freedom*. Urbana: University of Illinois Press, 2017.

Phillips, Christopher. *The River Ran Backward: The Civil War and the Remaking of the American Middle Border*. New York: Oxford University Press, 2016.

Pierson, Michael D. *Free Hearts and Free Homes: Gender and American Antislavery Politics*. Chapel Hill: University of North Carolina Press, 2003.

Piola, Erika. "The Rise of Early American Lithography and Antebellum Visual Culture." In "Representations of Economy: Lithography in America from 1820 to 1860," special issue of *Winterthur Portfolio* 48, no. 2/3 (Summer/Autumn 2014): 125–38.

Potter, David M. "The Historian's Use of Nationalism and Vice Versa." *American Historical Review* 63, no. 4 (July 1962): 924–50.

———. *The Impending Crisis: 1848–1861*. New York: Harper and Row, 1976.

Quigley, Paul. *Shifting Grounds: Nationalism and the American South, 1848–1865*. New York: Oxford University Press, 2012.

Quitt, Martin H. *Stephen A. Douglas and Antebellum Democracy*. Cambridge: Cambridge University Press, 2012.

Rable, George C. *Damn Yankees! Demonization and Defiance in the Confederate South*. Baton Rouge: Louisiana State University Press, 2015.

Randall, James G. "The Blundering Generation." *Mississippi Historical Review* 27 (June 1940): 3–28.

Robertson, Andrew W. *The Language of Democracy: Political Rhetoric in the United States and Britain, 1790–1900*. Charlottesville: University of Virginia Press, 2005.

Robinson, Michael D. *A Union Indivisible: Secession and the Politics of Slavery in the Border South*. North Carolina: University of North Carolina Press, 2017.

Rugemer, Edward Bartlett. *The Problem of Emancipation: The Caribbean Roots of the American Civil War*. Baton Rouge: Louisiana State University Press, 2009.

Scott, Joan Wallach. *Gender and the Politics of History*. New York: Columbia University Press, 1988.

Sheehan-Dean, Aaron. *Why Confederates Fought: Family and Nation in Civil War Virginia*. Chapel Hill: University of North Carolina Press, 2007.

Sielke, Sabine. *Reading Rape: The Rhetoric of Sexual Violence in American Literature and Culture, 1790–1990*. Princeton, N.J.: Princeton University Press, 2002.

Sinha, Mrinalini. "Gender and Nation." In *Women's History in Global Perspective*, edited by Bonnie G. Smith, 1:229–75. Urbana: University of Illinois Press, 2004.

Smith, Adam I. P. *The Stormy Present: Conservatism and the Problem of Slavery in Northern Politics*. Chapel Hill: University of North Carolina Press, 2017.

Smith, David T. *Religious Persecution and Political Order in the United States*. New York: Cambridge University Press, 2015.

Spurlock, John. "The Free Love Network in America, 1850–1860." *Journal of Social History* 21, no. 4 (Summer 1988): 765–79.

Stampp, Kenneth M. *America in 1857: A Nation on the Brink*. New York: Oxford University Press, 1990.

Taylor, Amy Murrell. *Embattled Freedom: Journeys through the Civil War's Slave Refugee Camps*. Chapel Hill: University of North Carolina Press, 2018.

Tetrault, Lisa. *The Myth of Seneca Falls: Memory and the Women's Suffrage Movement*. Chapel Hill: University of North Carolina Press, 2014.

Ulrich, Laurel Thatcher. *A House Full of Females: Plural Marriage and Women's Rights in Early Mormonism, 1835–1870*. New York: Alfred A. Knopf, 2017.

Varon, Elizabeth R. *We Mean to Be Counted: White Women and Politics in Antebellum Virginia*. Chapel Hill: University of North Carolina Press, 1998.

——. *Disunion! The Coming of the American Civil War, 1789–1859*. Chapel Hill: University of North Carolina Press, 2008.

Venet, Wendy Hamand. "'Cry Aloud and Spare Not': Northern Antislavery Women and John Brown's Raid." In *His Soul Goes Marching On: Responses to John Brown and the Harpers Ferry Raid*, edited by Paul Finkelman, 98–115. Charlottesville: University Press of Virginia, 1995.

Walther, Eric H. *The Fire-Eaters*. Baton Rouge: Louisiana State University Press, 1992.

——. *The Shattering of the Union: America in the 1850s*. Lanham, Md.: SR Books, 2004.

——. *William Lowndes Yancey and the Coming of the Civil War*. Chapel Hill: University of North Carolina Press, 2006.

Wardle, Lynn D. "From Slavery to Same-Sex Marriage: Comity Versus Public Policy in Inter-jurisdictional Recognition of Controversial Domestic Relations." *Brigham Young University Law Review*, no. 6 (2008): 1855–926.

Welter, Barbara. "The Cult of True Womanhood: 1820–1860." *American Quarterly* 18, no. 2 (1966): 151–74.

West, Richard S. "Wide-Awake Pictorial." Illustrated Civil War Newspapers and Magazines, n.d. https://www.lincolnandthecivilwar.com/SubLevelPages/WideAwakePictorial.asp.

Whites, LeeAnn. *The Civil War as a Crisis in Gender: Augusta, Georgia, 1860–1890*. Athens: University of Georgia Press, 1995.

Woods, Michael E. *Emotional and Sectional Conflict in the Antebellum United States*. New York: Cambridge University Press, 2014.

———. *Arguing until Doomsday: Stephen Douglas, Jefferson Davis, and the Struggle for American Democracy*. Chapel Hill: University of North Carolina Press, 2020.

Dissertations

Lynn, Joshua A. "Preserving the White Man's Republic: The Democratic Party and the Transformation of American Conservatism, 1847–1860." PhD diss., University of North Carolina at Chapel Hill, 2015.

Regan, John J. "Runaway Nuns, Runaway Bestsellers: Representations of Gender and Class in Antebellum Convent Captivity Narratives and Fictions." PhD diss., University of Rhode Island, 1999. http://proxy01.its.virginia.edu /login?url=https://search-proquest-com.proxy01.its.virginia.edu/docview /304525162?accountid=14678.

Reference Material

American Antiquarian Society. "The Early Nineteenth-Century Newspaper Boom." The News Media and the Making of America, 1730–1865. https:// americanantiquarian.org/earlyamericannewsmedia/exhibits/show/news-in -antebellum-america/the-newspaper-boom.

"Childs, John." In *Philadelphia on Stone Biographical Dictionary of Lithographers*. Library Company of Philadelphia, n.d. https://digital .librarycompany.org/islandora/object/digitool%3A78985.

"Clisby, Joseph." In *Georgia Info: An Online Georgia Almanac*. Digital Library of Georgia, n.d. https://georgiainfo.galileo.usg.edu/topics/people/article /journalists/clisby-joseph.

"Currier and Ives." In *Encyclopaedia Britannica*, n.d. https://www.britannica .com/topic/Currier-and-Ives.

Grisamore, Ed. "85 Things You May Have Not Known about the *Telegraph* and Macon." *Telegraph*. November 1, 2011. https://www.macon.com/news /article28623151.html.

"Kirtland, Ohio." In *Encyclopedia of Mormonism*, 793–98. New York: Macmillan, 1992.

"Magee, John L." In *Philadelphia on Stone Biographical Dictionary of Lithographers*. Philadelphia: Library Company of Philadelphia, n.d. https:// digital.librarycompany.org/islandora/object/digitool%3A79511?solr_nav %5Bid%5D=be202657ca03a9a4ff68&solr_nav%5Bpage%5D=0&solr_nav %5Boffset%5D=0.

PBS. "Utah." New Perspectives on the West. 2001. http://www.pbs.org/weta /thewest/places/states/utah/ut_salt.htm.

Reynolds, Donald E. "Cushing, Edward Hopkins." In *Handbook of Texas Online*. Texas State Historical Association. https://www.tshaonline.org/handbook /entries/cushing-edward-hopkins.

Index

"Cowardly Desertion of Capt. Brown by His Former Patrons, The" (*Brooklyn Daily Eagle*), 76
Crittenden Compromise, 132–33
Cushing, Caleb, 80, 123
Cushing, Edward Hopkins, 117, 124–25, 183n33

Davis, Jefferson, 105–6, 116, 123–24
DeBow, James D. B., 93
Declaration of Sentiments, 22
Delaware, 78, 93, 103
Democratic Party: conventions, 100, 102–5; division of (*see* Democratic Party, division of); on Kansas-Nebraska Act, 12–13, 64–71; manhood, understanding of, 154; mischaracterization of Republicans (*see* hyperbole, Democrats on Republicans; hyperbole, South on North); nominees of, campaign of 1860, 100–103, 105–6; northern vs southern (*see* Democratic Party, northern vs southern); platform of, campaign of 1860, 101–5, 123; on polygamy, 44–45, 58–63; on white patriarchy, 19–20; on womanhood, 28–29, 32–33, 86–92 (*see also* women)
Democratic Party, division of, 100–101; compromise and (*see* compromise, northern and southern Democrats); Constitutional Unionists and, 114–15; Democratic conventions and, 100, 102–5; Douglas and, 113–14; fire-eaters and, 124–27; free labor and, 105–9; free love and, 111–12; interracial relationships and, 118–19; secession and, 124–27; sectional differences and (*see* sectional differences); as warning on modern politics, 159–60; women's rights and, 109–13, 116–18, 121–23. *See also* Democratic Party; Democratic Party, northern vs southern
Democratic Party, northern vs southern: after Lincoln's victory, 129; on Brown's raid on Harpers Ferry (*see* Brown's raid on Harpers Ferry); on equality of southerners, 154; on Lecompton Constitution, 64–72; on popular sovereignty, 2, 58–61; on secession, 129–30; secession blame and, 130–31; sectional differences of (*see* sectional differences); on slavery, 36–37, 84–85; subservience of North to South, 108; unity of, 36. *See also* Democratic Party, division of
Dill, Benjamin, 141
divorce laws, 23, 62, 117, 183n33. *See also* free love movement
domestic institutions, 46–47, 67–71, 169n7; Buchanan on, 67; Democrats on, 58; Douglas on, 65–67; Lecompton Constitution and, 65–68; polygamy and slavery connection, 44, 51–53, 61–65
domesticity, 16–17, 23, 32–33, 89, 91, 143–44, 153
Douglas, Adele, 117–18
Douglas, Stephen A.: 1860 campaign and, 113–14; on affective theory, 135; compromise and, 180–81n8; on domestic institutions, 65–67; election of 1860 results and, 129; on Lecompton Constitution, 65–66, 71–72; on polygamy and, 52; on popular sovereignty, 45, 162n2; presidential candidacy and, 66–67; on secession, 120–21, 132; as slaveholder, 113–14; transcontinental railroad and, 12; on Utah War, 59–61; wife of, 117–18
Douglass, Frederick, 26, 76
Dowdell, James F., 135
Du Bois, W. E. B., 7

Hentz, Caroline Lee, 84, 91
hierarchy, southern, 121, 139–40. *See also* patriarchy
higher law, 112
Holden, William W., 151
Holmes, Emma, 130
Holt, Robert, 146
homes, plantations as, 122
honor, 124, 149, 154–55. *See also* manhood
Howe, Daniel Walker, 134, 182nn24–25
Howe, Julia Ward, 90
Hughes, James, 71
Hugo, Victor, 80
hyperbole, Democrats on Republicans: on abolitionism, 33–34, 74–78, 82, 144–45; on freedoms, 35; on free love movement, 29–32, 111–12; on northern fanaticism, 135–37 (*see also* radicalism); on slave rebellion after Lincoln's victory, 125–27; on slavery, 37; on women's rights, 23, 27–28
hyperbole, Republicans on Democrats: on free labor, 39–40; on northern men, 106, 108–9; on sexual violence of white women, 55–57; on white slavery, 40
hyperbole, South on North: on Brown's raid on Harpers Ferry, supporters of, 82–83; on interracial relationships, 118–19; northern invasion and, 146–47; on slave rebellion, 93; on women's rights, 116–17

Illinois, 45, 48, 119
independence, of white men, 133–34
independence, of women. *See* women; women's rights
Indians. *See* Native Americans
Ingersoll, Charles Jared, 77
insurrection, slave. *See* rebellion, slave

interracial relationships, 34–35, 94, 101, 112–13, 118–19, 145, 167n51, 179n46
isms, 115–16
Iverson, Alfred, 79

Johnson, Herschel, 114

Kansas, 46, 64–65, 69–72. *See also* Kansas-Nebraska Act
Kansas-Nebraska Act: Democratic support for, 12–13; domestic institutions and, 46–47, 67–68; Douglas and, 114, 162–63n2; Lecompton Constitution and, 64–69; northern Democrats on, 64–69; slavery and polygamy connection, 43–45, 51–52, 59, 61–62; southern Democrats on, 69–71; voting fraud in, 45, 64–65
Kentucky, 78, 154, 175n9

labor, free, 4, 37–40, 105–9, 138, 155
"Labor—Degrading!," 106
Lane, Joseph, 104
"Last Rail Split by 'Honest Old Abe,' The," 106, *107*
law, higher, 112
LDS (Church of Jesus Christ of Latter-Day Saints). *See* Mormonism
Lecompton Constitution, 45, 64–72, 173n54
"Liberty, the Fair Maid of Kansas," 56–57, *57*, 171n25
Lieber, Francis, 52
Lieber Code, 158
Lincoln, Abraham: on affective theory, 135; on Brown's raid on Harpers Ferry, 74–75, 83; cartoon depicting, 1, 106, *107*, 109–11, *110*, 156, *157*; Democrats on, 100–101, 125–27, 129, 145–46, 185n51; election of, 129; on interracial relationships, 119; manhood of, 106, *107*; radicalism and, 109–13,

and, 79–80, 92–95, 140, 145–48, 155, 157; of slaves, 140

Murray, C. D., 132

Nash, Theophilus, 137
nationalism, 78–81
nations, construction of, 139
Native Americans, 60
Nauvoo Legion, 48, 60
negative liberties, 114
newspapers, importance of in antebellum era, 8–9
New York, 100, 143
nominees, 1860 campaign, 100–103, 105–6
non-intervention, 114. *See also* popular sovereignty
North Carolina, 78, 114, 150–51
northern Democrats. *See* Democratic Party, northern vs southern
northern invasion, southern fear of, 146–47
Norton, Mary Beth, 117

Olsen, Christopher, 124, 138
Opposition Party, 38
orthodoxy, 140

patriarchy, 3–4, 165n35; abolition-
ism and, 125; Buchanan and, 20–21; control, 19–20; crumbling of, 117; Democratic Party and, 4, 9, 19, 34–35, 72, 133, 155, 162n12; Frémont and, 17–18; in Roman Empire, 19; secession and, 95–98; sexual segregation and, 119; slavery and, 26, 97, 101, 120–21, 125, 139, 144–45; threats to, 3, 23–25, 29, 31, 112–13, 125, 133, 136–37, 144–45; women's support of, 34–35, 142. *See also* manhood

Pickens, Francis, 140
Pierce, Franklin, 32, 56, 57, 58
Pierson, Michael, 5, 26, 44, 166n40
plantations, as homes, 122

Planter's Northern Bride, The (Hentz), 84
plural marriage. *See* polygamy, Mormon
poetry, 32, 37, 148, 151
Poindexter, George, 63
Polhill, John, 93–94
politicians, public vs private lives of, 113–14, 117
politics, women's involvement in: abolitionism and, 33–34; of Child, 86–90; conditional, 152–53; Democratic, 28, 140–44; of Douglas's wife, 118; of Frémont's wife, 16–17; northern, 90–92; secession and, 141–43, 188n26
polygamy, Mormon, 168–169n3, 171–72n33; as domestic institu-
tion, 51–53; federal interference in, 62–63; northern Democrats on, 58–61; political importance of, 43–44; as revelation to Smith, 48; sexual violence and, 53–54; slavery and, 44–45, 47, 51–53; southern Democrats on, 61–63
popular sovereignty, 162–63n2; campaign of 1856 and, 37, 39, 42; Constitution amendment for, 133; Democrats on, northern vs south-
ern, 2, 58–61; domestic institu-
tions and, 46–47; in Kansas and Utah, 46; Lecompton Constitu-
tion and, northern Democrats on, 64–69; Lecompton Constitution and, southern Democrats on, 69–71; manhood and, 101, 120, 122–23; moderates on, 116; as non-intervention, 114; as platform in 1860 campaign, 101–2; polygamy and, 44–45, 51–53; Repub-
licans on (*see* Republican Party, popular sovereignty and); sexual violence and, 53–57; southern Democrats on, 61–63
Potter, David, 64, 140, 146

poverty, 40

prison, Brown and, 86

propaganda. *See* hyperbole, Democrats on Republicans; hyperbole, Republicans on Democrats; hyperbole, South on North

property requirements, voting rights and, 39

Prophets, The; or, Mormonism Unveiled (Belisle), 50–51

protection, North's of South, 93–97, 138–39, 156

protectors, men as, 3–4, 18, 40–41, 80, 94, 97, 156. *See also* sexual violence

providers, men as, 3–4, 18, 23, 38

public vs private life, of politicians, 113–14, 117

radicalism: abolitionism and (*see* abolitionism); Brown's raid on Harper Ferry and, 74, 81–83, 85–86; causes of, 33–34; equality and, 35–36; fire-eaters as, 96–97 (*see also* fire-eaters); free Blacks, 81, 112, 118–19, 143; free love and (*see* free love movement); Frémont and, 13–14 (*see also* Frémont, Jessie; Frémont, John C.); gender, 2–3, 33–34, 74–78, 166–67n49; Lincoln and, 109–13, *110*, 129–30; in Maurer's cartoons, 1, 109–13, *110*; national family and, 97–98; northern, 85–86, 118, 135–39; sectional differences and, 4; slavery, influence on, 120; women and, 92 (*see also* women's rights)

raid, at Harpers Ferry. *See* Brown's raid on Harpers Ferry

rape. *See* sexual violence

rebellion, slave: at Brown's raid on Harpers Ferry (*see* Brown's raid on Harpers Ferry); hyperbole on, 75–76, 93, 125–27; Lincoln election and, 101, 125–26, 145–46,

185n51; in literature, 84; northern protection of South from, 93–97, 138–39, 156; post-emancipation, 155–56; southern fear of, 79–80, 92–95, 124–27, 140, 144–46, 157–58

Recollections of a New England Housekeeper (Gilman), 121–22

Recollections of a Southern Matron (Gilman), 121–22

Reed, William, 14–15

religion, 32, 59, 169n10. *See also* Mormonism

Republican Party, 12; Black, 110, 123, 129–30, 147, 151; on Brown's raid on Harpers Ferry, 73–75; mischaracterization of Democratic Party (*see* hyperbole, Republicans on Democrats); nominees, campaign of 1852, 106; platform, campaign of 1860, 106; popular sovereignty and (*see* Republican Party, popular sovereignty and); on slavery, 138; women, 14, 23–25, 92, 110 (*see also* women; women's rights)

Republican Party, popular sovereignty and: domestic institution and, 46–47; media portrayal of, 53–57, *56–57*; opposition to, 46; polygamy and, 51–53, 55, 57–58; sexual violence and, 53–58; slavery and, 47, 51–53

"Republican Party Going to the Right House, The," 109–13, *110*

Richardson, Catherine Martenet, 84–85

Richardson, John Smythe, 141

Roman Empire, patriarchal control in, 19

Ruffin, Edmund, 149

Russell, Mary Ellen, 90

Scott, Joan Wallach, 6

secession: 1860 campaign and, 124–27; blame for, 130–31; bravery, as reason for, 148; call for, 95–98, 103–4, 120, 124–27; compromise on (*see* compromise, northern and southern Democrats); Douglas on, 120–21, 132; first states of, 130; as manly, 127, 148; Southern national identity and (*see* Southern national identity); southern tactics to incite, 144–50; submissiveness and, 148–50; Unionist response, 78; of Upper South states, 150–53; violence, as reason for (*see* rebellion, slave)

Secret Six, 76, 90

sectional differences: literature on, 91–92; on marriage, 18–20; radicalism and, 4; social order, 139–40; societal, 82, 87, 91–92, 121–23; Wise on, 82; women and, 87, 121–23, 140–44

Seneca Falls Convention, 22, 26

Seward, William, 51, 83, 138

sexuality: Child and Brown claims of, 88; Democratic regulation of, 3; freedom of, 29 (*see also* free love movement); interracial (*see* interracial relationships); segregation of, 119 (*see also* interracial relationships); and wives, of southern soldiers, 153. *See also* sexual violence

sexual violence: cartoons on, *56–57*; compromise as, 123; Kansas-Nebraska Act and, 55–57, *56–57*; legal protections against, 158; nonspecific fear of, post-secession, 147; by northern troops, 146–47, 158; polygamy and, 53–54; by slaveholders, 26, 33, 54–57, 95, 122; slavery rebellion, fear of and, 79–80, 92–95, 124–27, 140, 144–46, 157–58

Seymour, Horatio, 154–55

slave code, 100, 102

slaveholders: sexual violence by, 26, 33, 54–57, 95, 122; and slave

relationship, 69, 89–90, 177n34, 190n48 (*see also* domestic institutions)

slavery: antislavery positions on, 1854, 12; cross-section fights over, 175n9; Democratic Party's demise and, 2; as domestic institutions (*see* domestic institutions); expansion of, 46–47, 76, 123, 162–63n2; flight from, 81, 92; free labor and, 37–39 (*see also* free labor); free love movement and, 29 (*see also* free love movement); interracial relationships and (*see* interracial relationships); in Kansas (*see* Kansas-Nebraska Act); marriage and, 26, 35–36, 45, 61, 64–65; as moral, southern thought on, 84–85; northern vs southern Democrats on (*see* Democratic Party, northern vs southern); prices of, 144; radicalism and, 120; rebellion of (*see* rebellion, slave); Republicans on morality of, 138; security of, 78; sexual violence and (*see* sexual violence); as shared economic interest, 187n18; southern society, effect on, 139–40; support for, as platform in 1860 campaign, 101–2, 105; westward expansion of, 38–39, 44–45; white laborers as, 40, 108; white patriarchy and, 97, 101, 120, 125, 144–45. *See also* slaveholders

Smith, Joseph, Jr., 47–49

Snowden, Edgar, 87–88

social classes, 37–39, 95

social institutions, 58–59

social order, of South, 139. *See also* patriarchy

societal differences, North vs and South, 82, 87, 91–92, 121–23. *See also* sectional differences

South Carolina, 98, 130, 132, 149–50

southern Democrats. *See* Democratic Party, northern vs southern

of, 34, 142; political involvement of (*see* politics, women's involvement in); polygamy and, 48–53 (*see also* polygamy, Mormon); protection of (*see* protectors, men as; rebellion, slave); rape of (*see* sexual violence); Republican, Democratic women on, 92; on secession, 148; secessionists on, 140–41; sectional differences of, 140–44; slaveholders, 87; southern, 140–44; southern, on Brown, 94; virtues judged by, 89; war support from southern, 152–53; white supremacy, support of, 34; wives (*see* wives); writers, 80–81. *See also* women's rights

women's rights: 1860 campaign and, 109–13, 116–18; abolitionism and, 26–27, 122; convention, 26–27, 116–17, 165n35; history of, 22–23; hyperbole on, 23, 27–28, 116–17; literature, 121–23; Maurer cartoon and, 110, *110*; mocking of, 23–25; Republicans and, 14, 23–25, 110; suffrage and, 23–26, 164n24. *See also* women

Woods, Michael, 7–8, 78, 135

"Worship of the North," 156, *157*

Yancey, William, 125–26

Young, Brigham, 43, 48, 52, 59–60, 63

CPSIA information can be obtained
at www.ICGtesting.com
Printed in the USA
LVHW111931290922
729619LV00002B/12

9 781469 671420